READING
THE
RIVER

JOHN HILDEBRAND

READING THE RIVER

A VOYAGE DOWN THE YUKON

THE UNIVERSITY OF WISCONSIN PRESS

The University of Wisconsin Press
114 North Murray Street
Madison, Wisconsin 53715

3 Henrietta Street
London WC2E 8LU, England

10   9   8   7   6   5   4   3   2   1

First published in 1988 by Houghton Mifflin Company

Printed in the United States of America

Cartography by Kevin Byrne

The author is grateful to Thomas Nelson and Sons, Ltd., for
permission to quote from *The Odyssey*, translated by W. H. D. Rouse

Library of Congress Cataloging-in-Publication Data
Hildebrand, John.
Reading the river : a voyage down the Yukon / John Hildebrand.
260 pp.   cm.
Originally published: Boston: Houghton Mifflin, 1988.
Includes bibliographical references (p. 242).
ISBN 0-299-15494-7 (pbk.: alk. paper)
1. Yukon River (Yukon and Alaska)—Description and travel.
2. Hildebrand, John—Journeys—Yukon River (Yukon and Alaska)
I. Title.
F912.Y9H55   1997
917.98'60451—dc21   96-49088

For
Sharon
and
Margaret

And I think over again
My small adventures
When with a shore wind I drifted out
In my kayak
And thought I was in danger.
My fears,
Those small ones
That I thought so big,
For all the vital things
I had to get and to reach.

And yet, there is only
One great thing,
The only thing:
To live to see in huts and on journeys
The great day that dawns,
And the light that fills the world.

—Eskimo song, translated by Knud Rasmussen
in *Intellectual Culture of the Copper Eskimos*

CONTENTS

PREFACE

I LEFT ALASKA TWENTY YEARS AGO with what seemed a pretty firm good-bye, rattling down the Alcan Highway with everything I owned in a pickup truck, my wife having already flown the coop. We had come North convinced that it was the best of all possible places, and when we stopped believing this, we left. But I keep coming back on my own, sometimes for short visits to friends in Fairbanks, and once for a summer-long canoe trip down the Yukon. That journey, the subject of this book, was partly a homecoming and partly an attempt to make the country feel strange and new again by entering it through the back door of the river.

The Yukon appealed to me because it's a river of such extremes, crossing borders and time zones, language families and ecosystems. It traverses the last great wilderness in America, yet also carries the freight of commerce and subsistence, and serves as a constant landmark in the traditions of those who live along its banks. It was the last major river on the continent to be explored by Europeans, and probably the first to be traveled by Pleistocene hunters. It's a river that begins in clouds over the coastal ranges of British Columbia and ends in salt marsh and tundra beside the Bering Sea.

After the first three hundred miles, the Yukon turns completely opaque with suspended glacial silt, so it's necessary to feel your way downstream. "Reading the river" is a canoeist's term for translating the flowing surface of water into hidden shoals or snags waiting underneath to capsize your boat or run it aground. Once, traveling through the night in the pilothouse of the towboat *Ramona* as she pushed barges from Tanana to Koyukuk, I asked the pilot how he could navigate in the dark. "Oh well, I just look at the outline of the hills," he said, "and know where I am." Just so, I tried to read the faces of people living along its banks to acquire a sense of the place, a sense of where I was. Two questions I always asked were "How did you get here?" and "Is this home?" Non-natives invariably had a vivid account of how they'd come to be at that particular bend in the river. But even if they'd spent a decade or more in that spot, I recognized a tentativeness about calling it home, as if they might pull up stakes and move on tomorrow.

To stay or to go?—these are the alternating currents running through our lives. On the road, we're in the enviable position of reinventing ourselves. "The soul of a journey," William Hazlitt wrote, "is liberty, perfect liberty to think, feel, do just as one pleases." Home, on the other hand, means being stuck with people who long ago got your number. Travel allows us to appreciate what we left behind by removing us from its daily grind until the journey itself becomes a drag, and we return to find home has become strange and new.

The last time I was there, Fairbanks had grown bigger and, if possible, uglier—new subdivisions sprouting from the spruce flats—though what had changed most was not the country but myself. I was back for a wedding on the summer solstice, a date of some importance in the subarctic. Every year the mother of the bride celebrated the summer and winter solstices, the twin poles of light and darkness on which the year turned. In winter, she cranked up Handel's "Messiah" and lit candles on a spindly black spruce to mark our climb out of the murky depths. In summer, a barbecue and interminable games of volleyball in the dusk reminded us that the scales were tipping again. But the celebration was a little muted this summer because the bride's mother was between rounds of chemotherapy, having postponed her next treatment until after the wedding. A steady rain canceled the post-nuptial volleyball game, so we gathered for a potluck at a sportsman's hall on the banks of the Chena River, filled our dinner plates with broiled salmon and roast moose, and watched tree stumps float down the swollen river. After a dance, I reminded the bride of parties that had swirled around her childhood when she'd fallen asleep in a pulled-out dresser drawer. But she didn't remember any of the names in that circle. "Funny how we're all caught up in time," she said. "How it changes everything." She didn't mean the new subdivisions.

Rivers give the illusion of outrunning time, at least the kind we're all swimming against, which is no small part of their appeal. Or maybe it's just that, being linear, they tend to connect things. Drifting down a familiar stretch of water, we're reminded of other trips and other rivers until memory and the present merge into one all-encompassing river that cuts through time and space and connects everything.

The Chena River is a tributary of the Tanana and, as such, connects Fairbanks with the Yukon. I've canoed it half-a-dozen times, and standing in the rain that afternoon, I wasn't thinking about the wedding but a recent trip far upstream near the headwaters. It was early October and the Chena was clear-running and shallow in stretches, skirting low spruce hills banded with yellow aspen. My canoe partner and I had made a circuit of Fairbanks bars the night before—The International, The Howling Dog, The Boatel—and now the crisp autumn air was tonic for our hangovers. We camped across from a high cutbank stratified into layers of gravel and dark silt. As sunlight warmed the frozen soil, sections of the bank periodically calved into the river, exposing ancient tree roots, which might had survived from the age of mammoths. The whole place gave off a strong, dank odor, like a cellar door thrown open. That night was very cold, and we stayed warm feeding a bonfire and catching up on old times—the glory days and missed opportunities—until there was a muffled roar across the river as part of the cutbank crashed down in the darkness, then nothing but the sound of water washing past.

READING
THE
RIVER

TRIBUTARIES

FOR A BRIEF PERIOD in my life I lived on a rock-stuffed creek, connected, through the logic of rivers, with the immense Yukon River. No wider than two hops across, the creek drained a narrow, incisive valley north of the outer mountains of the Alaska Range. It ran down the steep staircase of the valley into the braided, silty channels of the Nenana River, which flowed north into the Tanana, which flowed into the Yukon, which emptied into an Asian sea.

My wife and I traveled north in the early seventies, part of a migratory generation that has since buckled down to work and forgotten how to wander. We arrived in Alaska between the rival eras of homesteading and oil development. Under a state provision, we staked five acres on the south-facing slope of Panguingue Creek and began felling trees for the cabin walls. Close to tree line, the white spruce tapered quickly and had to be cut to length and peeled. With the cambium still moist, the bark peeled easily; the wood emerged pale and smooth as flesh and left my hands smelling pleasantly of spruce pitch.

We built up from the creek on a wooded bench to keep watch on the Outer Range and the weather that would hang itself on the peaks. The mountains rose vertically from the broad plain to five and six thousand feet, dark veins of spruce below the talus slopes showing the route of snow melt-off. Beyond these outer summits, the Alaska Range proper stood like a great white wall against storms blown north from the gulf. In the evening, the failing light bathed the slopes in alpenglow, and the valley filled with the rush of water over stone.

There was in all this the echoes of a very old life. Not far from the cabin, at Dry Creek, anthropologists digging on a bluff found the coals of ancient campfires and, mingled in the ashes, the bones of long-horned bison and Pleistocene horse. The last glacial epoch had not extended north of the Alaska Range, so while the rest of the continent lay under ice, these plains were green. Hunters newly from Asia trekked the foot of these slopes and ate their kill in the firelight of nights eleven thousand years ago. Eleven thousand years of these mountains, this sky.

A photograph taken at the end of that first summer shows me astride a logjam of thirty cabin logs, cut, peeled, and dragged uphill at the rate of one a day. Standing there with a doltish grin, arms akimbo, I posed with one leg bent, happier than I have ever been. I was acting out a vague dream of the North, a vision acquired mostly from books that promised that if we only lived simply our lives would be simple and carefree.

My wife paused often in her labors to document what she felt would otherwise pass quickly into reminiscence. But it didn't. Climbing out of the valley when the first snow was hard on the mountains, we left the cabin walls holding up nothing but sky.

I took a teaching job at the university in Fairbanks. From my office in a bleak new concrete building, I could watch the winter sun's brief arc in the sky between my morning and noon coffee breaks. My students were Athabascan Indians and Eskimos who came from villages where the old hunting life bumped up against the banalities of satellite television and oil pipelines — places as distant from me as the moon. Away from home for the first time, they felt either homesickness for open spaces or else great relief to be gone, because, as one dark-eyed Athabascan girl confided, there was nothing to do there.

In my office hung a wall map of Alaska, a wonderful thing in shaded relief, with buff-colored mountains and frazzled blue rivers. To keep track of my students, I stuck a red pin in each of their villages as if these were my branch offices. A line of red pins clustered along the ribbon of the Yukon River, villages with names that were evocative and beautiful to hear: Tanana . . . Nulato . . . Koyukuk . . . Emmonak.

An exchange was worked out. While I inflicted grammar upon my students, they taught me about the Yukon. In detail, they described separate pieces of the river, territories framed by their own particular uses. The boundaries might extend from a deep eddy beside a summer fish camp to a backwater slough heavy with moose in the autumn rut. The river provided both food and conveyance, a highway through roadless country, a constant landmark in their traditions. Assembled in my head, the composite river seemed awesome and mysterious. I traced my finger along the map and daydreamed a journey that would connect the pieces, a long drift to the sea.

But I never made the trip. In late spring, my wife and I returned to our own slender tributary to finish the cabin. Panguingue Creek still lay beneath five feet of ice, so I borrowed a dog sled and harnessed myself to haul lumber over the frozen creekbed for a roof and floor. We picked up our tools and worked as if the intervening winter had never happened. But winter *had* made all the difference, of course, and we found ourselves inventing side trips and excursions, idle days to cache away for the dark of the coming winter. Soon enough the cabin was heavily mortgaged with hikes and berry picking in the berm piles along the road. After a day of hauling boards for the roof, my wife just sat down in the wood shavings and said she was tired of it. Tired of the heat and the mosquitoes, tired of the work, but tired most of all of looking up these narrow valley walls and knowing that beyond them the briefest of summers was slipping toward a winter that would jump down from the mountains one morning and catch us unawares. She suggested a trip to the Gulf of Alaska where the salmon were running. We drove south for two days to the ocean, and when we returned, sure enough, summer had slipped by.

Each summer the cabin brought us back again from Fairbanks, even after we no longer shared the desire to return. When it was finished, nothing remained but to live there, and that was the hardest task of all.

"But there's nothing to do here."

Without her presence, I find myself taking her arguments: the isolation, the suffocating quality of the woods. Pregnant at the end of that third summer, she was often sick to her stomach, waiting out the rains and the overwhelming silence. The vision was fading, the reason for staying, but I was killing time until she delivered a child that would, I was certain, moor us to this valley.

Annoyed, I escaped to the creek to fish for grayling and Dolly Varden trout in the slick stretches between boulders. Sitting on a rock in midstream, I would sight down the valley toward its terminus, imagining myself a piece of flotsam drifting free with the current into the great network of rivers.

In midwinter in Fairbanks, she went into labor, three months premature. The early morning drive to the hospital remains fixed in my mind, an inversion of white landscape and black sky. I talked as I drove, full of an optimism she wouldn't share. Our son was born into the world at seven-thirty in the morning and died, nameless, an hour later. Not much time by any measure. A day later, driving back from the hospital, we said very little but understood that at the end of the summer we would be leaving.

In August she boarded a plane to California and flew off without a backward glance. The plan was for me to say the good-bys and tie up loose ends before driving south to join her. When the car was packed, I made a final trip to the cabin.

Along the creek, the willows had turned yellow and the blueberry leaves a bright crimson, but the days were unseasonably warm. No dusting of snow had fallen on the talus slopes of the Outer Range. I spent a few dreary days sorting out what to take and what to leave. Then, the cabin put in order, I shut the door on that life and headed for the mountains.

The ridge rose straight up from the Savage River, the mountainside flint hard except where rivulets bubbled from the loose rock. I paused to drink from them as I climbed the mountain. The climbing was hard, but the view opened up as I gained elevation: green glacial valleys, shimmering veins of river, and the stark white backbone of the Alaska Range, on whose high peaks winter was perpetual. The mountain leveled off at the top into a green ridge, windblown and covered with lousewort and primrose, a divide from which the world seemed to fall away. I climbed to a rocky cairn breaking out of the moss campion and could see to the north, among the brown hills, the narrow valley cut by Panguingue Creek. Holding on to the rock, I took the ashes of my firstborn out of a small box and let the wind carry them like snow onto the bare slopes. There was no service but the constant wind, the primrose, and the river below in the canyon.

In a week, perhaps two, winter would come to these slopes and stay. Walking back down the mountain, I felt a great sadness, knowing I would not be there in spring when the snow melted and ran off the slopes, freshening a watershed that fed the Nenana and the Tanana and the Yukon and flowed at last into an ocean that covers the world.

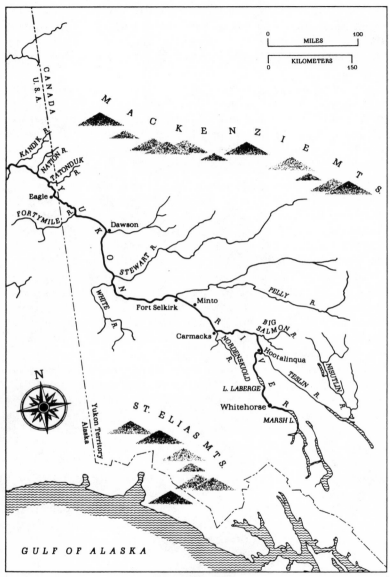

MACKENZIE MTS.

CANADA
U.S.A.

KANDIK R.
NATION R.
TATONDUK R.
YUKON
Eagle
FORTYMILE R.
Dawson

STEWART R.

WHITE R.
Fort Selkirk
Minto
PELLY R.

Carmacks
RIVER
BIG SALMON R.

NORDENSKIOLD R.
Hootalinqua

TESLIN R.
NISUTLIN R.

L. LABERGE
N
Whitehorse

Yukon Territory
Alaska

ST. ELIAS MTS.

MARSH L.

GULF OF ALASKA

Upper Yukon River

WHITEHORSE

THE PLANE BUMPED DOWN through the clouds until the land was suddenly very close, green, and patchy with sunlight. We followed the chalky line of the Alcan Highway north until the plane banked abruptly and I caught sight of the Yukon River tumbling out of Marsh Lake. Catching the sun, the channel flashed and then faded to a dull, metallic sheen, while beyond the white crescent bluffs a forest extended forever.

The airport lay on a high, flat terrace above Whitehorse and the river. In the grass between the runways, purple pasqueflowers bent into the wind. I grabbed my coat and stepped down the ramp into the wind and high sunlight of the Yukon plateau. Even now, in mid-June, snow clung to the saddles of surrounding hills.

A cab took me into town, racing along a pockmarked road that I had driven ten years before on my way south. Strange now to be back, no longer in my twenties, without a wife. The country seemed less changed than myself. I had grown a little older, a little softer, while the landscape seemed as hard-edged as ever. Pitching down the steep grade, the cab passed a sign that read WELCOME TO WHITEHORSE and another, a little farther on, a northern postscript: PUBLIC DRINKING PROHIBITED WITHIN CITY LIMITS.

Whitehorse is a squat town of wide streets spreading beneath a trellis of power lines. Assembled on the flood plain of the Yukon, it sprang up during the gold rush as a place for stampeders to dry off after running Whitehorse Rapids. But the town has long since turned its back on the river. Now the territorial capital is a city of car dealerships, government buildings, and unexpected seagulls wheeling in a slanting sky. The first impression is of the West rather than the North — of bald hills and flat-bottomed clouds. The men wear cowboy boots and deltoid sideburns and park their pickup trucks at oblique angles to the street. In the bed of every truck is a panting, mandarin-faced husky, a sort of reverse hood ornament.

Checking into a boarding house, I flopped down on the bed, exhausted from having spent the night on an airport couch in Edmonton. A television mumbled down the hall. On the floor next to my bed, I spread out a map of Alaska, the same map I'd hung years before in my office. It was perforated with holes but still showing the great blank spaces, the evocative names tied together by blue rivers. The North seemed to me now a foreign country, one whose news I no longer followed. I pored over the map, orienting myself to where I was going and where I had been.

My marriage had collapsed. The end had come slowly and then with the terrible suddenness of waking in a strange bed alone. There had been deep, unspoken fissures over the years, but when things finally came apart I was stunned. As my equity in the divorce settlement, I agreed to take the cabin on Panguingue Creek. It was a white elephant, a nod to a past we'd both lost the heart for. My lawyer thought I was a fool. But it seemed important, necessary even, to salvage something from those days.

Those days. So much of the back-to-the-land movement struck me now as slightly ludicrous. There was a pious smugness to it, an upside-down Calvinism in which brown rice and patched jeans and scabies somehow imparted a higher karma. We were all so new to the country that real knowledge was hard to come by. Scratch the work rags and earnest folksiness, and you'd find another pilgrim from the city. "What *are* these funny black specks?" a woman once asked me, peering into her sack of raw oats and not recognizing mice turds. Well, it was not such a bad ambition — living by one's own hand, following the cycle of seasons — but finally, for most of us, it wasn't enough — or maybe it was too much. People went into the woods looking for themselves and found nothing more or less than that. Afterward, emerging from isolated cabins and squatters' shacks, they awoke from that dream as if from a long hibernation, wide-eyed and exceedingly hungry.

My own life had narrowed in all the predictable ways. But the essential problem remained: how to live decently and keep one's head above the crapola. It was never easy. What came easy was everything else — career, house, a comfortable boredom. When a little credibility was called for, I trotted out my cabin-building as an after-dinner anecdote until even I no longer believed it. It was somebody else's story, not my own. When the divorce swept everything clean and I found myself thrown out on my ear, homeless and alone, I whimpered at the unfairness of it, all the while nursing a secret exhilaration. The world had opened wide again and seemed filled with possibilities.

One possibility was to go back to Alaska. I was still haunted by my original vision of the North — the nightless summers and long winters of solitude. But I had no desire to spend a lonely summer in my cabin. I was more curious about the sort of people who had stayed behind, leading a life I frankly couldn't manage. We need our dreams even if we don't live up to them. Flying back now, I meant to find the North that had eluded me before. I needed to verify that the life I had imagined had a counterpart in actuality, that, after all these years, it had not simply been the wrong dream.

First I needed to relearn the country. The choice of routes was important. I lacked the necessary innocence to rumble up the Alcan Highway again in a beat-up van, seeing the landscape in a haze of desire. Whatever mystique the Alcan once held for me had long since disappeared behind cracked windshields and caravans of Airstream trailers. Besides, the road would dead-end in nostalgia, and it was other people's pasts I was after, not my own. Then I remembered the river trip I had once day-dreamed to the sea. The Yukon River was the original highway into the country, the main artery, the broad sum of all the northern streams and creeks, including my own. Floating down-river, I could sample a little of each tributary. The Yukon also appealed to me not only because it traversed one of the last great wildernesses of North America but, more important, because it was a working river, where people followed, or tried to follow, a very old cycle. A voyage down the Yukon would be a journey through time as well as geography, back to the world as it used to be. Along the way, I could rub elbows with the survivors of many winters, the pioneers and the veterans of my own generation. Hitching a ride on the river, I could drift into other lives, people I might have become.

In the late afternoon, I left the hotel and went looking for the river. The street beside the railway station was being torn up and the wind blew dust against the shop windows. An Indian girl cradling a boom box brushed past me on the sidewalk, lost in music.

In a riverside park, I fell in step with a group of schoolchildren touring a dry-docked steamboat. Proportioned like a shoe box, the paddle-wheeler had three balustraded decks and a single smokestack rising behind the glassed-in pilothouse. On the saloon deck, rattan chairs ringed a circular observation room, just the place to sit with a drink in your hand and watch the treetops slide past. The boat had been beached in the early fifties when the completion of an all-weather road linked Whitehorse to Dawson. In a single stroke, the road had eliminated steamboat traffic on the Yukon, relegating the surviving boats to museum pieces and the river itself to no more than a painted backdrop. But the kids were too fidgety to listen to the tour guide. Swarming over the decks, they turned the open staircases into monkey bars while their teacher shouted after them: "Stay in line! Keep your hands off that! Get down from there!"

After he herded the kids back on the bus, I climbed down the grassy bank for a closer look at the Yukon. I found it sliding beneath a highway bridge, a swift-flowing river the pale, oxydized green of weathered statuary. A truck rumbled overhead and swallows poured from the bridge shadows. I sat down on the bank and skipped a stone across the water. Not so wide as I had imagined, the river looked faster, barreling like a freight train between white clay bluffs, heading north.

In the morning I rented a car and drove south on a gravel road along the river. No one agrees on the Yukon's exact beginning or its length. One source is a glacier above Lake Lindeman in the Coastal Mountains of British Columbia, a scant few miles from tidewater. But if measured from its farthest tributary, the Yukon rises in the headwaters of the Nisutlin River in the Pelly Mountains of the Yukon Territory, two thousand miles from the Bering Sea. (For that matter, one could say that the river begins in the clouds.) But for my purposes the river started at the head of navigation below the tailrace of a hydroelectric plant, a strange beginning for a wild river.

At the power plant beneath the dam, the chief engineer, a short, bearded man with a pocketful of pens, showed me around. He was in charge of the river, at least the first hundred miles before tributaries swelled it. From a control panel of computer terminals and breaker switches, he could fine tune the Yukon into kilowatts and megawatts.

"Most of the river's water comes from glaciers. If it rains up in the hills or we get hot weather, the glaciers melt and raise the level of the river."

The temperature that day was in the high seventies. Someone flicking on a light switch in Whitehorse would tap into voltage the far end of which was blue glacial ice. In the heat of summer, the glacier's melt water flowed from a string of mountain lakes through Miles Canyon and into the reservoir of Lake Schwatka to drop into lightless penstocks that led beneath the power plant.

We put on hard hats and left the quiet of the chief engineer's office for the humming center of the plant. The floor gratings vibrated from the turbines spinning beneath them.

"We're standing," the engineer shouted, "over the tail end of Whitehorse Rapids."

The rapids took their name from the foam-tipped waves that resembled the flying white manes of horses. In the first summer of the gold rush, seven thousand rafts and ripsawed scows and bateaux drifted down from the mountain lakes until the river narrowed abruptly in Miles Canyon a few miles above the rapids. Those who didn't portage around the canyon risked drowning in its sucking whirlpool and still faced the roaring cascades of Whitehorse Rapids.

Now the canyon was itself drowned, and the rapids had been transformed into the very heart of the dynamo. Standing over the turbines was a disquieting sensation, all that compressed violence, as if someone had stoppered up a fearsome storm in a bottle and invited you to peek down the neck.

We strolled outside past bulldozers and dump trucks moving earth for a new turbine that would double the Whitehorse dam's generating capacity. This was the only existing dam on the Yukon, but there were proposed dam sites already on the books, waiting for the right circumstances to turn the river into a chain of flaccid lakes.

At the edge of the tailrace we watched the river plunge over the spillway. You could lob a message in a bottle here and conceivably expect it to be picked up by a Bering Sea Eskimo. Across the river, the long flume of a fish ladder ran along the shore for half a mile so migrating salmon could reach their spawning grounds on the other side of the dam.

"They start off from the Bering Sea the first week in June," the engineer said. "When they arrive here in the middle of August, they've only got another fifty miles to their spawning beds."

By that time, I thought, I would be at the river's mouth.

The perpetual northern twilight kept me awake at night, so I wandered out for a drink. I wanted rattan chairs and a view of the river but settled for a gloomy lounge that smelled of spilled beer and pinged with video games. A dance band began to play, but nobody danced. The lead vocalist sang in a lilting prairie accent.

> "I'm glad I'm Canadian
> I'm glad I'm free"

Another voice, lower but more insistent, was not at all glad. It belonged to the man sitting next to me at the bar. He was drunk and talking to himself in the mirror above the row of bottles. "I'm so fucking bitter," he moaned to his reflected image. "My fucking car's broke down in my fucking yard. It's enough to piss anyone off."

He had a furrowed, angry face, a face nobody would want to talk to, and then I realized he was talking to me. I picked up my drink and moved to a table.

"This band is good," the woman at the next table told me. "That's why we're here. The last band didn't leave for eight years."

She and her girlfriend were celebrating pay day. I asked if I could join them.

"Thank God you're not German," said the tall one. "All summer in Whitehorse all you see are German tourists with their buck knives and funny get-ups."

Marge was her name. When I told her about my river trip, she suggested places to stop and places to avoid.

"Stay out of Carmacks," she advised. "My brother got beat up there once trying to stop a fight. Fighting's recreational in Carmacks."

Marge had tanned, muscular arms from working as a flag man for the highway department. She was from Edmonton and her friend Annie from Toronto. They were part of the melting pot that had come north for the good wages and got stranded.

"Anybody who can't make it down south comes up here," Marge said, not excluding herself. She was only staying six months until the union job ran out and then she'd kiss this place good-by and fly south for the winter. She had enrolled in a ceramics course in Mexico.

"I don't want any more academics," she said, slamming down her drink. "I just want to learn pottery. But they're always making you write a fucking essay, you know?"

I knew exactly what she meant.

Her friend Annie was going camping over the weekend and invited me to stay in her apartment while she was gone. "Stop by tomorrow and I'll give you the key. You can't miss the place. It's the only three-story log cabin in town."

The next afternoon, I lugged my duffel bag to the cabin, which turned out to be a local landmark — the log skyscraper of Whitehorse. With overhanging eaves and a three-tiered catwalk, it looked more like a log pagoda. The whole structure swayed as I climbed the three flights to Annie's apartment. She wasn't home yet, so I dropped down to the second story apartment where Marge lived. She answered the door in her bathrobe, a black cat crooked in her arm.

"Everybody has dogs in this town," she sighed as we went inside. "They don't like cats."

There was just one room. With a single step, you could land in the kitchen, a living room chair, or the bed. I landed in the chair.

"In the winter it's really cold," Marge said. "I'm constantly chinking between the logs because the cat likes to play with the insulation. Then in the summer, tourists stare at you through the window. It's weird."

She'd had an edgy day at work. It had been a scorcher, and she'd drawn hoots and catcalls from the men on the highway crew by wearing a T-shirt. And she still had a hangover from the night before.

She brought us both cold beers, then got out a stack of photographs of places where she'd lived — Fairbanks, Victoria, Dawson, Teslin — an itinerary of starts and stops. It was a mixed bag of memories. Teslin had been heartbreakingly beautiful, a long headwaters lake rimmed with Swiss mountains, but working there as a chambermaid had been a disaster.

"They called me the snaky white lady with the shit-brown hair and the shit-brown eyes. One old Indian woman thought I was stupid just because I didn't know how to tan a moosehide. For three weeks I drank all the time because it was so normal there. I mean, you could drink all you wanted and feel perfectly normal."

Marge put the pictures away. They had left us both depressed. Still, she was not without hope. In the winter she would go to sunny Mexico and make pots. She'd never been to Mexico before; it was terra incognita.

Hearing Annie thump up the catwalk, I grabbed my duffel and left poor Marge in her bathrobe to contemplate Mexico.

Annie's apartment, even sparer than Marge's, looked like a diorama of the sixties: a mattress on the floor with a batik bedspread, a bookshelf with titles on Sufi, Zen, and self-healing. A caribou skin was splayed against one wall like an enormous duncolored moth.

Annie had frizzy brown hair and a sweet, freckled English face. She worked in the library and couldn't make up her mind whether she liked Whitehorse or not.

"Two years ago I left, vowing never to return. I came back and then left again. Then I was broke and needed a job, so here I am. Actually, I don't mind the winters so much. You tend to stay indoors and have lots of potluck suppers."

She gave me the key to her apartment and I gave her a bottle of wine for the trip. There was a familiarity implied in these gestures, an undercurrent of domesticity. She also gave me the name of a retired Mountie to look up: G. I. Cameron. It would make a nostalgic start to the trip, more an epilogue than a beginning.

"Don't worry about the cat," she said.

I hadn't seen a cat.

"She's just dropped a litter, so she's a little shy. You probably won't even see her."

From the recesses of the kitchen cupboard I could hear kittens crying.

After Annie left, I was sorry she was gone. She'd looked very appealing in her woolen camping outfit. I stretched out on the bed and fell asleep reading a book called *Healing Yourself.* In the middle of the night I awoke to find a shaggy white cat draped around my neck like a scarf.

Gordon Irwin Cameron lived in a tidy house across the river with a mountain ash growing in the yard and potted geraniums on the front steps. We shook hands at the door. Wearing a tartan shirt and bolo tie, he was a big, ruddy man, but trim for someone in his eighties.

It was the day after the Camerons' fifty-fifth wedding anniversary. Bouquets and cards were arranged on the living room side tables. There were crochet covers on the easy chairs and the usual northern landscapes in oil hanging from the walls. An exercise bike stood in the center of the room. As we sat down, Cameron's wife, Martha, called from the dining room.

"Now don't let him bend your ear."

But that's exactly what I'd come for. I'd had enough of the

new North, the whining over wages and discomfort. Cameron was the old North; he'd been a Royal Canadian Mounted Policeman when there was still some romance attached to the job. He spoke with a clipped British briskness, constantly undercutting his own adventures, making it all seem a jolly time. Retired now, he served as sergeant-of-arms of the territorial legislature, a kind of official greeter to remind the legislators who they were and what they had been.

I told him I was heading down the Yukon that afternoon.

"Really? How far?"

"All the way to the sea."

He was leading a party down the river himself in a few days, taking a twenty-foot riverboat of his own design. Perhaps we would meet. Of course, the Yukon was all changed from when he'd been stationed along it.

"The steamboats were the lifeblood of the river, you know. When they stopped, a whole way of life ended." He launched into a whistlestop tour of downriver settlements, most of them now abandoned: Lower Laberge, Hootalinqua, Big Salmon, Little Salmon . . . His voice trailed off.

"You can go down the river a hundred times," he said, "and it's always different. Different stage of water, different time of year. It's never the same."

He'd first made the trip by steamboat in late May of 1925, a young constable on his way to Dawson. The 460-mile downriver passage took a day and a half. Standing on the deck, he watched Indian villages and wood camps drift past along the wooded shore. The country seemed alive with people, and most of them stood on the banks gawking back at him, as this was the first boat of the season, as much a sign of spring as the lengthening days.

Dawson had fallen into a slumber following the gold rush. By 1925 mammoth steam dredges had taken over the pickax work of extracting gold from the hills, and much of the rough-and-tumble crowd had grown old or departed for other stampedes. Police work was mostly administrative: recording mining claims, collecting royalties on furs and gold, enforcing game laws. "In those days you knew everyone in the territory," Cameron said. "And the worst of it was, they knew you!"

Occasionally there was some of the old adventure — shoot-outs and long pursuits through the snow. The principal characters in these episodes were winter, the darkness and isolation, and an unhinged miner. Shortly after Christmas one winter, a miner at Sulphur Creek went off his rocker and began taking potshots at anyone who passed. Another Mountie was already on the scene when Cameron and a teamster arrived from Dawson. They devised a plan for Cameron and the teamster to circle around the back of the miner's cabin and get the drop on him. But the ruse failed, and the miner pinned them down behind a woodpile. It was a beautiful night, clear and cold, the winter sky tracked with constellations. For an hour they lay in the snow with only their sweaters to keep them warm. Suddenly the miner rushed them. Cameron's hands had gone numb from the cold, and the one shot he got off went wild. As in a dream, Cameron watched the miner cross the yard, trip in the snow, get up again, and point his rifle directly at him. There was a flash and an explosion. Surprised to find himself alive, Cameron looked across the gap of snow at the miner, who was even more nonplussed. Then everyone beat a quick retreat. Reinforcements arrived the next morning and a final ultimatum to surrender was extended to the miner. "But he started shooting again, so we really peppered the place." Inside, they found the miner shot through like a sieve, the cabin floor littered with metal filings. Falling the night before, the miner had plugged his rifle barrel with snow, and when he'd fired at Cameron the muzzle had burst. All night long, he'd been filing away at the barrel.

Cameron's final assignment was to Fort Selkirk, a village on the Yukon midway between Whitehorse and Dawson. Selkirk had two traders, a telegraph operator, a pair of missionaries, and a floating population of Indians who moved with the seasons. There was little crime beyond family quarrels and the occasional brawl. But as sole representative of the government in a territory the size of Maine, Cameron made several patrols a year. In winter he traveled by dog sled. In summer, he would load a square-stern Peterborough canoe on a steamboat headed upriver and then drift down, stopping at Indian fish camps and miners' cabins. "There were no doctors. I'd look after them if they were sick, or else bury them."

One summer, a friend of Cameron's named Bill Hartnet drowned in the Yukon near Carmacks. His canoe had overturned, and when he'd tried swimming for shore in the frigid water his muscles had cramped and he'd gone under. Hartnet's body wasn't recovered until late October, revolving slowly in a slough, "after the gulls had been chewing on him." Cameron was told to bring the body to Dawson. The steamboats had stopped for the season and there was slush ice running in the river. Cameron loaded his friend's corpse into the Peterborough canoe and started downstream. The intense cold kept the stench down but numbed Cameron's hands so that at hour intervals he had to stop and build a fire on shore to thaw out. Night fell a few miles above Dawson as the ice closed in. Listening to the canoe creaking and groaning as pressure built against it, Cameron wondered if it might hold two corpses by morning. Then, in the darkness, he heard people walking along Dawson's boardwalk and called for help.

The clock on the mantel chimed. I looked up at the exercise bike in the middle of the living room and reminded myself that I was listening to an old man recollecting events from half a century ago. Still, it was a horrific story and I wondered if the telling had touched an old nerve. But Cameron went on, speaking matter-of-factly, so that you could see that the episode had become, after all, just a story.

Most of the memories, though, were pleasant — warm days with picnics by the river and hand-churned ice cream. The pioneers of Cameron's generation didn't go to the bush to test themselves but to live as comfortably as possible; there were enough hardships to go around without inventing any. But the old life was fading. Mail that had been delivered once a week by dog team was soon arriving by airplane. And when the Camerons departed Selkirk in early May of 1949, they left not by steamboat but in a float-equipped Fairchild, flying over the river and the still frozen lakes. Their departure anticipated Selkirk's general abandonment by four years.

"The boats stopped in 1953. Once that happened, the people

moved off the river and up the road to Pelly Crossing. The store closed. And *that*," he said, "was the end of Selkirk."

I spent my last day in Whitehorse buying provisions for the trip and mailing last-minute letters. At RCMP headquarters, I filled out a wilderness travel permit, an official form listing my Canadian itinerary so if I failed to show up at Dawson, next of kin could be notified. The desk sergeant pointed out Five Finger Rapids, three ominous slash marks on the map.

"Two years ago a party of Germans drowned here. They took the wrong channel and their boat went under. None of them had worn a life jacket. But don't worry," the sergeant added cheerfully, "you'll make it fine. Just stay to the right." I nodded and marked down the rapids, wondering if he'd given the same advice to the Germans.

My voyage down the Yukon would be the length of an Atlantic crossing, with the difference that I could stop on dry land for the night. In ten years of marriage, even in Alaska, I'd spent surprisingly little time alone, and it was the prospect of a summer in a small boat by myself that was both attractive and unnerving. But traveling alone was the only way to really see the country. Two people in a canoe soon become a society; observations are filtered through the partner, and you end up learning more about the partner than about the landscape through which you're passing.

At Lister's Motor Sports, Ltd., I picked out a boat. I wanted a shallow-draw craft to skim over hidden shoals but with enough freeboard to ride out any rough chop. Also, I needed something cheap. I settled on a square-stern canoe, 15 feet 8 inches long, that would take a small outboard but could be paddled if the engine conked out. The Yukon was a hefty river and I had no intention of paddling eighteen hundred miles to the sea, so I had brought along a 4.5-horsepower outboard to carry me briskly with the current. The boat itself was not as lovely as the cedar-ribbed freighter canoe I might have daydreamed myself in. The hull was forest green and constructed of a "high-molecular-weight polyethylene," the immutability of which the company advertised by pummeling its canoes with boulders. But the boat's lines were clean enough — the sides flaring out from the skinny transom to a forty-inch beam, then narrowing to a V-shaped bow. When the salesclerk loaded it in the bed of his pickup for the ride down to the river, the canoe hung over the tailgate like a coffin riding on a gun carriage.

The sky was a brilliant blue. A few onlookers watched as I waded around in gum boots, loading gear and clamping the Johnson outboard to the transom. I tied down spare paddles and trimmed the canoe so it rode evenly in the water. There was just enough room for two fuel jugs, a duffel with tent and sleeping bag, and a small footlocker with my clothes, shotgun, and food inside. Nosed up on the landing, the boat looked absurdly small.

I walked the canoe into the river, letting the current catch the bow and swing it around while I fiddled with the motor's choke. It had been years since I'd run an outboard. I yanked on the starter cord. The engine coughed once and then settled comfortably into idle, the air filling with a heady mixture of gasoline and oil fumes that transported me to early mornings on a lake and the immense mystery of fishing. I slipped into forward gear and turned the throttle grip wide open for a big exit. The bow raised up momentarily and then planed off. Steaming down the sunlit river, I turned around to wave, but the onlookers at the landing had already dispersed. Two men sharing a bottle on the shady bank behind the railroad station shouted something as I passed, their words unintelligible over the burble of the outboard. Good luck? Go to hell? It didn't matter. I was under way.

A WAKE OF SEAGULLS trailed behind the canoe as I followed the river out of Whitehorse. Beyond the banks, a boatyard slid past, then the jumbled roofs of a shantytown and sagging power lines, until the last remnant of city fell away. The river was the color of jade, a fence of blue hills defining the valley's northward course. I liked the compactness of my canoe, the snug fit of its stern seat, the exhilaration of being self-contained and self-propelled. To get the hang of steering with the tiller arm, I weaved from side to side as the river flowed through high clay banks perforated with the nests of cliff swallows. With the engine revved up, the canoe threw two perfectly expanding lines of waves washing against the pebbled shore. This is so easy, I thought. All I have to do is keep my eyes open.

A few miles below town, the Takhini River entered at a right angle from the west, briefly clouding the pale green Yukon with silt. Then the valley widened, and the banks lowered to a swampy alder flat, and the current became negligible as I entered the head of Lake Laberge. Rotted pilings stuck up above the water line, the remains of dikes built in the steamboat era to keep the channel firm as it entered the lake. Thirty-one miles in length and five miles wide, Laberge had the windblown look of a Scottish loch, a long glacial laceration through barren highlands. Bordering the lake was a range of rounded hills with bare limestone summits that gleamed like snow.

Before the delta, Lake Laberge is the widest stretch of open water along the Yukon, and it has a reputation for dangerous sudden squalls. The lake ice is the last to break up in the spring and the first to form in the fall. Steamboats were sometimes trapped in the lake at freeze-up. Such was the fate of the *Olive May,* a boxy little steamer that froze at the head of Laberge in 1900. A Dr. Sudgen, sent to investigate reports of a miner sick with scurvy, found instead a corpse and used the *Olive May's* firebox as an impromptu crematorium. Years later, the doctor told the story to a young bank clerk named Robert Service, who turned the grim business into "The Cremation of Sam McGee."

Today seemed bright and fair, so I rigged a line and trolled for lake trout. I started along the eastern rim until the shoreline began to recede and I found myself out in the middle of an enormous lake. Far from shore, the illusion of speed was lost; the canoe seemed almost stationary. The wind had picked up, and now I noticed a storm front rolling in from the west, the hills beneath starkly illuminated against the darkening clouds. The blue lake turned ashen, its surface minced into triangular waves. Running open-throttle for the leeward shore, the canoe lurched and the outboard kicked out of the water with an awful whine. I had hit a sandbar. The little boat rocked wildly in the waves and threatened to overturn until I poled it to deeper water and restarted the engine. Bounding through the chop, I pictured Cameron's drowned friend, the one who'd ended up a floating island of gulls.

In the slanting rain I rammed the canoe onto the rocky beach of an island sticking up in a small bay. A bower of spruce trees sheltered me as rain lashed the lake. All of this — the sudden squall and hidden sandbars — seemed premonitory, a warning not to take the river too lightly.

When the storm passed, I lugged my gear to a high, mossy shelf overgrown with violets, wild rose, and yellow cinquefoil. Among the flowers were mounds of old bear shit, withered and white as talc. I prefer to camp on islands; the breeze keeps the mosquitoes down and water surrounds you like a moat. After a hot supper of canned stew, I set up my tent on level ground with a view of the lake and its rim of distant hills. Then I crawled inside the small nylon dome of my tent, my home for the next few months. The tent had been a gift from my wife. I remembered setting it up in my living room and watching it take shape among the furniture. House and furniture were long gone, but the tent had weathered that storm. Already it seemed cozy and homelike inside. I lay down in the warm, still air and listened to the muffled sound of rollers crashing against the beach.

I was up early the next morning. The sun was still low, the woods in long shadows, and at my doorstep was this vast blue lake. Laberge had calmed overnight into an altogether different lake, a smooth mirror reflecting high-masted clouds. I scavenged a driftwood board from the beach and fitted it between seat and transom as a backrest, so I could work the tiller arm with my elbow. Now, steaming along the western shore, I was free to watch whatever hove into view: seagulls on a white-splattered rock, a bald eagle swaying in the crown of a spruce tree, nine roan horses in a sedge meadow at the water's edge. As Laberge narrowed to its northern outlet, the current revived, almost imperceptibly at first, then with the rushing momentum of flood water into a culvert. The lake bottom abruptly tilted upward through the apple-green depths, and a mosaic of bouldery reefs rushed to make contact. Frantically, I cut the engine, hauled it up against the transom, and paddled into the swift channel.

The river commenced again beside the abandoned Indian village of Lower Laberge, where I put ashore to nose around the ruins. The weathered hulk of a stern-wheeler, half sunk into the beach, carried a cargo of river gravel. Back in the willow, a dirt-roofed telegraph-relay cabin stood knee deep in bluebell and wild rose. Inside, nothing was left but a cast iron stove, too bulky to move, standing in the window light; otherwise, the cabin held only heat and a heavy silence. Beyond the open doorway I could see the river surging with light and motion.

Old cabins interest me, partly because of my own clumsy efforts at building with logs. Fashioning a house out of the woods is a beguiling notion. Compared to the complexities of modern life, anything as elemental as stacking logs together to form a shelter seems thoroughly manageable. Luckily, log architecture is simple enough; there are only a few ways to frame a corner.

But the task of cabin-building only forestalls the larger question of exactly how one is going to live in the woods.

Rummaging through an abandoned cabin, I want to invent lives to be lived there and stories for why people left. The builder was often an amateur who improvised on the spot and lived with his mistakes, his own image caught in the cabin's tottering lines like a copper-tinted daguerreotype. This place seemed thoroughly humorless. The fellow had built it low to the ground with saddle-notched corners and a single window to catch the southern exposure. The cabin would have been pleasant enough in the summer with the river racing past. But the winters must have been bleak, with long silences between messages tapped out on the telegraph and a wind howling off the frozen lake. So why did he leave? Something better came along or something went wrong. Whatever — the stories always end the same way, the bowed roof and empty walls being proof of that.

Back in the canoe, I let the current sweep me along. After the wide-open expanses of Laberge, the Yukon narrowed into a steep-walled canyon, transforming itself into exactly the swift, intimately proportioned stream I'd always imagined it to be. Looping through switchback bends, the river revealed itself in quarter-mile sections. Spruce hills gave way to high silt bluffs with wind-carved hoodoos on the outside curves. Steamboats pushing barges down this stretch of Yukon used to "jackknife" through the turns, winching their barges at a right angle to conform to the curve. At the sharpest of these, U.S. Bend, the river bore through an S curve so tight my canoe seemed momentarily headed upstream. Out of the corner of my eye I watched an owl glide into the dark timber of the next hillside.

There were no rapids but plenty of riffles. Sunlight permeated the greenish water clear to the cobble bottom, magnifying it so that the river always appeared shallower than it really was. The chief obstacles were fallen trees, or sweepers, that yawned over the water on the inside bends. Undermined by the swift current, a row of sharp-tipped spruce had toppled into the river like a breastwork, their branches sweeping the surface with the sound of heavy rapids. I skirted them and steered down the channel's center lane. Farther on, in mid-river, I plowed the canoe into a boil, an upwelling where the current sweeps over a submerged boulder and billows upward in a satiny pillow of water. The prop spun without purchase, the canoe pivoting and yawling as if caught in an invisible turnstile before getting free. After a few encounters, though, I learned to discern the sweepers and boils and, reading the river for its hazards, pick my way downstream.

Until the middle of this century, Canadian charts showed this segment of river not as the Yukon but as part of a tributary called the Lewes River. The Yukon proper was not considered to begin until the juncture of the Lewes and Pelly rivers, three hundred miles below Whitehorse. This confusion in nomenclature often resulted from the river's piecemeal exploration, during which overlapping names were laid down for the same territory. The Russians, who ascended from the Bering Sea, called the river by its Eskimo name, *Kwikpak,* while the Hudson's Bay men, working downriver from the mountain headwaters, called it the *Youcon,* an Athabascan term meaning the same thing: "big river." But the Yukon's biggest name dropper was an American army officer named Schwatka.

The same year *Huckleberry Finn* was first published, another narrative of a raft voyage down a mighty river appeared in print. Lieutenant Frederick Schwatka's account of his journey down the Yukon River combined a boy's adventure story with the patina of serious exploration. As in Twain's novel, there was a long raft trip away from civilization, the rough company of men, and the river, immense and quixotic, sweeping Schwatka and his party to the sea. The book was a best seller. It was as if Huck, grown to manhood, had lit out for Indian territory and returned to tell the tale.

At thirty-three, Schwatka no longer had the lean look of a West Point cadet. His hair was thinning; he wore a pince-nez and a goatee. At midnight on May 22, 1883, Schwatka and his party of six men sailed from Portland, Oregon, on the steamer

Victoria and up the Inside Passage to Alaska. Anchoring in a Tlingit village at the head of Lynn Canal, Schwatka hired native packers to carry the expedition's three tons of supplies over the Chilkoot Pass. The Tlingits had zealously guarded the pass as their own until a U.S. gunboat firing blank rounds from a Gatling gun convinced them otherwise. Two of the packers stayed with the expedition as interpreters. One was a young half-breed named Billy Dickinson, the other an older Tagish Indian who later took Schwatka's name as his own.

In the mountain lakes where the Yukon rises, Schwatka's men constructed a raft, "a great gridiron of logs," 16 feet by 42 feet, with corduroy decks of pine poles fore and aft and a sail rigged from a wall tent. Pegged together with wooden pins and christened the *Resolute,* the raft heaved in the rough water of the open lakes like an accordion.

Descending the river, Schwatka blithely ignored both Indian and Hudson Bay nomenclature and dispensed his own. He christened rivers and mountains for fellow explorers, geographers, politicians — anybody, it seemed, whom he admired or owed a favor. Thus the Chilkoot Pass became Perrier Pass after a member of the French Geographic Society, the Little Salmon River became the Daly River after a chief justice who'd funded Schwatka's earlier Arctic expedition, and the Teslin River became the Newberry River after a New York professor. Certain topographical features must have suggested corresponding personalities, but the associations are often oblique. Occasionally, however, one seems pointedly transparent, as near the mouth of the Thirtymile where Schwatka located "an isolated and conspicuous butte which I named after M. Charles Maunoir, of the Paris Geographic Society."

For days the rafting party drifted downriver without seeing another human being. Occasionally they passed an isolated Indian grave, a rough box of hewn boards surrounded by a fence of carved palings like a miniature house, on the edge of a high bank along the river.

Rounding an island below the mouth of the Pelly River, the expedition encountered the largest Indian encampment of the trip. Nearly two hundred Indians lined the beach and swarmed

toward the raft in canoes. Schwatka ordered his men to ready
their rifles in case of attack, but the Indians were merely curious. Taking a line ashore, they pulled the raft onto the beach
and then broke out in a low, monotonous song of greeting.
Surveying their weapons, Schwatka counted only bows and
arrows besides a few ancient Hudson's Bay Company flintlock
muskets and noted that the Indians bore "a most decided He-
brew cast."

They were Northern Tutchone Indians who had come down
from the Pelly River to fish the Yukon for salmon. A riverine
people, the Tutchone defined their territory only as far as it
extended along the major streams. Their dome-shaped brush
huts smelled of drying fish and were attended by hordes of
ravenous, scratching dogs. They bore nothing but curiosity toward the white men who had drifted into their midst, men with
blanched skins the color of dead salmon. In their worst dream-
visions they could not have imagined that before long a thousand score more white men would follow the same route into
their country, looking for gold.

Early the next morning, Schwatka's party stole out of the
village and began the long drift into American territory. After
weeks negotiating the labyrinthine channels of the Yukon Flats,
they abandoned the raft at Nuklakayet, thirteen hundred river
miles from where they'd started, and purchased a schooner to
carry them the rest of the way to the sea.

Schwatka's Yukon voyage, self-promoted as "the longest raft
journey ever made, in the history of geographical science," con-
tributed little in the way of scientific knowledge, but it did cap-
ture the popular imagination and revive interest in Seward's
Ice-Box. When the army refused Schwatka leave to go on a new
expedition, he resigned his commission. In 1886, financed by
the *New York Times,* he led an expedition to the Saint Elias range
in southeast Alaska. By this time, Schwatka weighed over 250
pounds, and the explorers spent only ten days away from the
beach. Schwatka's final journey north was to the headwaters of
the White River, but he never got the chance to publish the
results.

Early on the morning of November 2, 1892, a policeman in

Portland, Oregon, found Schwatka slumped in the street, a half-empty bottle of laudanum, a mixture of alcohol and opium, by his side. Supposing the lieutenant intoxicated, the policeman took him to the St. Charles Hotel, "where he was placed in a chair." When his condition worsened, Schwatka was rushed to Good Samaritan Hospital, where, despite great efforts to save him, he died. He was forty-three. An obituary in the next day's *New York Times* explained the explorer's use of laudanum as relief for an ailing stomach, a condition brought on by a life "marked by such a degree of convivialities."

Not all of Schwatka's names stuck, thank God. The broad tributary entering from the right beneath a bluish mountain with a cocked peak was not called the Newberry but the Teslin, a more precise Indian term meaning "long waters." The Teslin was a straight, north-running river that flowed from a narrow lake at the foot of the Cassiar Mountains. It had been the last leg of the murderous Stikine Trail to the gold fields, and the Mounties built a post across from the confluence to keep an eye on the river traffic.

I beached the canoe below what was left of the post at a place called Hootalinqua. The view of deep, adjoining valleys was unfailingly beautiful. With the sun dipping behind the hills, I walked down to the riverbank to catch supper. Fish were rising in the smooth water below a riffle, dimpling the surface of the pool like the first drops of rain. Flipping a spinner into the deep, green pool, I began a slow retrieve. A grayling struck, jumped once, and after a brief, heartening run was suddenly alive in my hand. With its high dorsal fin, the Arctic grayling looks like a sailfish grafted to a brook trout. Far-ranging fish, they lead brief summer lives in tiny creeks, then bolt for the mainline rivers before winter freezes them out, like so many people I've known. A rap on its skull with the back of my knife, and the fish went rigid. I laid the grayling down on the river gravel to admire: iridescent silver sides flecked with black, the dorsal fin tipped with carmine. In the low light the colors were still vivid.

Another cast, and the line went taut. I swung the rod back and set the hook, the rod bending as I worked the fish against the current and, without a landing net, hauled it ashore. Another grayling, a little larger than the first. Then I called it quits. Faced with such easy pickings, there's an inclination to be greedy, but two fish were all I cared to kill or clean. I fried them up nicely in a skillet until the flesh pulled easily from the pearly bones. My hunger was unreasonable.

Later, down at the beach to clean my dinner dishes, I found a dozen or more grayling, fileted of their meat, washing up against the shore. A party of sportsmen had cleaned their catch here, then thrown the offal into the shallow water, where it slowly undulated in the current. In the warm weather, the beach smelled like a fish house.

The thought that bears might be drawn by the ripe odor made me forgo the tent and sleep in a trapper's cabin dug into the hillside below the old Mountie post. An old dog sled hung from the roof beams and there was barely room to stand upright. A year ago, a work crew of Indians from Little Atlin Lake and Pelly Crossing, descendants of the tribe that had pulled Schwatka's raft ashore, repaired the cabin. They had left behind a ledger and signed their names on the first page: Sam Silverfox, Eddie Tom Tom, George Johnny, Roger Alfred. Subsequent entries were by canoeists who had arrived via the Teslin River and were overwhelmingly Teutonic: Reinhard, Kurt, Karl, Willi, Walter, Erwin, Ernst, Rudolph.

> May 24 Jurgen and Werner Ritau — West Germany — We have found a deadt brown bear in the River. Wheather isn't ok, We are on Trail Johnson Crossing to Dawson.

I unrolled my sleeping bag on a wooden pallet, beside which I had assembled, in order of likely need, some reading material, a flask of bourbon, a notebook, and a twelve-gauge shotgun. In Whitehorse I had obtained a sundry permit to carry the shotgun, along with a field guide to bears written for the Yukon placer mining industries. In the dusky window light I read the chapter entitled "Reacting." "It should be emphasized that a very small proportion of Bear attacks result in fatalities or serious disfigurement. People are usually knocked over and perhaps bitten before the Bear runs off."

I closed my eyes and tried to forget what I had just read.

What I remembered instead were bear stories. When I first came to Alaska, I listened to every blowhard with a gory tale to tell. The stories were standard campfire fare and largely interchangeable, the bear always playing the role of primordial serial killer, the fanged grizzly of the outdoor magazines. As a result, I always felt some foreboding, some menace lurking in the woods. A menace I wasn't above sharing. Once, with malicious glee, I regaled a visiting friend with the latest atrocities just to watch him tremble in his sleeping bag. Now, with no one to tell me the tired tales, the maulings and the mutilations, the half-fables and outright lies, I told them to myself.

My only encounter with a bear in the wild, however, suggested an animal of a different stripe. It was a meeting so vague and anticlimactic that it hardly seems worth the telling. I was hunting in the hills behind Panguingue Creek and had descended an alder swale on my way back to the cabin. I parted some branches and revealed a glistening pyramid of bear shit steaming in the cool autumn air. Blood pounded in my ears, and the rifle I carried suddenly felt puny and insubstantial. Breathless, I turned to flee, and ran toward a clearing, where I found the ground torn open and the dirt heaped in mounds as grizzlies will do when digging for ground squirrels. Looking around wildly, I heard a deep, sharp grunt. The sound appeared to come from behind every tree. Yet there was no attack, nothing to report of the meeting but my own dread. Later, retelling the incident, I emphasized my cool head in the face of terror and not the beast that had coughed so politely, like a man entering a room, to announce its presence.

A rustling came from a corner of the cabin. I sat bolt upright and searched in the dimness for the looming shadow. A mouse scampered over my sleeping bag. When another mouse chased after the first, I hurled my boot at it. The scampering stopped. But in a minute it began all over, accompanied by a high-pitched trilling. In the end there was nothing to do but dig deeper into my sleeping bag and listen to the mice frolic.

The Teslin River entered the Yukon just across from Hootalinqua, muddying the water and widening its avenue. Beyond the terraced valley, the Semenof Hills, spring green with leafing poplar, rose to five thousand feet. Linear stands of spruce defined the lines of drainage on the hills, while patches of snow still lingered in the high saddles.

I stopped on an island in the middle of the channel, where a canopy of alders grew up around an old stern-wheeler. The three-story boat had been pulled ashore for repairs and left to decay. Its roof had slumped into the staterooms on the upper Texas deck and branches probed the pilothouse. The riverboat had been operated by two owners under different names, so *Norcom* had been painted above the water line on one side of the bow and *Evelyn* on the other — like a sailor with a tattoo for each romance.

Wrecked steamboats and old cabins were fragments of a history that wanted to be deciphered. Instead, I let the river carry me downstream. There was no hurry. I was traveling on river time now. My itinerary was fixed by the river's course, and the current set my timetables. River time has nothing to do with Greenwich Standard. It is a circular flow, a cross-section of past and present, cutting through time and space just as the river itself wears down its banks. Drifting down the Yukon, one sees the same river that G. I. Cameron saw on patrol, that all the other river travelers saw. Beyond the next bend, just out of sight, is Schwatka's heaving raft; around a farther bend, a flotilla of Tutchone canoes. The changes are infinitesimal against the backdrop of mountains and woods. Alterations tend to be cyclical: the regeneration of forests, the seasonal migrations of fish and birds, the extremes of weather. To fix one's place in river time, everything must be cross-referenced, like counting growth rings on a salmon's scales. The time lines are horizontal as well as vertical — history, geology, the mythology of the Distant Time — all of them tributaries flowing together to form this single, ongoing river.

Reaching the abandoned Indian village at the mouth of the Big Salmon River, I found three boatloads of Germans already encamped. In their big-pocketed brush pants, they lounged around a campfire like healthy young *Wermacht*. One of them wore a mosquito net on his head like a lamp shade. I recalled that Jack London's books, with their blond, blue-eyed heroes, were very popular in Germany. Perhaps that was why I often had the feeling the Yukon was a tributary of the Rhine.

Lazily, the Germans watched as I pulled my canoe ashore and walked to the fire. The one who seemed to be the leader was a strapping fellow with a big blond beard, who wore wooden clogs on his feet. With him was a sunburned, toad-faced woman, apparently his wife, who followed him everywhere. He watched me paring an apple with my Swiss Army knife and produced his own knife, prying open the blades and gadgets, slowly, one by one. It was an informal challenge. So I opened the rest of my blades.

"Ah, you see!" he shouted. "Yours has no corkscrew!"

One of the younger Germans who'd been casting from the bank asked if I would motor him a short distance up the Big Salmon to fish. His name was Joaquin, and as we headed against the current he confided that the blond fellow was not of their party. In fact, they had been trying to lose him for days.

"No one likes him. He is, you know, all the time talking."

The river was low and reedy, and Joaquin flayed the water to no effect. He appeared to be growing a beard, but when he slapped his cheeks the bristles became mosquitoes and flew away. When I offered him repellent, he shook his head.

"I have an allergy."

He'd had much better luck the day before, he said, catching sixty grayling in a deep green pool below Hootalinqua.

I wheeled the canoe around and took him back to shore.

While the Germans brewed tea over their campfire, I made the rounds of the empty village. The cabins were arranged in a ring facing the confluence and the hills beyond, half a dozen in all, framed with dovetail notches, their roofs overgrown with luxuriant grass. Canoeists had left a collection of liquor bottles on the floor of one of the cabins, but the original inhabitants had left behind very little. There was none of the attendant rubbish of a quick departure. At the turn of the century, Big Salmon had a population of fifty Tutchone Indians, who cut wood under contract for the steamboats and trapped in winter. The main purpose of the steamboats had been to haul ore from the silver mine at Keno, and when the highway made it cheaper to truck the ore, the big boats stopped running. With no way of getting freight, the people simply moved to the highway, which was a river of another sort, only dusty and smelling of diesel.

A line of dark clouds was spilling through a gap in the hills to the west. The wind picked up, and the Germans moved their gear into the tighter cabins. Not wanting to be holed up with this bunch, I pushed on down the river for Little Salmon. But the rain overtook me, and for three hours I motored on in a steady downpour until I came to the head of a sandbar where two men shrouded in rain ponchos stood over a smoldering fire. I beached the canoe and joined them at the campfire. They were Germans as well, a social worker and a tall, bearded architect. Digging into their food sack, they came up with a tin of corned beef, so I dug into my sack and came up with a packet of instant hot chocolate, and in this way we shared supper.

They were generous with their food and tent space, and I liked them very much. The two were bicycling around the country, picking up work when they ran out of money. This was their second trip down the Yukon to Dawson. They kept coming back to the Yukon, they said, because things were ruined at home.

"In Germany there are rivers," the architect explained, "but the water isn't clean, and you need permission to camp on the shore. Once I went to Scandinavia on holiday and saw these beautiful, clear blue lakes with no fish in them. The water was like vinegar."

Here on the Yukon, he said, one didn't mind the rain and the mosquitoes and the bad dreams about bears because this was wilderness, perhaps the last true wilderness left.

As the architect said this, we heard the whine of a truck gearing down on the long grade to Carmacks. The spell was broken, and we slipped quietly into our tents to sleep.

4 ⫽ PIONEERS

THE KLONDIKE HIGHWAY parallels the river for several miles before crossing it on a two-span iron bridge at Carmacks. I camped beside the bridge and listened all night to trucks rumble overhead. The intervals between their passage were musical with night bird songs and swift water piling against the footings. Built too low to accommodate high-stacked steamboats, the bridge had assured Carmacks' survival while sealing the fate of other settlements downstream. The bridge also linked the town with an Indian village across the river. A satellite dish and Indian spirit houses, equally pale in the twilight, faced each other from opposing hilltops, sending and receiving vastly different messages.

The next day a steady stream of Indians crossed over the bridge from the village. The foot traffic was all one-way. On the road into town, an old woman asked me to light her cigarette, cupping my hand shakily as she leaned her face into the match.

I spent the heat of the day on a bar stool in the air-conditioned Carmacks Hotel and drank beer with one of the truck drivers. He'd driven from Whitehorse in as many hours as it had taken me days by canoe. His cap was tilted back on his forehead, and he hailed everyone who came into the bar by asking, "What the hell are you doing here?"

After the trucker left, I asked the barmaid if anybody remembered what the town had been like before the bridge. She made a face when I suggested talking to someone in the village.

"They're ignorant," she said, swabbing the bar with a damp rag. "I don't like them. They won't talk to you."

If I really wanted to talk to a genuine pioneer, I should see Frank Goulter. "He used to work on the steamboats," she said, and gave me directions to his cabin.

It was a hot day for walking. A swallowtail butterfly fluttered ahead of me down the gravel road. I passed a boarded-up log roadhouse and crossed a wooden bridge over the Nordenskiold River, a dazzling little stream, before realizing that I'd messed up the directions. I leaned against the bridge railing, trying to figure out where I'd gone wrong, when a rain shower came up suddenly. I ducked into a gap-toothed cabin partially hidden under a roof of willow suckers and long grass hanging from the eaves. The cabin had no floor, and I had to share the place with swarms of mosquitoes. But it was dry inside, and when the rain cloud moved on, so did I.

The Goulter cabin stood on a bend in the Yukon, waist deep in rhubarb, its arched gable posts painted bright red. As I made for the porch, a snarling elkhound lunged at the end of its tether as if wanting nothing more than to tear out my throat.

A broad-faced man in a blue checked shirt stepped onto the porch.

"Oh, hush up!" he said to the dog. Then to me: "He's tied, so he can't hurt you. Are you lost, or did you want to see me?"

"You," I said. "I wanted to ask about the steamboats."

Frank Goulter was shy and friendly in the manner of older bachelors. When I told him I was traveling down the river, he asked me inside.

The cabin was as densely furnished as a Victorian drawing room. Butterfly collections in lacquered frames hung from the papered walls. There were burgundy throw rugs on the floor, a bowl of toffees on the round Hepplewhite table, and potted geraniums on the windowsills. A stuffed grouse, smoky with age, stared down from the top of a china hutch along with a great ticking clock.

As a boy, Frank Goulter had decked and fired the boiler on the *Casca II*, flagship of the Yukon stern-wheeler fleet. He was on the downstream run to Dawson in 1936 when the *Casca II* struck the wreck of another ship in Rink Rapids and sank in two and a half minutes. Frank and the crew spent the next two weeks rowing a dinghy inside the broken hull in water up to the bulkheads, trying to salvage the two hundred tons of freight aboard.

When I pressed him further about the past, he suggested I talk to his mother.

"She's not feeling too well. But I'll see if she'll talk to you."

He disappeared into a back room and returned with a very, very old woman hobbling on a crutch. Ida May Goulter wore her hair in a long silver braid that hung down to her waist. She had a shrunken mouth, but her eyes were clear and gray and sly. Sitting with one hand on her lap, the other resting on her cheek, she said that she had cancer. She planned to move to Whitehorse soon because the winters here were too cold for her. The cold came right up through the floorboards. She called her son Frankie, and they argued over the date the *Casca II* sank. They each had their own television set.

The elkhound was still baying in the yard. When I mentioned how it had terrified me, Ida seemed enormously pleased.

"We found that if you had a *really* mean dog," she said, "he'd make the best work dog you could imagine. Indians would say, 'Frankie Goulter's out on the road!' And they wouldn't go near because of his dogs. Oh, they'd fight with other dogs and bite people, but they made such a wonderful team!"

Frankie must have come by his shyness from his father, because Ida Goulter was tough-minded and talkative. When I asked about the old days, she fixed me with a contented, sphinxlike smile before going on to describe a world that had utterly closed behind her.

Ida's father had come north in the first wave of the Klondike stampede, leaving behind a wife and daughters in Minneapolis. He lost one of his party, a doctor's wife, crossing the Chilkoot Pass when an avalanche buried her sled, but he rafted the rest safely through the canyons and rapids, having learned to run rough water as a lumberjack on the St. Croix. After the hoopla of the gold rush, he and his brothers stayed on to prospect and cut cordwood for the steamboats. Four years after he had left, he sent three hundred dollars in an unsealed envelope to bring his wife and daughters north. Carried from hand to hand, the envelope arrived in Minneapolis a year later still unsealed, the money inside.

"We were living out in the country on a farm when the letter came. Momma said we were going up north and gave away our nice summer dresses. She had a dressmaker make us red flannel underwear and heavy serge dresses, which she packed in a big trunk."

Ida was nine years old when her family boarded a train to Seattle in 1903. From there they traveled by steamer to Skagway, and then by train over the White Pass to Whitehorse, where the family boarded the steamboat *Selkirk*. On a late summer's evening, the boat eased to a stop in mid-river and lowered the gangplank onto a woodcutter's island.

"It was pitch dark and the steamer had to find the landing with its searchlight. Mother said, 'I'm not going to get off in these woods.' But the boatman said, 'Don't worry. They'll be someone along shortly.' We saw a torch coming through the dark woods. It was my Uncle Frank. He'd grown a beard, and my mother said, 'Oh look, there's a tramp!' "

They lived at the wood camp across from Eagle Bluff for four years. Ida and her sister studied arithmetic, music, and recitation from books packed in the steamer trunk. (She recited for me the first few lines of "A Storm on Lake Michigan.") There was another woodcutter on the river, a one-armed man, who would walk to their cabin every Friday to sing with Ida's father and uncles all night long.

Listening to Ida recall her youth was like trying to remember the details of a dream. There was the same baffling mixture of the familiar and strange. What struck me was not so much the trappings of the past, the commodes and dog sled teams, but how fundamentally our lives have changed. It's not just that the pace has quickened, but that we have so many more choices and want to try them all. In science fiction, the time traveler always fumbles with gizmos and inventions, when the real adjustment would be to the human heart. Geography has kept the Yukon to a slower pace, so that if I wasn't exactly traveling backward in time, I often had the illusion of drifting more slowly in the present. The cheerfulness of the old people I'd met made me think it was easier to inch forward, dragging along memories of horse-drawn cutters and all-night singalongs, than it was to go in the opposite direction as many of us did, improvising a past we'd never known.

At eighteen, Ida had married an ex-Mountie, a square-jawed Englishman who'd soldiered in the Boer War. The whole town turned out for the wedding, and afterward her husband brought her home to this cabin on a sharp bend in the river. The Goulters ran a silver fox farm and raised two daughters and a son. At that time the government wouldn't pay for a permanent teacher unless a settlement had at least seven white children. Between them, Ida and her neighbors only had five, so they recruited two Indian children to make up the difference. But somebody snitched, and the government took the teacher away.

Now she felt the tables had been turned.

"The government's been too good to the Indians. They've ruined them with free housing."

She didn't approve of mixed marriages, of white women "shacked up with Indians." She recalled with nostalgia the old days when she could look out the window and see an entire Indian family — squaw, kids, dogs — floating down the river on a log raft.

"They didn't care where they landed. They just made camp and used the logs for firewood."

This reminded Frankie of a joke about an old Indian who was rafting down the Pelly River. "He hit a snag and fell in the drink. When they pulled him out, they asked, 'How long were you under the raft?' And the old Indian said, 'Oh, 'bout two 'owl.'" Frankie slapped his knee and repeated the punchline, but I still didn't get it.

"Two hours," Frankie explained. "The old man thought he'd been under two hours." It was a dialect joke.

Sometimes Ida's recollections were unexpectedly poignant, as when she'd describe a person, long dead, in the flush of youth. She talked about her sister, who had married a stableman at the roadhouse and lived just down the road. As a wedding gift, Ida's father had built them a lovely cabin beside the Nordenskiold

River. "Oh, there was a wonderful garden there," she said. "But that's all gone to trees now." It was the same ruined cabin I had ducked into that afternoon to escape the rain.

Back in the present, Ida said she was feeling tired and limped back to her room. I heard the television switch on as Frank Goulter walked me out to the yard. He asked when I was getting back on the river.

"Tomorrow."

"When you hit Five Finger Rapids, take the right channel. Hit it head on and you'll have no trouble."

The party of Germans who perished in Five Finger Rapids two years before had attempted the middle channel and capsized their canoes. One managed to cling to his canoe, then tried to save his pack and lost his life with the others. The rapids were not terribly difficult, and all down the Yukon one heard theories about why the Germans had drowned: they had been drinking; they had been asleep in their boats; they had not understood the directions given them. Whatever; the Germans, who were just passing through, had by drowning entered the mythology of the river.

Rounding a bend in a steep sandstone canyon, I heard a sound like wind through trees and then saw the looming, digital islands splitting the river into five separate channels. Close up, the islands looked like stone pilings from a ruined bridge. The navigable channel lay between the last island on the right and the sheer rock bank, an alley just wide enough for a stern-wheeler to squeeze through. Bucking the racehorse current, steamboats had winched themselves through the rapids by attaching an anchored cable to a windlass on the deck.

I swung the canoe hard to the right. The narrow turnstile of water between the island and bank seemed a fairly straight shot. As the sun fell behind a cliff, the air turned cool and damp. The river contracted, accelerating into a smooth tongue of water as it entered the chute. With no place to go, the water piled into a sawtooth ridge of foamy swells flanked by powerful side eddies. The first wave caught the canoe under the bow. The canoe lifted momentarily, then slammed into the green trough as if descending a staircase. Was this how the Germans had awakened — a sudden lurch and then into the drink? A second wave broke over the bow and drenched my gear. When the canoe crashed into the next wave, I looked for the shore in case I'd have to swim for it. Then suddenly I was in the clear. The river leveled off and the roar was behind me. I felt that sudden absolution of fear typical of takeoffs and landings, the quick prayers quickly forgotten.

Below Rink Rapids, where the *Casca II* had come to grief, the Yukon broadened into sluggish, island-choked flats. Along the cutbank ran a continuous band of white volcanic ash, several inches thick and sandwiched between layers of alluvium. The ash came from an ancient eruption in the Saint Elias Range. Carried east by the wind, the powdery band had been deposited centuries ago in a blinding snowfall of ashes. The Indians who must have witnessed this extraordinary storm left no record either of it or of themselves, so the only history of the event was written here in the cutbank.

At Yukon Crossing, I caught a northern pike in a slough and cooked it for lunch in a clearing where the old Overland Trail disappeared into a vault of prickly rose. Feeling well fed and indolent, I stretched out in the grass beside the fire. The rapids were behind me now, and tomorrow the unimpeded river would deliver me to Fort Selkirk. A straight shot. I had been so many hours in a canoe that the ground under my back seemed to rock slightly. I looked up at the sky, through overhanging branches. Along the riverbank the cottonwoods were in seed. The slightest breeze filled the china-blue sky with a blizzard of cottony fluff that fell to earth like snow, like ashes carried on the wind.

Today was the summer solstice, the longest day. I'd nearly forgotten. Days on the river tended to run seamlessly together. But in Fairbanks, after the long winter, I had always celebrated this date with a pagan fervor. It was the pivotal point on which the year turned, at once the apex of sunlight and start of the long slide toward darkness. Every summer, a woman I knew threw a solstice party at her cabin. A volleyball net was strung up in the dusty yard, and we'd play into the next day. Teams were not rigidly fixed, and there was a constant flux of substitutes; at any one moment, the net arbitrarily divided husbands and wives, friends and lovers. A player might unintentionally spike the ball into an opponent's face, but as a rule the play was good-natured and unaggressive. Nobody bothered to keep score.

After a winter's lull, it was reassuring to see the same faces, everyone still in their twenties, still content to drift along in life. When we gathered in T-shirts and jeans to play another game, it wasn't just to celebrate another year's passage but to show one another that we had remained unchanged.

We'd play for hours without tiring. The constant twilight made for limitless energy. The volleyball game seemed to operate on the ritual principle of imitation: as long as the ball stayed in motion, the sun wouldn't set. At most it rolled behind the bordering woods. And even then, enough light remained to faintly see the small white ball on its erratic flight over the net.

Today was the summer solstice. How could I have forgotten?

On the globe I owned as a child, Fort Selkirk appeared in the same bold type as Boston and Dublin. The North seemed crowded with metropolises, until I learned that mapmakers merely dislike empty splashes of color. During the gold rush, Fort Selkirk seemed destined to become the territorial capital, located as it is halfway between Whitehorse and Dawson. A garrison of soldiers was barracked here to show the flag to American prospectors. Streets were laid out, a township plotted, a railway surveyed from the railhead at Whitehorse. But nothing came of it. The history of Fort Selkirk was one of missed opportunities.

Fort Selkirk's founder was a Scottish sheep farmer's son from Perthshire named Robert Campbell. (Hudson's Bay Company had a penchant for staffing its lonely outposts with Scots, who could be counted on to endure the miserable weather and miserly wages.) Campbell had already made a reputation for opening up new country to the fur trade as well as displaying a cool head and astonishing endurance. But the posts he established at Dease Lake, Frances Lake, and Pelly Banks were only jumping-off points, for the jewel in the crown was yet to come.

In June 1843, Campbell and a mixed crew of Indian and

French-Canadian *engagés* descended the westward-flowing Pelly River in a birchbark canoe. On the sixth day, they followed a high basalt cliff on the right bank until they reached a large greenish river flowing from the southwest. Campbell mistook the larger river for a tributary of the Pelly and named it the Lewes. He had, in fact, become the first European to glimpse the upper Yukon.

Five years later, Campbell returned to the forks of the Yukon and Pelly and established a trading post named for Lord Selkirk, sponsor of the Red River Settlement. The local Tutchone Indians were eager to trade, but Campbell had brought only a paltry outfit and spent the fall building the post and hunting meat for winter.

Distance made the logistics of the fur trade exceedingly complex. Seven years normally elapsed between the time goods were shipped to a post like Selkirk and the time the furs purchased by those goods reached the market in London. The first half of the circular route was as follows: across the Atlantic to York Factory on Hudson Bay; by river and portage to Norway House, a trading post on Peel River; across the mountains to La Pierre's House; and then on to Fort Selkirk in the fourth year. Campbell, although an intrepid explorer, proved a poor businessman. His records were a shambles. His other posts, difficult to maintain and unprofitable, were abandoned one by one. At Selkirk, he was undersupplied by the company and undersold by his competitors, the coastal Tlingits.

The Tlingits had exercised a virtual trade monopoly on the upper Yukon before Campbell's arrival. They controlled the mountain passes, acting as middlemen between Russian and British traders on the Pacific and the interior tribes. With the virtual extermination of sea otters on the coast, the inland fur trade took on increased importance. Late each summer, the Tlingits scaled the Chilkoot Pass and rafted down the Yukon to barter with the local tribes. Then, strapping hundred-pound bales of fur on their backs, they tramped back to the coast. To the Tlingits, even a little competition was too much.

On August 19, 1852, Campbell and a handful of men were cutting hay across the river from Fort Selkirk when five rafts of

Tlingits hove into view. The timing could not have been worse. The Tutchone, whom Campbell relied on for protection, were downriver and half his own men were on a trading trip. Pickets for a stockade had been cut but lay useless in the grass.

Campbell and the men paddled quickly back to the fort, but the Tlingits had already gained the upper hand. All night he watched helplessly as armed Tlingits wandered about, trying doors and windows on the storehouse. In the morning, the storm broke. Roaring like fiends, the Tlingits began smashing everything in the storehouse. They seized Campbell and his men as if to massacre the lot. In his diary, Campbell wrote: "Our sins must have been great ere our merciful Creator gave us to these unmerciful savages."

But the Tlingits only rousted their prisoners to the riverbank and cast them off in boats. For a day and a night, Campbell and his men drifted downstream, stopping to pick up others who had fled into the woods. Reaching a Tutchone camp the next noon, Campbell persuaded the Indians to return with him to Selkirk. But they arrived to find that the raiders had already fled and what had not been carried off lay "smashed into a thousand atoms." Campbell, his heart bent on revenge, called for pursuit. But the Tutchone prudently declined.

Campbell then embarked on a legendary and pointless journey. Traveling to Fort Simpson, he begged for men and supplies to avenge the attack and rebuild Fort Selkirk. But his supervisor would not authorize a reprisal and advised Campbell to file a report and wait. It was now November. Determined to plead his case in person to the Hudson's Bay Company governor, George Simpson, Campbell set off alone on snowshoes in the dead of winter. With only dogs to carry his supplies, he traveled three thousand miles through uninhabited country, stopping only at scattered posts, until he reached the roadhead at Crow Wing, Minnesota.

Arriving at Simpson's winter quarters near Montreal in late March, Campbell repeated the story to his old mentor. Although personally sympathetic, Simpson privately held Fort Selkirk to be a losing proposition. (The Hudson's Bay Company did not reopen a store there until 1938.) To soften the blow, he persuaded Campbell to take a furlough back to Scotland since he'd come this far. Campbell never again saw Fort Selkirk. As for the Tutchone, they had no recourse but to resume trade with the Tlingits. Perhaps they already had a premonition that white men would come and go.

I drifted down to Fort Selkirk through a maze of alder islands and rocky shoals. The Pelly River entered from the east, along the base of a high tableland of black columnar basalt skirted with scree. I could see the old settlement just downriver from the confluence, a row of cabin roofs showing above the gravel bank. A shirtless workman on a scaffold was hammering cedar shakes onto the steeple of the Anglican church. The staccato of hammer blows seemed disconnected, the sound reaching me just after the nail had been driven.

I tied the bow painter to a tree root and climbed the cutbank. Selkirk lay stretched out along the grassy bank, a ghost village heat-wavering under the midday sun.

In its latest incarnation, Selkirk was being restored as a historical park. When the steamboat era had come to an end, the Indians from Selkirk moved upriver to Minto and then to Pelly Crossing, where the government built them houses. Now the government was rehabilitating their old homes for tourists like myself to poke around in. The result was a sanitized village with no heaps of old sleds or broken-down snow machines in the yards, no rich confusion of smells of drying fish and motor oil, and no villagers except a caretaker and the seasonal work crew. Most of the crew were Indians from Pelly Crossing — sons of families that had abandoned Selkirk when the highway was built. Some of the men had brought their families and even a few horses along for the summer. A pair of black-haired children were playing beside their grampa's collapsed cabin. When I asked what they did for fun, one of them grinned and said, "Frisbee!"

I pushed open a cabin door to a dim, square room smelling damply of old bedding. A yellow china cabinet stood in a corner and white muslin sagged from the log walls. Hanging on one wall was a montage of tinted holy cards strung together with cotton twine. Under the colored pictures were captions like

"Jesus Enters Jerusalem" or "St. Peter Delivered from Prison." One card, entitled "An Eskimo Learns of the Child King," showed a slack-jawed youngster in a caribou parka. I turned it over to read the Bible lesson on the other side. "Question: Where was the Holy Child King born? Answer: The Holy Child King was born in a stable in Bethlehem."

I pictured an Indian child passing a dreary hour in Sunday school. Would he have thought of the king born in a stable, or of the other king, the one with a pointed beard who lived in Windsor Castle?

In the cook tent, Eric Clapton's "Lay Down, Sally" blasted from a tapedeck, while the young bullcook tapped out a rhythm on the counters with a knife and spoon. He'd been *chef de parte* at the Banff Springs Hotel, carving centerpieces out of ice and butter, but liked camp work better. "You cook one thing," he said. "You don't have to diddle around all day."

He pulled a rhubarb pie with a delicately fluted crust from the oven. When it cooled, he sliced us each a piece to eat with our coffee. The rhubarb tasted sweet and tart, having been cut that morning from the shady spot beside an old cabin.

The cook had a limitless supply of off-color stories that always began, "That reminds me of a joke." He also had a girlfriend who sang at the Palace Grand Theatre in Dawson. "She's the pretty one," he confided. But when I asked about the old Selkirk, he said I was barking up the wrong tree.

"Talk to Danny Roberts," he said. "Danny's never really left."

Danny Roberts found me before I could find him. Born in Selkirk, he was an Indian who had stayed on after the town's abandonment. He wore a Chinaman's beard, rainbow-colored suspenders, and a visored cap with "Yukon Parks" written above the bill. He carried a ledger, which he opened to the current date.

"Going to be another hot one today," he said, looking off while I signed my name. Since the early sixties, he'd been employed by the territorial government as caretaker to scrape snow off the roofs and keep the vandals at bay.

"Not many people coming through this summer," he said, and took the ledger back.

We walked over to the cutbank, where he was building

a plywood riverboat, using the work crew's generator to run his saw and planer. The boat lay inverted on sawhorses, a flat-bottomed craft with flaring sides and a slant front. He worked without plans, following blueprints that existed only in his head.

Until the workmen came in the summers to renovate, Danny Roberts and his wife were the only residents of Selkirk. He had been a riverboat pilot on the *Casca III* and made a living as a woodcutter, floating hundred-cord rafts down to Dawson. He was downriver cutting wood when Selkirk was abandoned, in 1952. When the Robertses returned, Selkirk looked as if it had been swept by a plague. Tables were set with china, tools abandoned in the grass; furniture, stoves, bedding — everything that couldn't be carried had been left behind because of high shipping rates. So the town became Danny's by default. He found himself sole proprietor of the one-room school he'd attended, the RCMP post, the Taylor and Drury Store, the log cabin he'd grown up in, and all the houses of his neighbors.

Roberts stayed on because his trap line was here and he saw no reason to leave. He netted King salmon below the bluff in summer and trapped across the river in winter. There were only a couple of weeks on either side of winter when he could not cross the Yukon by boat or snowmobile. After freeze-up, he crossed the ice like a tightrope walker, carrying a long pole to tap on the ice for thickness and to catch him if he broke through.

The winter before, Roberts's wife had died. A daughter lived thirty-eight miles upriver at Pelly Crossing but he rarely visited. "Too much drinking in Pelly." Twenty years had gone by since Roberts visited Dawson. The last time he had gone to Whitehorse was 1956. Unlike the whites I'd met along the river, Roberts did not view his own life as adventurous because he'd never lived anywhere else nor wanted to, which seems extraordinary enough these days.

In Carmacks I'd heard plenty of white-Indian disparagement. Much of it stemmed from pending settlement of Native land claims, which some Yukoners look upon with the same unease with which Southerners must have viewed Reconstruction. But

relations between the races tend to swing on a pendulum. In narratives of exploration, individual Natives figure prominently because the explorer depended upon their good graces and often married into the tribe to cement good relations. (Campbell mentions two helpful Tutchone chiefs, a father and son with the marvelous names Thlin-ikik-Thling and Hanan, who warned him of attack if he proceeded downriver.) To the indigenous population, however, the pioneers' transition from explorer to settler signaled their demotion. Arriving at the end of a long journey, the newcomer saw himself as the hero in an unfolding adventure; the Indians were merely part of the scenery. In diaries of pioneers, they emerge as little more than a nuisance, squatters who fade nameless and faceless into obscurity.

In the afternoon, a caravan of three powerboats landed below Selkirk. The party included the commissioner of the Yukon, a Mountie, several Alaskans, and its leader, G. I. Cameron. While the others held his boat steady, Cameron jumped ashore, but he insisted on lugging his own gear up the steep bank. He wore his trousers stuffed into rubber Wellingtons and the same tartan plaid shirt he'd worn the morning we'd talked in Whitehorse. Aware that this was a sentimental return, the rest of the group clicked away with cameras as Cameron gained the riverbank.

The commissioner, who'd been momentarily eclipsed by Cameron as the center of attention, inspected the grounds. He wore his hat cocked on the side of his head and walked with a sailor's rolling gait. He squinted up at the Maple Leaf snapping at the end of the flagpole.

"Remind me to send them a new flag. That one's a disgrace."

The group arrived in an ebullient mood at the old RCMP post, its front yard overgrown with fireweed and foxtail. Standing in the center of his former home, Cameron blocked out the vanished furnishings.

"Dining room here. Bedroom there. Big heater right over here. Kept the whole place warm except when it got down to seventy below and ice started coming through the walls."

The kitchen floor in the rear of the cabin had buckled. Cameron pointed out where the fruit cellar had been.

"We ate moose and caribou. Salmon in season. Bought fresh beef from the riverboats until freeze-up. We'd keep eggs cool in the fruit cellar, turning them around all winter so they'd keep better. Oh, they had a wonderful taste by spring!"

Someone asked, "Where was the jail, Cam?"

"The living room. When I went on patrol, I'd just tell the wife, 'Now if they get out of hand, just sit on them!' "

"Where did you hang 'em, Cam?"

It was a facetious question since Selkirk rarely had a crime worth hanging someone for. But Cameron had seen men hung in Dawson; the hangman had been imported from the East to do the job. He remembered one prisoner's words, just before being strung up: "Okay, make it snappy."

I attached myself to the commissioner's party as they followed a worn path into the woods behind the town. Segments of telegraph wire lay on the ground or dangled from poles, part of a line that once connected Dawson to Vancouver. Then the woods opened up to a log church standing in a clearing. The walls were chinked with mud and straw, its belfry weathered to a fine silver. French-Canadian oblates had built the church to overlook the river, then changed their minds and skidded it back here, away from the Anglicans. When the work crew arrived, the church had badly slumped on its foundation. The crew replaced the rotten sills with fire-killed timber that was already aged and presented no problems with shrinkage.

Doug Whooton, a retired contractor, was in charge of the reconstruction.

"We're not restoring at this point. We're just underpinning floors and roofs — I hope in time to restore the old wall and floor coverings. The eventual aim is to turn this place into a kind of museum."

Behind the church, an Indian cemetery stretched into the woods. The graves were contained behind wooden fences, the hand-carved palings diamond shaped or squared like bedposts. In the rising heat, we walked among them, stooping down to read names and dates sunk into gray wood. Many of the dead had been children, cut down by an influenza epidemic that swept the Yukon in 1918. Spruce trees had sprouted within some of the palings and blanketed the graves with a fine layer of needles and tiny pine cones.

The temperature was 87 degrees in the shade. Stripping down to running shorts, I plunged into the river. The water was a cold shock! The current piled against me, undermining the loose gravel beneath my feet. Riding in a canoe on the surface gave no hint of the river's sheer power. Give it half a chance, you think, and the river would sweep you to the sea. The current was too strong to fight, so I let it carry me feet first past the cutbank and row of cabins until I emerged at the far end of town, dripping wet and out of breath. By the time I hobbled back to my tent, I was dry again.

After dinner, there was an impromptu party outside the guest cabin. Cameron's group supplied the Scotch, rum, and beer, while Doug Whooton donated ice cubes from the camp's generator-powered freezer. I brought my flask of bourbon and helped myself freely to the rest. The commissioner, Whooton, Danny Roberts, Cameron, the camp cook, and myself — the past, present, and foreseeable future of Selkirk — assembled around a picnic table by the riverbank. Except for the cook, I was the youngest, and felt exuberant being in such accomplished company, so many doers. These days we're encouraged to stay young, when the real trick is to grow old without becoming apologetic or defeated. Roberts and Whooton were the same age, fifty-seven, and both widowers. In the coming winter, they alone would remain here, running trap lines while the rest of us were comfortably home. For Roberts, this life was a familiar groove, but for Whooton it signaled a new start. Whooton had bought a pair of walkie-talkies so the two of them could chat through the long, dark months.

As the evening wore on, the last of the light climbed the basalt cliff across the river. The battered surface of the water turned a shade of lapis lazuli, and mosquitoes hovered above the picnic table. Danny Roberts blew them away as if exhaling smoke rings. With the sun gone, the temperature fell twenty degrees. I began to shiver and quickly put on a sweater and a wool shirt. The others held out longer, engaged in an unspoken test of endurance to see who could outlast the cold. Finally Cameron pulled on a jacket, then Whooton and Danny Roberts, leaving the commissioner as undisputed iron man. He wore a yellow T-shirt with a slogan stenciled across the chest: SAVE GAS — FART IN A JAR.

At one in the morning, the picnic table was crowded with dead soldiers, a good share of them mine. Loosened up, I babbled more than I had in days.

"That reminds me of a joke," the cook said, testing the waters with a story that hinged upon a honeymoon couple, hunting season, and a broken-down bus. A lull followed; people got up to leave.

Cameron started naming the steamboats that once stopped at Selkirk to put off freight and pick up wood: the *Casca*, the *Whitehorse*, the *Aksala*, the *Klondike*. In summer they ran like trains, on time and belching black smoke. When the big boats drew up to the bank, Cameron would change out of his work clothes and into his scarlet dress uniform to greet the passengers.

"It was just about this time of night," he said, recalling a 1926 voyage on the *Casca*, "that we came on caribou crossing the river below Selkirk. The captain blew the whistle, and people came out of their staterooms just as they were."

Cameron went on, painting Selkirk as he remembered it, a village filled with people, the hills alive with game. Occasionally, he would glance at Danny Roberts for collaboration, although Roberts would have been just a teenager when Cameron was the village policeman.

"Caribou used to come through by the thousands. I've seen fifty to a hundred go right through town here, Indians shooting at them with .22s, just like buffalo on the prairie. Remember, Danny?"

Danny Roberts nodded and blew away another mosquito.

5 | "TO
BUILD A
FIRE"

THE DAY AFTER the party, I slipped quietly out of Selkirk and drifted down the long corridor of river. The valley rose up green and steeply canted, with castellated cliffs like those on the upper Hudson. Stacks of driftwood were heaped at the heads of islands in great bonfire piles, whole trees stranded high and dry, tap roots radiating like spokes. I watched a dust devil swirling along the long white spit of a sandbar. Every so often a creek came in, thick with alder and willow, a riverboat tied to the bank and a path winding back to a cabin. But I kept on without stopping.

I felt talked out. River travel made for an edgy blend of isolation and company. Days passed when I spoke to no one. Then, falling in with a party, I'd talk myself silly. The hard part was the transitions, as abruptly felt as barometric changes, these sudden swings from being too much alone to being caught in a crowd. I kept moving between silence and noise. The ghetto blasters that you see everywhere in villages along the Yukon aren't used to create space, as they are in cities, but to fill it in. Here the country is so immense, so full of space, that it soaks up sound. After a long, solitary drift, I wanted company and hearty campfire chatter; a few hours later I'd be ready for some trackless sandbar and life as Robinson Crusoe.

Homesteaders must view the summer with mixed feelings. After a winter of counting whole valleys their own, they have to share them with canoeists who drift by, jabbering in English and German, poking around, asking questions. When I talked to some soft-spoken pioneer in the quiet of his cabin, my voice was so amplified, by comparison, that it seemed to issue from a bullhorn. Behind the questions about trap lines and steamboats, what I really wondered was: Are you happy? Is this enough? Trying to read their faces was like reading the river. Nothing showed on the surface except a wry grin like a two-way mirror that said: Of course we're happy or we'd have left long ago. But also: Why are you here?

Below the mouth of the Selwyn River, I passed a cow moose and calf swimming along the shore. The cow moose had an ungainly, Lincolnesque head with soulful eyes and a pendant beard. Stilt-legged, she scrambled up the willow bank, but her calf couldn't get purchase and drifted down the river with me. The cow didn't care much for this arrangement. She crashed along the shore until the calf found a low bank and climbed from the water. I waved good-by. The cow only shot me an incendiary look and turned, big-hipped, into the willow.

The Yukon was changing day to day, shifting gears, picking up momentum. The White River, entering from a gap in the hills to the west, doubled the size of the Yukon and ruined its clarity. I climbed a hill to see the T-shaped confluence; the mouth of the White was a maze of braided channels with driftwood logs stranded on the sandbars. Robert Campbell named the White for the milky sediment it carries down from glaciers high in the Wrangell Mountains and Saint Elias Range. The Tlingits called it the River of Sand: the water was exactly that buff color. You couldn't tell it from the sandbars except for its pulsing movement. For maybe a mile, the two rivers flow side by side until the White dissolves its glacial load into the Yukon, turning it into a yellow cement wash. From here on, the Yukon is opaque with silt except in winter, when the glaciers stop melting and the river runs clear under the ice. Now at the height of summer flow, the silty water makes a slightly abrasive sound, like sandpaper, against the canoe's hull.

In late afternoon, I watched three big cumulus clouds towing rain and blue shadows across the valley until they jammed up downriver. A flash of lightning, thunder rolling over the hills, and I bumped onto the nearest sandbar. There was the rush to put up the tent and rainfly, then the long wait inside as the heat gathered. The storm when it came broke like a fever, bringing a cool breeze and an end to the quiet. Raindrops fell heavily at first and then settled into a steady drumming on the tent.

A sudden bout of loneliness, nameless and unexpected, overtook me like the rain. It was accompanied by a tightness in the chest and the conviction that I was, literally, shrinking. I lay on my sleeping bag hugging my knees to my chest until the ache passed. Isolation has a scouring quality. While it had left people like Danny Roberts with lilting smiles, having worn down the rough edges, it must wear others down until there's nothing left. I often wondered how I'd do here if left to my own devices. Badly, I think.

Lately, I'd missed my ex-wife, which surprised me since there were more recent women to dwell on. Now, instead of the fights and recriminations, what I remembered were pleasant moments: reading to each other in bed, picking berries, long talks. I would rather have remembered the fights. After a divorce there's an inclination to shift geography and start fresh, but at every bend this place reminded me of her and how it had felt to be young in a new country. The irony was that she grew to hate the North and would never have dreamed of coming back. But in my memory she was forever stuck here. I'd hear the four-note song of a fox sparrow or pick up the jackknife she'd given me, and it would all come back — the good years together and all the things done badly.

For lonely nights, I devised a form of tent therapy. First I poured a drink and mixed it with boiled river water, which gave the bourbon an ashy taste. Then I unscrolled a topographical map, the country in miniature, on the tent floor. Canadian charts are very beautiful, rivers a brilliant azure flowing through chartreuse valleys and ranges of sienna mountains. With my fingertip, I traced the Yukon and arrived by dead reckoning at a likely spot below the White River. It was comforting to fix my position, to locate myself at certain quadrants, to say I occupy this precise point in time and space. Here.

The sun reached its zenith by mid-morning and turned my nylon tent into a hothouse. Feeling drugged and thick-headed, I crawled out on my hands and knees to fix breakfast. Coffee was the only antidote. Beneath the sun's glare, the sand and gravel island held a terrible radiance.

In a torpor, I gathered twigs and dry grass stranded from highwater. Scooping a depression in the sand, I laid down a gridwork of tinder and driftwood and struck a match, playing out the pivotal scene in Jack London's "To Build a Fire." As a boy, it was my favorite story, the first one I read without coaxing, and the particular details remained fixed in my head: the amber streak of tobacco juice on the prospector's beard; the brindled, pragmatic sled dog. In the throbbing heat of summer, it was hard to imagine a man freezing to death. But from where I sat, gazing downriver toward the confluence of the Yukon and the Stewart rivers, I looked out over the very country that had inspired the tragedy.

Jack London spent his only season in the North on a spruce-covered island at the mouth of the Stewart River. A square-shouldered youth of twenty-one, with curly brown hair and deep-set blue eyes, he watched from his cabin doorway as the winter sun rose late in the morning over one range of hills and disappeared a few hours later behind another. In London's stories, it was always winter, the temperature falling, the country a sprung trap. Darkness, silence, the unearthly cold — these were the perimeters of London's North.

The year before, Jack had toiled as a work beast in an Oakland laundry, having dropped out of the University of California for lack of funds. His deliverance came when the northern steamship *Excelsior* docked in San Francisco, laden with gold and the first news of the Klondike strike. His brother-in-law, a man of sixty with a heart condition, offered to grubstake the two of them in exchange for Jack's strong back. Eleven days later, they boarded the *Umatilla* bound for the Yukon.

London's brother-in-law, complaining of rheumatism, turned back soon after the boat reached Skagway, but Jack had already joined company with four other stampeders, all his senior. Instead of paying fifty cents a pound to Tlingit packers, Jack lugged his own outfit over the Chilkoot Pass, later bragging of "outpacking many an Indian." At Lake Lindeman, the party hammered together two whipsawed skiffs, rigged them with square sails, and sailed down the mountain lakes into the Yukon River with Jack at the tiller of the lead boat. They drifted past Indians at Little Salmon wearing rings through their noses and, farther on, boatloads of mounted policemen headed for Dawson.

It was early October. With slush ice from the tributaries running in the Yukon, the two boats landed on an island at the mouth of the Stewart River. Stampeders called it Split-up Island since so many partnerships were dissolved there, and London's was no exception. London and his partner decided to stay, while the other boat continued on to Dawson, eighty miles downriver. The decision to stay was logical. Stewart River had been the site of an earlier gold strike and there were abandoned cabins on the island; at Dawson they would have had to settle for a tent on the beach.

The inhabitants of Split-up Island were a far-ranging crew: a German, a Swede, a French-Canadian, a Stanford football star, and an alcoholic physician. The only woman the men saw that winter was a redhead who lived across the river with a ferret-eyed man twenty-five years her senior. Her paramour was a crack shot. Once he took a Winchester from the wall when Jack was visiting and treated him to an impromptu display of marksmanship by putting ten bullets in a piece of tin nailed to a tree.

One of the men had found "colors" across the Yukon on Henderson Creek, and, with the others, London staked five hundred feet of streambed on the left fork of the creek. (This was the destination of the ill-fated *cheechako* in "To Build a Fire.") But the hard work of thawing and digging at the frozen muck didn't appeal to Jack, and the claim went unworked. He was content to spend the winter in the smoky confines of the cabin, playing whist, arguing socialism, and reading. He had carried Milton's *Paradise Lost* and Darwin's *Origin of Species* over the Chilkoot Trail and borrowed a copy of Kipling's *Seven Seas*. Earlier, Jack had devoured the writings of Herbert Spencer, whose biological determinism offered a rationale for his own racial theories. In Jack's eyes, the Yukon was a northern Galapagos, an isolated and harsh proving ground where only the fittest survived. Hadn't the white man taken the Indian's country as his own, besting him at his own game as Jack had "outpacked" the Tlingit packers? In London's most popular book, *The Call of the Wild*, Buck the "outside" dog comes to the North, like Jack, from California and by brute strength and cunning soon dominates the native huskies. The novel, at one level, is an allegory of colonialism, and Buck a stand-in for London's Anglo-Saxon supermen.

But by the end of his first winter, London was barely surviving. A steady diet of bacon, bread, and beans had left him bent double with scurvy. His joints swelled and ached, his skin grew pale and puffy, his teeth rattled loose in his mouth. He resolved to leave the Klondike as soon as the river was open.

Spring came late that year. Balmy May winds blew into the valley from the coast, and the river began to rise. Then with a cataclysmic roar the ice broke, great blocks of it crashing along the shore, scouring the banks. With the river open, Jack and his partners tore apart their cabin, built a raft from the logs, and floated down to Dawson, where they sold the wood for six hundred dollars. The muddy streets of Dawson were filled with dogs, mosquitoes, and new arrivals. Jack met up with two other men ready to quit the country, and together they purchased a "homemade, weak-kneed, and leaky" skiff for the voyage down the Yukon.

They set off from Dawson late in the afternoon, camping the first night in a light rain. The open boat was outfitted with a portable cook stove and a sleeping bunk amidships made of pine boughs and blankets, so the men could travel without stopping to cook or find a place to sleep. Days were tropically hot; in the evenings a smudge fire kept the mosquitoes away. Drifting with the stream, the trio played cards, shot at passing ducks, and took turns at the helm.

Jack preferred the night watches, sailing along beneath the northern twilight while his companions snoozed under mosquito netting. He kept a log of the voyage, the only notes he made of his Klondike experience. He recorded the stern-wheelers passing in the night, bound for Dawson, and how the miners in the camps along the river besieged him for news of the Spanish-American War and the outcome of the Sharkey-Jeffries fight.

In the villages and fish camps on the Yukon, London was both fascinated and repelled by the miscegenation of whites and Indians, the mixture of primitive and civilized blood. In his diary he wrote: "Squaw three quarter breed with a white baby" and "Traces of white blood among the papooses everywhere apparent." From these fleeting glimpses, he would fashion the improbable Natives of his fictions, doomed and brutal characters like Nam-Bok the Unveracious, or Makamuk, the shaman of "Lost Face."

London's scurvy worsened as the trip wore on. At Anvik on the lower Yukon, he obtained fresh potatoes and a can of tomatoes, noting in his diary how the Episcopal missionary had implored them to stay "at least one Christian Sunday." Jack proved to his own satisfaction the shallowness of the Natives' conversion by trading them a pack of playing cards for a crucifix. The party sailed through the Apoon Channel of the delta and up the Bering Sea coast to the port of St. Michael. Jack signed on as a stoker on a steamship bound for home, where he would shortly sit down at a writing table and reinvent the North. He wrote his final diary entry on June 30, three weeks after having departed Dawson: "Leave St. Michael's — unregrettable moment."

Stewart Island, at the mouth of the Stewart River, was probably London's Split-up Island. I landed there below a steep cutbank. A manicured lawn led back from the riverbank to a tin-roofed house painted cerulean blue, like a chunk of sky that had tumbled onto the grass. Behind the house, a middle-aged woman pegged white sheets to a clothesline. The scene was unexpectedly suburban for an island in the midst of a wild river valley. The woman came out to meet me and we talked beside the cutbank. Yvonne Burian wore tinted glasses and had a habit of glancing upriver.

"I didn't see you land," she said. "Usually I can spot a boat well before it gets here."

She couldn't say for certain whether this was the island where

Jack London had wintered, but even if it had been, the cabins had long been lost to the river's slow attrition.

"There was a big meadow there," she said, and pointed into the swirling water. "But it's gone now. The river took it. Some years the river takes ten to twelve feet. One year we lost sixty feet."

Whenever the Yukon gobbled up their front yard, the Burians put the buildings on skids, hitched them to a tractor, and hauled them farther back into the cottonwoods.

"We've had to move the house back. The store's been moved twice. The warehouse three times."

Yvonne's father had been an agent for the White Pass Railway when Stewart Island was a transfer point for barge traffic on the river and the small settlement here was optimistically called Stewart City. There were two roadhouses, a store, a telegraph post, a full-time bootlegger, and a summertime Mountie. Yvonne and her sister were the only children, except when a relief telegraph operator brought his family along. While there were few playmates, the roadhouses filled, in summer, with steamboat passengers and trappers in from their creeks, and being the only fair-haired child on an island of homesick men made her a kind of star. In 1940 she married Rudy Burian, who had come up from British Columbia with his brother to cut wood for the steamboats.

When the big boats stopped running, the Burians bought the Hudson's Bay store for their home and stayed to raise five children. In the winter, they trap and chat on the shortwave with neighbors on creeks up and down the river. Summers, they run a small clapboard store and rent cabins to canoeists and rafters, letting visitors drift to their doorstep.

Over my shoulder, Yvonne spotted a canoe and hurried to finish hanging the laundry. The canoeists turned out to be the big German in the wooden clogs and his toady wife. The river was a small world: you were always running into the same people. The Germans set up their tent on the front yard, and I headed for the store.

Where his wife was plump and kinetic, Rudy Burian was lean and creased as a walnut, possessed of a woodsman's economy of movement. He wore oily coveralls, like a mechanic, which is what a woodsman has to be these days. Inside, the store shelves were stocked with the Burians' own groceries, as well as the candy bars and soda pop they sold at cost to visitors, since the store was less a business than an excuse for company. Like Danny Roberts, the Burians kept a guest register, which I signed.

In winter, Rudy covered his trap line, up to two hundred miles, by snowmobile. He leased the trap line or "trapping concession" from the territorial government for twenty dollars a year, and he could pass it on, like an inheritance, to his children. He shipped the furs he trapped to auction sales in Ontario but kept a few for the store, "for people to look at," although canoeists these days didn't want to see a pelt without the animal in it. One countertop was lined with pelts of animals Rudy had trapped last winter: mink, marten, red fox, cross fox, lynx, wolverine, wolf, and beaver. The beaver pelt felt the softest, the brindled wolf the deepest. Price tags dangled from desiccated muzzles, and the vacant, slanted eye holes gave the skins the stern expression of ceremonial masks.

"Wolf is about the hardest thing to trap," Rudy said. "They'll see the toggle line and walk around. Best time to catch them is when there's a fresh snowfall. The most I've ever got was a dozen when they were real thick. This winter I only got one. He went up and down my trail, pulling the bait, so I set an extra trap beside the one he'd hit. A blind set. Finally got him on the last trip."

The door swung open, and I heard the clump, clump of wooden clogs on the floorboards. The big German wanted to buy beer, but the Burians had none, and this launched him on a long tirade about liquor laws. His wife glanced around and fixed upon the furs on the counter with a look of horrific disgust.

Outside, Yvonne Burian led me through the cottonwoods behind the store to a frame building, which they had turned into a museum. It had a wonderful collection of old bones and tools, more like someone's attic than a museum. Finding an old, fallen-in cabin, Yvonne would figure out where the fellow had thrown his garbage and start digging. There were old china plates, porcelain conductors from the telegraph line, a woolly mammoth's tusk, rusty guns, a blacksmith's bellows, a hay saw, old bottles tinted lavender from the magnesium in the glass. There was the leg bone of a Pleistocene horse pulled from the tailings of Henderson Creek where Jack London's unworked claim had been. There were skulls of lynx, wolf, and marten and the massive, bony dome of a grizzly bear.

"I'd like to get more of a collection of skulls," she said wistfully, "but no one wants to clean them."

We walked back to the store, past a ripe-smelling shed that held dried fish and haunches of bear meat. I wanted to rent one of the small cabins for the night, but the commissioner's party had arrived and made a clean sweep.

I climbed back into the canoe and waved to Yvonne on the bank.

"Maybe next time."

"We'll be here as long as our health holds out," she said. "Or until we get washed away."

MYSTERIOUSLY, my outboard trembled and died below the mouth of the Sixty Mile River. I cleaned the spark plugs, adjusted the fuel mixture, and pulled relentlessly on the starter cord. Nothing happened, and I found myself floating sideways downriver in the overwhelming silence. Tilting the motor up, I tried a stint of paddling. But without power, the canoe rode through the water like a sunken log; even the driftwood kept pace. Luckily, Dawson could only be a few hours downstream, so I stowed the paddle and let the current carry me. The canoe passed beneath an overhanging bluff, and cliff swallows poured from their gourd-shaped nests like blue smoke. They filled the sky, a whirling matrix of wings, skimming along the water so close that at times bird and reflection seemed to merge. Then, in a single impulse, the flock funneled back into their mud nests, and I drifted away.

Around a bend, I spotted the landslide scar on a hillside above Dawson, a bald white patch like a huge hide stretched to dry. The scarred dome had been a beacon for the thousands of summer sailors who descended the Yukon during the Klondike rush. Bobbing upon the river in ripsawed boats and rafts, they whooped and hollered, tears in their eyes, because Dawson had been the point of it all, the pot of gold at the end of the rainbow.

The only tears in my eyes were from paddling into a stiff headwind. Dawson spread out on the east bank, but the current was too strong against me, so I decided to make for a campground on the west shore and take the ferry over. While I was struggling downstream, a scaled-down paddle-wheeler, its balustraded decks lined with tourists, steamed easily upriver. I could hear the tour guide describing the sights, one of which was me. The stern-wheeler loomed larger and larger, until I realized we were on a collision course. A woman on deck snapped my picture while I paddled frantically to get out of the way. The stern-wheeler swept past at the last minute, orange paddles threshing the river. As I roiled in the boat's wake, the voice of the tour guide boomed over the loudspeaker: "I want to thank all you people for joining us on the river today!"

Dawson looked like a town given over to summer stock. Store clerks done up like Gibson Girls clomped along the boardwalk in full skirts and feathered hats. Sway-backed buildings with false fronts and Victorian gingerbread leaned gregariously against each other like folks who'd stayed too long at the party. At every turn, Dawson reminded itself of a past not lived up to, a brief moment when it was the largest Candian city west of the Rockies. There was the '98 Drive-in, the Gold Nugget Motel, the Sluice Box Lounge, the Sourdough Saloon, the Eldorado Hotel. Old-time Dawson was not being merely reconstructed but re-enacted in a summer-long charade. After I showered and shaved at the Klondike Gold Camp Trailer Park, I stood outside Robert Service's former cabin with a crowd of tourists waiting to hear an actor recite the old hokum. Service, a teetotaling bank clerk, had missed the Klondike rush by several years; but his table-thumping verse was what people associated with Dawson's heyday. At 10 A.M. sharp, a man with the battered face of a bar fighter strode out of the cabin, hooked his thumbs behind his lapels, and began in a hammy Irish brogue: "A bunch of the boys were whooping it up at the Malemute Saloon . . ."

The streets had been wet down in the morning to hold the dust, but the Westour and Grayline buses that rolled in by afternoon raised billowy white clouds that hung in the air. The tourists stepping down from the buses into the dry heat were dressed for the coast, in Chilkat sweaters and raincoats, and wore colored lapel pins to identify their tour groups. They were usually overseen by youthful, smiling guides. Mostly retired people, they looked frail and somehow poignant to me, walking up and down the dusty streets, peering into windows, sifting through memories not their own but their grandparents'.

I couldn't work up much enthusiasm for Dawson's wax-museum version of its past. The gold rush had been so quirky and ephemeral a movement anyway, over nearly as soon as it began. In 1897 the nation still languished in a depression, and the frontier, hitherto a good escape from tenements and sweatshops, had been declared officially closed. Against this backdrop, the discovery of gold on an unmapped river in a far country must have seemed just the ticket. People quit their jobs, abandoned their families, sunk their life savings to go off on a fool's lark. Most of the thirty thousand farmers, store clerks, and cowboys that sailed down the Yukon in the summer of 1898 found the good claims already taken. After a miserable winter of chopping through frozen ground with pickaxes, they skulked home with nothing to show for their troubles but the trip itself. In two years, the rush was over, a last fling before the century closed and modern times began.

Across from the Red Feather Saloon, I found a small engine repair shop. Engine parts were strewn all over the cramped office, tools spilling out of an oak buffet. The young owner agreed to have a look. We drove down to his boat and raced across the river to the campground where I had left the stricken outboard. Removing the engine cowling, he fiddled with the spark plugs, then realized he'd left the proper manual back at the shop. When he returned, I was cooking dinner beside my tent. Another hour passed before he finished tinkering with the motor.

"I don't know what was wrong with it, but it's fixed."

Apprehensively, I asked what I owed him for two hours of shop time.

"Oh, I don't know," he said, lifting the lid off my steaming pot of noodles, canned chicken, and wild chives. "What are you having for dinner?"

In the evening I bought a ticket for the Gaslight Follies at the Palace Grand Theatre, an opera house built during the gold rush by a cowboy-entrepreneur named Arizona Charlie Meadows. From my seat in the third balcony, looking down upon the stage was like peering down an elevator shaft. The Follies combined the more sentimental elements of *Spoon River Anthology* and *Our Town*. Led by a strutting, long-haired Arizona Charlie himself, the ghosts of Dawson sang and danced upon the stage. When the curtain dropped, the audience stumbled out into the unaccustomed evening twilight, there joined by the actors, still in grease paint. I talked with one of the actresses, the girlfriend of the cook at Selkirk. She was a college girl from Edmonton with a pretty soprano voice and, on close examination, deep green eyes and a feline face.

"Are you going to Diamond Tooth Gertie's?" she asked.

"I hadn't thought about it," I said, wondering if she was really the cook's girl. "What are your plans for the evening?"

"A bath and early to bed."

So I went alone. Most of the audience had already surged up the street to Gertie's, where there were legalized gambling and dancing girls. I wandered among the gaming tables and watched the floor show, which was as naughty as a church bazaar. The high point of the evening came when the cancan girls descended into the audience and fetched men back to the stage to participate in a dance contest. The men rolled up their pants legs and high-kicked to the music, while the audience cheered to indicate their favorites. The winner was a fat man who won unanimously by falling over on his back.

A pale light outlined the hills as I stumbled down to the riverbank to wait for the ferry, the river sliding past like mercury. A scruffy bunch squatted by the landing with rucksacks and walking sticks. The night had cooled, and their breath appeared in quick clouds of frost. They were complaining about inflation.

"I pay a hundred dollars for a lid of B.C. green, seven hundred for a gram of fucking coke, a hundred twenty-five for Hawaiian thatch, twenty for mushrooms."

A kid with a curly mop and the face of a Hobbit shook his head.

"I wouldn't pay ten dollars for that shit."

Aware suddenly of my presence, the little group perceptibly stiffened.

"Are you a cop, eh?" the Hobbit asked. "You look like a cop."

What a difference a few years and a haircut make! Time was

when they would have passed me a joint. Now I looked like bad news.

"If that's true," I said, rocking on the balls of my feet, "then you're all busted."

Nobody laughed, but then no one took me seriously either. A bottle of beer was passed around and I took my swig with the rest. Summer people, like myself, they spoke with solemn awe of the coming winter.

"I've been up to Yellowknife. It gets cold there."

"The coldest fucking place in the world is Siberia, man. A hundred and seventy degrees below zero," somebody said, shivering in running shorts and a tank top.

"What?"

"I said the coldest fucking place in the world is Siberia."

"Oh. I thought you said Sudbury."

The ferry landed and a tanker truck rumbled off the ramp. While the little throng climbed into the bed of a pickup for the ride across, I found a corner of the boat to myself. The ferryman hooked a chain across the ramp and we labored into midriver. The ferryman stood beside me at the railing and watched the river unfurl. I asked him if business was good.

He frowned. "All the mines have shut down. And now the government wants to close the placer miners down too because they say they're hurting the salmon run."

"Are they?"

"Look at the river," he said, nodding at the turgid water. "That's not from mining. That's silt."

The next morning I had coffee at the Eldorado Hotel with its manager, Peter Jenkins. He was in his late thirties and wore the standard emblem of success in the Yukon, a gold watchband festooned with nuggets. Jenkins was currently on leave of absence as mayor of Dawson.

"All we're selling here," he said, "is nostalgia for the Geritol set."

Jenkins had recently been reelected mayor by a healthy margin while serving a six-month jail sentence for perjury. He was a booster, a go-getter, and only seemed pushy if measured against the lassitude of small northern towns. He'd brought cable television to Dawson, improved the streets, lowered his own salary, and accepted the occasional investigation because, as he said, "It just takes somebody with balls to take the risks."

Aside from tourism, the Yukon's economy was in a terrible slump. The big gold dredges had shut down in the late sixties, and more recently the lead-zinc mine at Faro and the asbestos mine downriver at Clinton Creek had closed. All that kept Dawson afloat after the tourists went home were the gold placer miners. And now the government in Ottawa was trying to shut them down, and all because of the salmon.

"We are probably the most overgoverned area in Canada," Jenkins complained. "There's Social Welfare and Game Management and the Federal Department of Fisheries, for starters. The Fisheries people have more power than the police force. They think they sit on the right hand of God the Father Almighty!"

The Department of Fisheries had charged that placer mining was destroying the water quality of salmon spawning grounds in the Yukon. Placer miners used bulldozers to ream out entire sections of streambed and then ran the gravel and soil through a sluice box to separate out the gold. The run-off that resulted left an otherwise clear stream muddied and brown. Yukon River King salmon migrate from the Bering Sea in their fourth or fifth year back to their home stream to spawn, a distance of two thousand miles in some cases. If the stream were polluted for as many years, no salmon fry would be hatched to remember the way home. The circle of stream-to-sea-to-stream would be broken, and the stream would cease to produce salmon. So the government had proposed new guidelines, five volumes' worth, requiring miners to file extensive environmental impact statements and assess gold deposits before they could lift a shovel.

"The new guidelines," Jenkins said, "will probably result in fifty percent of the placer miners being shut down. That's by the government's own estimates."

He and the city council had submitted a brief to the federal government in support of the placer miners. But at the moment, Jenkins had his own problems. He was on leave from the mayor's office while being investigated for tampering with the electric meters at the Eldorado (the charges against him were eventually dropped).

"I've always been high profile in this town," Jenkins said, leaning over his coffee in a conspiratorial tone. "In a small town, there's always someone out to get your ass."

It was another scorcher. Ravens croaked from the power lines as I walked south along the riverbank. At the end of town, I came to a shallow green river that rushed over a bed of white stones. Rising in small streams on the west flank of the Ogilvie Range, the river flowed a hundred and fifty miles to empty into the Yukon. For a long time I watched an old man below the cutbank gathering driftwood from the gravel bars.

At one time, before gold dredges had consumed its lower portions, this tributary had been among the great spawning grounds for salmon ascending the Yukon. The local Han Indians had fished here by hammering stakes into the riverbed to hold their salmon nets. They called the river the *Con'dik*, meaning "stone-for-driving-in-fish-trap-poles river." The Han, whose villages ranged as far north as the Charley River in Alaska, belong to the great Athabascan-language family that occupies nearly the whole of the Yukon watershed. Their name, "Han," is a shortening of *Han Gwich'in*, or "the people of the river." In the mid-nineteenth century, they wore caribou-skin leggings and long-tailed skin shirts and moved to the river each spring to catch salmon in large quantities to dry and store for the winter. Unlike the coastal tribes, the Han lacked the rich resources of the sea. There was only this one season of plenty when the salmon migrated upriver to spawn.

When the vanguard of the salmon run approached, a lookout posted on the riverbank, usually a child or old man, would spot the ripple of salmon below the surface and sound the alarm. At the lookout's cry, the village men launched slender bark canoes into the river and shagged King salmon with long-handled dip nets. Borne ceremoniously back to the village, the first salmon of the season was boiled in a spruce-root basket. The resulting broth was then shared by all in the village, except those women nursing or sequestered by menstrual taboos, and the fish bones were carefully replaced in the river so as not to offend the salmon's spirit.

By some circumstance, the Han were absent from the Con-'dik late in the summer of 1896 when two Tagish Indians and a squawman named George Washington Carmacks arrived to fish for chum salmon at the river's mouth. Carmacks preferred the company of the Tagish to his own kind and took an Indian's stock in the visionary quality of dreams. He had decided to fish here after dreaming of a pair of King salmon with gold nuggets for scales and gold coins for eyes.

But the salmon run proved poor, and the three men poled up the clear tributary to look for saw logs and do a little prospecting. In a buggy side creek, one of them dipped his hand in the water and pulled out a thumb-sized nugget. The gold lay in the creekbed, Carmacks would later say, as thick as cheese on a sandwich. As word of Carmacks's strike quickly fanned across the country, prospectors left their own diggings to descend upon the valley of the Con'dik. But in their mouths the Han name for the river emerged with a sharp, Yankee twang. They called it the Klondike.

I sympathized with the plight of the placer miners. But as a fellow river traveler, I was more interested in the salmon. I also had a prior loyalty to them. Years before, I had worked a season in a Puget Sound cannery. Cannery work was the lowest rung on the ladder of commercial fishing, fishermen being at the top, but I loved to be around saltwater and boats. In the early morning dark, I'd climb into the clammy hold of a purse seiner to unload salmon for the cutting tables. The salmon I tossed around were oceangoing fish caught early in a comparatively short spawning run, but I couldn't help wondering at their destination and feeling a little sorry they hadn't made it. The King salmon that migrate to the Yukon River and its tributaries were veterans of the longest and most perilous spawning run. Following the chemical memory of their natal stream, they picked their way through a ganglia of side streams and channels, past nets, fish wheels, logjams, bears — past a thousand deaths — to reach the very stream where they had hatched, there to spawn and die. In its elements of homecoming, mating, and death, the salmon migration was a reminder that life itself was a journey.

The first salmon of this summer had been caught the day before. A twenty-five-pound King salmon in rosy spawning hue had ensnarled itself in a gill net twenty miles downriver from Dawson. It had been swimming upriver for the better part of a month, averaging fifty-two miles a day against a swift current. It had taken no food since leaving saltwater and had traveled fourteen hundred river miles only to run afoul of a nylon gill net and drown.

Preparations for the arrival of the main run of King salmon were under way at the new Han fish processing plant on Front Street. The plant was jointly owned by the Dawson and Old Crow Indian bands, but chiefly financed by the federal government, which understood the historic cachet in putting the Han back in the salmon business. Above the plant door hung a bright red, totemic rendering of a salmon, hook-jawed and tailwalking.

The plant manager showed me around. The walls and floor were coated with Fiberglas, the floors sloped for drainage. What I remembered from my cannery days in Puget Sound was a disassembly line of rubber-aproned workers lopping off salmon heads and pulling out viscera, and the great whirlwind of seagulls that arose at the end of the day when we hosed out the place. But the rows of stainless steel tables that gleamed under these lights were still awaiting the arrival of the patient. The main thrust of migrating King salmon would not cross the border for another week. When it did, a twin-engine Han collecting boat would make a sixty-five-mile run down the Yukon early each morning to pick up salmon at isolated fish camps, most of which were at the juncture of tributaries: Cassiar Creek, Sunset Creek, Fortymile River, Cliff Creek. Back at the processing plant, the salmon would be slid down the wet surface of these tables, beheaded, eviscerated, and otherwise reduced. Flash frozen at minus forty in a blast freezer, the salmon would then be loaded onto freezer trucks coming back empty from Innuvik and shipped to Vancouver and Seattle. Given the coastal location of Han's markets, it was like carrying coals to Newcastle.

"We took about four thousand salmon last year," the manager

said, "and didn't make any money. This year we'll try to break even, and by the fourth year we should be in the black."

Aside from the manager and a secretary, all of the employees at the Han plant were Indian, and all of the fishermen who sold to Han were white. It was an intriguing cultural reversal and said something about the grass being greener: the Indians took the wage jobs in town while whites were strung along the river, trading their salmon for cash. The low men in this arrangement were often the fishermen. Since Han was the only local buyer and its main purpose was to provide Indian employment, the fishery could set its own price. This summer, Han was paying fishermen forty cents a pound for King salmon, half what they'd gotten the year before.

When I told the manager I was heading downriver the next day, he gave me the names of two fishermen at Cliff Creek, the end of the collecting boat's run. So far, the Yukon had seemed an antiquarian stream, lined with old-timers and musty cabins. I was looking forward to a change of pace: a working river.

7   THE
    SALMON
    ROAD

THE CREAKING of a water pump woke me. Summer mornings this far north, I always awoke with the sun blazing overhead and the suspicion of having overslept. I crawled from the tent and found the campground tables covered with a mantle of cottonwood lint, the spangled river moving through the trees. My watch said 5:30.

The trio in the next campsite were pulling up stakes. They worked like men possessed. Collapsing their tent, they stomped on the billowing canvas, then heaved it into the back of an ancient Ford truck. Their leader came over to proudly show me the shiny claim plate to gold diggings he was going to work. Thuggish in a greasy beard and Mexican serape, he might have been heading out for the Sierra Madre. He'd bought the mining claim the summer before and worked it himself with only a shovel. This time he had returned equipped with a hydraulic pump, a homemade sluice box, and two stooges who were busy sweeping up the rest of their camp.

"Gotta get a move on!" he shouted.

"Where to?"

A wave of foolish cunning swept his face. "Oh, just back in the hills," he said, and waved an arm in a vague direction.

The truck fired up and, as it wheeled around, the passenger door swung open and the leader hopped in. Then they were off, jouncing down the road and out of sight. The Klondike played out each summer to diminishing returns.

By noon I was back on the river. Dawson fell away and the

valley rose up in a V-shaped formation called the Tintina Trench. The river looked deep and fjordlike. The rise in surrounding elevation lent an exaggerated sense of the river's gradient. Rounding a bend, I stared down the long stretch of water, expecting a staircase of rapids that never came. Under the shadow of a steep bluff, the river boiled as it swept over submerged rocks, the tiller arm suddenly paralyzed by the upwelling. Then the canoe broke free and I steered back into the slot of sunlight falling between the valley's rims. To the east, beyond the nearly perpendicular spruce hills, soared the snowless brown summits of the Ogilvie Range.

Floating in mid-river, a piece of driftwood caught my eye. Why was it moving crosswise to the current? A pair of semaphore ears twirled about, and the snag transformed itself into the head of a bull moose. Disembodied by the silty river, the moosehead seemed to have floated loose from the wall of some smoky lodge hall. As the gap between us narrowed, the enormous head reared back, eyes wide with panic. The Han used to hunt moose by canoe, leaping onto the moose's back to slit its throat, then steering the floating carcass to shore. I wasn't hunting, of course, but the moose swam as if propelled by a residual fear of men in boats. When it reached the far shore, the rest of the moose emerged, looming larger and larger until it stood six feet at the shoulder. It looked back for a moment, as if trying to recall my face, then disappeared into the surrounding willows.

I hauled the canoe onto a flat tongue of land formed by the confluence of the Yukon and the Fortymile. Thickets of wild rose and bluebells, telltale signs of habitation, grew up around a cluster of tumble-down cabins. Gold had been discovered at Fortymile when Dawson was still a mudflat. A thousand prospectors living in cold, stooped cabins had once been strung the length of this tributary, waiting for the big strike. When the strike came, it was not here but on the Klondike. Back in the cottonwoods, I found an old Anglican church and an RCMP post slowly moldering, floors rotted out.

I got out the twelve-gauge shotgun that I kept disassembled in my footlocker, to be put together each evening in the tent. The new ethic was to enter the wilderness with an open heart and empty hand, but I had no intention of killing anything. I'd brought the gun along for the same reason I'd kept a glow-in-the-dark crucifix in my room as a child: it helped me sleep at night. At any rate, I needed some target practice and this place seemed isolated enough. Fitting the stock and barrel together, I loaded the shotgun with a round of double-aught buckshot. "I've seen a grizzly hit with this," the gunshop owner in White-horse had assured me, "and it'll pick 'em right up and sit 'em right down." I paced off fifty feet from a log that I had set on end to imitate a boar grizzly charging out of the tall grass. It still looked like a log. There was a tremendous clap, the shotgun bucking hard against my shoulder, and the log keeled over. I examined the grouping of pellets in the mortally wounded log, then slunk away feeling as if I'd pulled a schoolboy prank.

To the east, anvil-shaped thunderheads, slate gray at the base and pearly on top, were piling above the Ogilvie Mountains. Filaments of lightning played over the summits. The air felt dense and charged, ready to storm. I picked out the snuggest cabin of the bunch to wait out the rains. It had a corrugated tin roof and a faded green sign hanging above the door:

GENERAL STORE
David Swanson
— Prop. —

Inside, wallpaper was peeling from the logs to reveal strata of overlapping layers — stripes, flowers, paisley — that proceeded from the wainscoting up to the sloped ceiling. A geology of wallpaper. I unrolled my sleeping bag on a creaky iron cot and made the day's entry in my journal. While I wrote, a green bottlefly buzzed against the window pane.

This place reminded me of my own tin-roofed cabin, with its view of moving water and mountains beyond. It reminded me of how contented I'd been to do nothing in the face of such beauty. Living off the land would have been a more practical proposition on a big river like the Yukon, instead of a pretty tributary creek. This was a perfect spot. I wondered why, when people willingly live in the ugliest places, no one lived here. More pointedly, why hadn't I settled along the Yukon in the first place? The simple truth was that I had lacked the nerve. To drift down a great river and put up a cabin requires a high level of resolve, especially when freeze-up ends any graceful exit. I never was that certain. Building within three miles of a road system had been a way of hedging my bets. If things didn't work out, as indeed they didn't, I could pull out easily. But even then it hadn't been that simple. How would it feel to leave a river like this behind? You couldn't stay long in a place this beautiful without it haunting you the rest of your life.

Dust motes swirled in a shaft of light where the stovepipe had been. The fly had stopped buzzing. I looked out the open door, the river flowing past like a memory, and wondered how David Swanson, Prop., was getting on in the world.

Two men and a freckled, auburn-haired woman sat on metal folding chairs around a driftwood fire. The furniture casually arrayed upon the beach — chairs, card table, a child's playpen — suggested a pleasant tale of shipwreck.

I walked up from my canoe and shook hands. The two men were about my age, the one blond and ruddy-faced, the other tall and angular. For fishermen, their names had a Biblical ring: Timothy and James. They were cooking their midday meal, the first salmon of the season.

"Had your lunch yet?" Tim asked.

I hadn't, so they brought out another chair and placed it in the circle. The fire burned a bright orange against the buff-colored sand and gave off a searing heat. Tim's wife, Andrea, laid an iron skillet and coffee pot on an enormous grate balanced on two piles of rocks. Sweeping her long hair behind her back, she leaned over the fire and dolloped lard into the skillet. Then she laid out thick salmon steaks that sizzled in the grease until the meat faded to the color of the fire.

We ate the salmon off tin plates, washing it down with the strong, hot coffee. The salmon tasted oily and delicious. We ate quickly and then had seconds, picking the bones with our greasy fingers. A blue-eyed child in the playpen began to fuss. Andrea fed him bits of salmon from her plate and whispered to him in French. I felt particularly happy to be included in this group.

There was something wonderful and vaguely ceremonial about sharing a meal of the first fish pulled from the river.

The King salmon run had only just started and would last for another month. At the height of the run, Tim and James would check their nets every six hours to untangle fish and driftwood. They had two nets in the river, set at the upstream end of eddies. The most productive was a two-hundred-foot nylon gill net strung off a jutting cliff where the river swirled in small vortexes and back eddies, a place where salmon could rest against the current. There were three distinct salmon runs up the Yukon. After the Kings came the summer chum or dog salmon, and then the fall chum or silvers, which ran until the river froze. By then, the novelty of salmon for lunch would have worn thin.

"Are you Canadian or Yank?" Tim asked me.

By temperament he seemed the group's natural leader.

"American."

"No offense," he said, "but you Yanks are making a big effort to shut us down by taking every fish in the river. People on the delta have been fishing for a month. The only fish they allow through are what they consider necessary to maintain their own stock."

James agreed. "It's true. Fish definitely seem to be on the decline."

But Tim could scarcely contain his anger. He looked down-river toward the border, simmering at people he'd never seen, people more than a thousand miles away setting their nets in *his* river, hauling in *his* fish.

"The U.S. has got the upper hand," he said. "And right now you're killing us!"

It was the pure anger of an expatriate. Tim Gerberdine and James Bouton were ex-Yanks themselves. They had linked up in Colorado and hitchhiked the Alcan Highway, arriving in Fairbanks roughly the same time I did. Fairbanks in the early seventies was a clearing-house for people coming north, a place to get one's bearings before trying out more difficult terrain. Our paths must have crossed, we realized, and we backtracked until we found they had: at Nine Mile on Chena Hot Springs

Road, a place known locally as Hippie Hill. My wife and I had stayed there briefly with a friend of hers, a serious young woman who'd changed her name from Terry to Trees. My memories were of a steep, washed-out road lined with junked cars, squatters' shacks in the woods, and packs of loose dogs.

James's recollections were kinder. "A wonderful place," he said. I tried placing him among the crowd that had shuttled through Fairbanks on their way to other places. Then I saw the James of ten years ago, an outlandish figure, tall and thin, stalking down the hillside dressed like a buffalo hunter, long hair falling from under a broad-rimmed hat. I wouldn't have cared for him back then. Our ambitions were too similar. I would have seen only another seeker, part of the general costume party. But if he'd started out playing at homesteader, after a decade that's what he'd truly become. Secure now in our different lives, we were just people reminiscing, smiling fondly at each other's memories like old friends at a reunion.

There was another connection. Tim and James had staked open-to-entry land on Bear Creek about twenty miles north of my cabin. I had looked over the same land but passed it up because the creek had a tendency to run dry in late summer. They had spent a month building geodesic domes for what was to be a commune, then failed to meet the application deadline and had to forfeit the land. They headed for the Yukon Territory.

"There were no citizen requirements then," Tim said. "The Yukon was less populated. Fewer roads. Wilder country."

He built a raft on the McQuesten River, rode it down to the Stewart River, and then slipped into the broad, heady Yukon. At Dawson he built a second raft and floated to Eagle. By that time he'd already decided this was the prettiest stretch of river on the Yukon. That autumn, Tim started building a cabin at Cliff Creek.

"There were six of us that fall. As it turned out, all the others flaked off in November, never to return, except James, who stayed until December. That was the winter that got down to forty-seven below the second week in November."

James returned the following summer, and they'd been partners here, more or less, ever since. Their lives were divided, according to season, among garden, salmon nets, and dog team.

Last year the Han collecting boat had picked up their catch right at the beach, but this summer Tim and James were boycotting Han. They stored the salmon they caught in a box submerged in a bouldery, refrigerant creek until they could be taken to market.

"We haven't set a price yet," Tim said, "but we agreed it wouldn't be Han's price."

They had convinced other fishermen on the river to join the boycott and were trying to line up freezers in Dawson. The problem was that within a week they would catch more salmon than they could ever hope to sell on their own. Eventually they would have to pull their nets.

Andrea sounded more conciliatory. "We can survive without fishing, but it sure raises our income. It's just so easy to sell fish when the boat picks them up. You don't even have to clean them."

The baby began to fuss. Andrea pulled him from the playpen and set him down on the sandy beach. *"Reste là, mon ange,"* she said. And then to me: "There's no way he'll learn French unless I speak it to him."

Andrea came to Dawson from Quebec on a summer holiday, never intending to stay. She met Tim at a friend's birthday party. He wooed her and brought her back to Cliff Creek. That was five years ago. Last winter, she had returned to Quebec to finish a degree in anthropology, only to discover she was pregnant.

The baby had been born last September on a stifling Indian summer day. The silver chum salmon were running in the river, and Tim had stayed behind to pick the nets while Andrea waited in the Dawson hospital. She was in labor when he finally got to the hospital. He walked into her room, his clothes bloodstained and reeking of fish, and she screamed at him to get out. Cleaned up, he stood by her in the delivery room as she bore down on the pain. But the close heat and lack of food and sleep began to work on him. The room filled with light and his knees began to buckle. A nurse told him to lie on the floor. At the moment of birth, Andrea called, "Look, Tim!" He raised his head briefly to see his new son and smiled before passing out.

We focused our attention on the baby, who scuttled crablike from the circle of chairs, heading on hands and knees toward the water.

"He's going to be a real river person," Tim said. "In a couple of years he'll be driving those outboards, booting it down the river. I just hope there are some fish left to net."

Children seem the surest sign that people have settled in and put down roots, although I wondered if Tim and Andrea's son wouldn't grow up to leave for other horizons, as his parents had. The attractions of a river life were certainly lost on the present generation in their twenties, who had better things to do than play Swiss Family Robinson. Each summer fewer people floated down the Yukon; even fewer stayed on. But I felt close to Tim and James if only because we had started in the same place. This was the path not taken; these were the people I had not become. It was tempting to look past the brief, light-shot days and imagine their lives in another decade, shaped by the poverty of long winters. Surely, time was on the side of those of us who had stayed in school, worked in offices, harnessed ourselves to details. But sitting here in the sunshine, I envied them. That their lives had remained so remarkably intact while mine had not was strangely cheering. I liked to think someone had kept faith with their dreams even if I hadn't.

The baby meanwhile had edged closer to the river. He stared at the water lapping against the shore as if encountering for the first time a new element, one that moved in smooth sheets of reflected light. His mother got up from her chair to bring him back into the circle. But before she could reach him, he lowered his blond head into the river and took a long drink.

The Canadian Department of Fisheries maintained a field station on a small island six miles above the international border. Two young biologists sat on lawn chairs, waving away mosquitoes as I climbed the cutbank. A pair of water-skis leaned against a nearby tree. The biologists didn't look like the sort of people who sat at the right hand of God the Father Almighty. When I told them that, the younger one laughed.

"There's enforcement and there's biology. In the biology end you don't have to wear a uniform, and people don't have to take you seriously."

They were studying the migration of King salmon in the upper Yukon River Basin. They trapped salmon in fish wheels, then tagged and released them, monitoring their upstream movements by radio telemetry. The head biologist, a tall and intense man, believed that half to three-quarters of the Yukon River King salmon spawned in Canadian waters, yet only a fraction wound up in Canadian nets.

"Overfishing on the Alaskan side accounts for it. A treaty was negotiated for the Stikine and Taku rivers, both transboundary rivers like the Yukon, but the governor of Alaska wouldn't sign it."

He held out what looked like a vacuum tube in the palm of his hand. It was a lithium-powered radio transmitter, weighing twenty grams, which emitted a bubbling signal, like water dripping from a faucet. In a few days he would insert it into the stomach of a live-trapped King salmon before releasing the fish. Eavesdropping by boat and airplane, the biologists would follow the salmon upriver, marking vectors on their maps to determine travel rates and spawning sites.

Anadromous fish, salmon lead a double life, migrating from the ocean to spawn in the freshwater streams of their birth. In the open ocean, schools of salmon travel in predetermined circuits, tracing elliptical journeys of up to ten thousand miles. They grow sleek and torpedo-shaped on a diet of shrimp and herring. In their fourth to sixth year, King salmon move along the Bering coast, following an internal compass and timetable, to the outlet of their home river.

Gathering in the brackish water of the Yukon Delta, the salmon undergo a transformation. Their coloring changes from bright silver to muddy red; their stomachs shrink as they cease feeding. Already they've begun to die from the tail up. The stored fat in their bodies will sustain the salmon until they reach the spawning grounds, unless they are delayed. There is no return journey.

Male salmon, called "cocks," usually precede the female "hens" on the run. Against the current, the salmon swim in starts and stops, keeping to deeper water and resting in the eddies. They move upriver with a single-minded purpose, their destination mapped out in their brains. As the school ascends the river, groups break off to follow separate tributaries, until each salmon finds the exact stream in which it was hatched.

The most astonishing aspect of the salmon's homing run is that it is learned rather than genetically programmed. Navigating up the maze of a river system, the salmon retraces, in reverse, its earlier passage to the sea years before. This "memory" is composed of essentially olfactory cues — the chemical characteristics of a given water and streambed — as well, perhaps, as current, turgidity, and temperature. The salmon's mental map of the river is not complete or even linear, but made up of critical junctures such as tributaries — a kind of directional shorthand of where to turn and where to go straight, like directions we might give to someone's house.

Not all salmon reach their spawning grounds. The biologists found one badly chewed transmitter by Minto, in a pile of bear-killed fish. Another they found on the beach at Tim and James's fish camp after the salmon had been fed to Tim's sled dogs. Once they wired a whitefish that promptly headed downriver and tangled in a net across the border at Eagle. The fisherman who found the transmitter thought it was a Russian listening device.

The day before, the biologists had implanted a transmitter in a King salmon, kept it alive in a submerged box for a few hours, and then dissected the salmon to check for internal damage. There was none. The victim was a hook-jawed male. Males were considered more expendable since a single male could service several females upon the spawning bed.

For supper we ate the post mortem, fried in butter and served up with tossed salad and cold beer.

Next morning we jumped in a snub-nosed boat and roared upstream to check the fish wheels. The river had dropped a foot overnight. On the far shore a long tattoo of wolf tracks meandered up the newly exposed beach.

The first fish wheel was moored to a steep rock cliff, eight feet from shore. It was a hollow, square raft with a pair of mesh scoops, bolted radially to a log axle, rotating in the current. The contraption worked on the order of a perpetual-motion machine. As one scoop lifted into the air, the other plunged into the river. It resembled a Ferris wheel caught in a flood. Migrating salmon typically follow the curve of the shoreline and cannot see the onrushing scoop in the silty water until it hoists them into blue sky. As the scoop reaches a vertical position, the fish slides down an angled trough into one of two partially submerged holding boxes.

"Here we are!" the assistant biologist cried as we lashed the boat to the raft. "The Wheel of Fortune!"

The motion of the raft was dizzying. The two scoops revolved clockwise at a rate of four and a half revolutions per minute, while the river raced below in a countermovement, and the catwalk shimmied back and forth. It was all I could do to keep from falling overboard.

The first holding box was empty, and the second held only a single whitefish, which the younger biologist dropped back in the river.

The other fish wheel was a mile upriver, churning beside a soaring hillside. We cleared away driftwood from the weir that funneled salmon into the scoops and then climbed aboard. As the raft rose and fell, a pair of dorsal fins appeared and disappeared in the first holding box. The young biologist straddled the box, made a sweep with the landing net, and came up with a heaving, speckle-backed King salmon, iridescent in its roseate spawning colors. He passed the fish to his partner, who measured it from tip to tail and plucked a scale from the salmon's back. Salmon scales, like the cross-sections of trees, have concentric growth rings that can be counted to determine the fish's age. The biologist threaded an orange strand of plastic tubing, printed with a number and address, through the salmon's dorsal fin and dropped the fish back into the slot of river as if posting a letter.

After sulking a bit, the tagged salmon would proceed upriver, traveling at a mile and a half an hour. In three days it would reach Dawson, and beyond that, who could say?

Moving to the other box, the younger biologist made a sweep with the net and seemed to connect with a fire hose. The salmon whipped the water into a froth and punched a hole through the mesh. The biologist tried to get a grip around the King's thick middle, but the salmon, a good forty pounds of muscle, quickly broke his hold. Finally, the biologist cornered the salmon with the gaping net while his partner tagged it, half submerged in the water. A grid of blue bruises was etched across the salmon's head from an earlier encounter with a gill net. With its pincer mouth and silver eyes, the salmon looked angry, impatient with our delays.

"You want to get them back into the river as quickly as possible," the chief biologist said. "Salmon have a biological imperative and a set amount of energy. If you delay them too long, you reduce their chances of spawning successfully."

The last thing any of us wanted to do was hold up a salmon's journey. There was a keen sense of urgency, a seriousness in the endeavor, because propagation of the species, not their own survival, propelled the salmon upriver. Still, it was the individual fish that you rooted for. Even if salmon have no choice in their movement, the effort seems heroic. The poignancy of the migration was not that it ended with mating and death, but that the salmon were so eager to get on with both.

At last, sliding one hand under the salmon's belly and another around its tail, the assistant hefted the King up and dropped it into the river like a chunk of stone.

Back at camp, I changed into dry clothes and loaded my canoe.

"Try to get the chance to see a spawning bed," the head biologist said by way of good-by. "It's really quite moving — all those fish spawning and fighting and dying."

I pushed off, letting the current sweep me away from the island. A few miles down, I crossed the 141st meridian, the international boundary marked by a blazed line cut into the wooded hills. There was no customs house, no gate at the border, and so, undeclared, I drifted home.

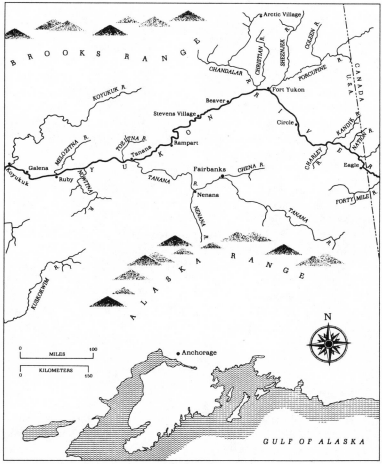

Middle Yukon River

8 | AN
AMERICAN
RIVER

The yukon poured out of Canada into a bowl of blue-
rimmed mountains. The first settlement on the Alaskan side of
the river was Eagle. Actually, there are two Eagles, one Indian
and one white, each with a different posture toward the river.
The Han Gwich'in village of Eagle squats along the cutbank in
a jumbled row of log cabins, as if watching for the first salmon.
Three miles farther on, Eagle City stretches back from the high
bluff in a Jeffersonian grid of shady streets and white frame
houses. American miners, disgruntled over Canadian taxes and
Mounties, had chosen the town site with an eye to its perfect
view — a horseshoe bend in the river framed in mountains.

While other roaring camps withered after the gold rush,
Eagle prospered into respectability. A federal court and a military garrison were established to police the gold fields. Later,
when mining fell off, the soldiers of Fort Egbert laid a telegraph
line to Valdez on the coast and fought their last campaigns
against muskeg and alder swamps. The completed line linked
Eagle to the outside world and brought the town its most celebrated visitor.

On December 5, 1905, two dog teams racing south along the
frozen Yukon left the ice and climbed the steep bank to Eagle.
The temperature was 60 degrees below zero. Even in the pale
winter twilight, one driver was easily recognized as Arthur Har-
per, the mail carrier from Circle. The other, a tall, dour man,
was dressed conspicuously in an Eskimo parka, the skin turned
inside out. He had wintered the past three years in the high

Arctic. His men and his sloop, the *Gjoa,* still lay locked in the Beaufort Sea ice at King Point. For forty-two days he had been traveling by sled and ski, traversing the eastern Brooks Range, then following the Colville and Porcupine rivers to the Yukon.

In a thick accent, the stranger inquired where he might send a wireless message and was directed to the telegraph office inside Fort Egbert. There he sat down and composed a two-hundred-word telegram, addressed to Fridtjof Nansen in Christina, Norway, and signed "Amundsen." The line to Valdez snapped in the intense cold before more details could follow, but the gist of Roald Amundsen's message was that he had navigated the Northwest Passage.

Eagle must have impressed the explorer because he lingered here for two months in a trim bungalow on First Avenue before hitching up his dogs and mushing back to the Arctic.

A monument to Amundsen's visit stood outside the Eagle post office. Otherwise little had changed but the seasons. Birch trees drooped in the midday heat. People still filled water jugs at a clapboard well house down the street. A yard sale was in progress across from the general store. If Dawson had seemed overdressed and entrepreneurial, then Eagle was by comparison chaste and lovely. No tour buses rolled into town from the spur road, and nobody wore costumes.

The mail plane had just landed, and the line at the post office extended into the street. Waiting my turn in the small foyer, I read Wanted posters and a list of events for the coming Fourth of July celebration. I decided to stay in Eagle for a few days. It seemed just the place for a man on the run to lie low.

"Just arrive?"

"An hour ago, by canoe."

Two middle-aged men with shovel-billed caps and sunburned necks were sitting outside the P.O. when I came out.

"Now that sounds like fun," the skinny one said, tucking a pinch of snuff under his lower lip. "Hey, Red, I'm going to try that myself someday."

They were retired policemen and brother Masons who'd driven up from Ohio to spend the summer panning gold. They were renting a house out by the boat landing.

Earl spat a thin stream of tobacco juice into the dust. "Plenty of room," he said. "Come out if you feel like sleeping indoors for a change."

I went by in the afternoon. The house was a litter of beer cans, mining pamphlets, and paperback westerns. The Ohioans were playing cards with their landlord, the owner of a gold mine and a fellow Mason. Neil had prematurely silver hair and a self-propelled laugh that rang out with every good hand. He'd bought the gold mine three years before and was in the process of losing it in the courts. The way things were going, Neil needed a laugh when the cards went his way.

While the courts decided the mine's fate, Neil invited his Ohio friends to pick through tailings that had been mined twice already. Earl and Red's claim was spread all over the kitchen counter in plastic margarine tubs filled with different gradations of sediment, from pea-sized to fine flour, the end result of sluicing through forty tons of muck. Now they were in the process of sifting through the smallest particles with an artist's brush, looking for gold flakes. A sneeze could have wiped out their holdings.

"Exactly how much gold have you found?" I asked.

Earl held up a water-filled vial holding perhaps an ounce of gold flakes.

"Maybe four hundred dollars' worth. Hell, we spent twice that just driving up from Ohio!"

After the card game broke up and Neil left, I spread my bedroll on the floor while Earl took his turn on the couch. He lay silhouetted against the drawn curtains, balancing an empty beer can on his chest for a spittoon. The endless northern dusk kept him up, so he tried talking himself to sleep. He talked about a rowboat he'd taken down the Ohio River with his best bird dog. He talked about two men he'd shot with his service pistol in a Kentucky tavern. He talked about walking the line and wanting a little on the side. Talking about women did nothing for his insomnia.

Earl pulled a worn snapshot of his ex-wife from his wallet. The small, dark-haired woman in the picture wore a black swimming suit and smiled guilelessly at someone she loved.

"Now, honestly, does she look like a woman who's almost fifty?"

She honestly didn't.

Early Sunday morning, Neil drove up to the house and was shocked to find everyone asleep.

"But you're going to church, aren't you?"

We piled into his truck and bounced down the road to a lovely old log church beside the river. Built by Episcopalians, the church was now run by the Central Alaskan Mission. We took our places in the back pew, and the service began with a comely pianist thumping out " 'Tis So Sweet to Trust in Jesus." The church stood at the end of the old Fort Egbert parade ground, now a runway. Halfway through the hymn, our voices were drowned out by a Piper Cub that hurtled down the field and roared off the riverbank into thin air.

"Now, I ask you," the young, bearded minister said, shrugging his shoulders. "Do I look like a preacher?"

In his checkered shirt and blue jeans, I supposed not. But you only had to close your eyes to recognize the modulated voice and practiced folksiness of a radio evangelist.

"Once I knew a fellow who was quarterback on the St. Louis football team, a mountain of a man. But if you set him down in Eagle, why, he'd be just one in a crowd. And if you looked at a road map of Alaska, you'd see that Eagle is just a tiny little old speck. And if you looked at a globe, Alaska would be just one patch of color. And if you looked at the solar system, you'd see that Earth is just a dot. And that solar system is just a tiny part of the Milky Way galaxy, one of many galaxies! Makes you feel pretty small, don't it?"

I could see where this was going. Having sluiced us down to pea size, he offered Jesus as a remedy to our insignificance. The minister's voice was soft and reassuring, but his text was stringent Old Testament. Samuel to the Israelites: "But if you still do wickedly, you shall be swept away."

"Christ tells us," the minister went on, "that Christians are fishers of men. We're like a fish wheel in the river: we need to be out in the current or we're useless. Just as a fish wheel has a

steel cable to moor it in the current, we need our guidelines —
fear of the Lord, obedience to his commandments — or we'll be
left on the rocks."

The river running through the homily didn't resemble the
one I'd ridden into town. Instead, it was a swift, venial torrent
of possibilities, against which the best defense was to be tied
down, securely anchored, moored in place. With the Yukon
River just a sharp right turn at the door, the congregation probably heard this advice every Sunday. Living in a small town
surrounded by a vast wilderness presented a paradox. On the
one hand, people were drawn to Eagle by its unfettered setting;
yet wilderness also suggested temptations to be guarded against.
This was the classic frontier dilemma: to choose absolute free-
dom, and with it the potential for anarchy and lawlessness, or
accept the nullifying restraints of civilization. It is the problem
Huck Finn faces at the end of his tale, deciding whether to stay
on the raft or move to town and let Aunt Sally "sivilize" him. In
Eagle there were a lot of Aunt Sallys.

We finished with "The Battle Hymn of the Republic," and the
minister invited visitors to rise and introduce themselves to the
congregation. Two tow-headed missionaries from Minnesota
stood up shyly to applause. They were nice-looking teenagers,
the kind who appear in soft drink ads. Then it was my turn. I
bobbed up briefly, smiling like an idiot because I felt like a
fraud. For a traveler, church attendance is a form of endorsement, like wearing a Masons' ring. It's an affidavit that you're
not a Philistine, that back home you're just like them. But I
didn't want to be one of the minister's fish wheels, anchored in
midstream, scooping errant souls into a suffocating sky-blue
heaven. I'd rather take my chances with the salmon.

After services, a pickup softball game started at the end of the
runway. Outfielders squinting into the sun had to look out not
only for fly balls but incoming airplanes. Most of the people
from church were here, swinging a bat or shouting encouragement as someone rounded the bases. It would be easy, I
thought, to be drawn into this net. In the bottom of the ninth,
the game was called when a sudden rainstorm turned to hail. It
was an isolated storm, blown off the river and surrounded by

blue sky, so that, except for the shadow over the field, the rest of the valley was in bright sunshine. I crouched under the church eaves while hail clattered against the tin roof. The hailstones grew bigger and bigger, pelting the green field as if heaven had been emptied of fly balls.

In the evening I helped Red carry a crock of baked beans to the potluck dinner and later took in a movie at the log cabin library. Sitting in a folding chair, I watched *Superman II* flying between the aisles of books. Each time the lights went on for a reel change, the audience turned around in their seats to chat or thumb through a book. I was reading *A Dog Puncher on the Yukon* when someone tapped me on the shoulder. It was a woman who'd recognized me from Sunday services.

"Ain't this place great?" she said enthusiastically. "We moved here last year and the kids just love it. I'd never think of going back to L.A."

The lights dimmed and we settled back into the movie. A trio of henchmen from the planet Krypton were making life unpleasant for the Man of Steel. When things got to be too much for him, he flew off to the North Pole, which looked suspiciously like the outskirts of Eagle in December. There were other parallels. You could sense the mixture of sympathy and contempt the audience felt for their movie counterparts in the city — overrun by aliens, taking whatever the villains dished out. You could almost hear the audience thinking, Why do they take it? Why don't they just get out?

After the final reel, we staggered outside into a cool drizzle, feeling somehow smaller. The neon lights of Metropolis were fading into green hills and distant blue mountains.

The morning of July fourth broke hot and windless. Too late for the flag-raising at the courthouse, we joined the stragglers, including a man on stilts dressed as Uncle Sam, walking to the old school grounds. A row of stalls draped in red, white, and blue crepe stood in a grassy field ringed with pickup trucks. The carnival was a homegrown affair, without shrieking rides or sullen roustabouts. But kids lit off noisy bottle rockets and firecrackers, and the small midway offered games of chance, trinkets to buy, and plenty of good things to eat. The wonderful, greasy smells of popcorn, burritos, and fry bread wafted in the air. It was a perfect summer day, and Eagle seemed less like the Last Frontier than it did small-town America re-created from a Norman Rockwell cover.

I bought a ticket for the cakewalk and promenaded around the one-room schoolhouse to a record, but when the music stopped I emerged cakeless as ever. The contestants at the pie-eating contest each got an entire pie to themselves but had to eat it with their hands behind their backs like pigs at a trough. The winner turned out to be one of the young missionaries from Minnesota, who had rooted happily through a lemon meringue. Finally I bought a hunk of sweet fry bread and sat down at a picnic table with Earl and Red to watch the balloon toss and three-legged race. We seemed to be the only familyless men in Eagle. Everywhere you looked were children, red and white, underfoot or crooked in someone's arm, waving miniature Stars and Stripes left over from the parade.

Some of their parents sat cross-legged in a circle on the grass, strumming guitars and drinking beer, although Eagle was officially dry. None of them was a churchgoer, so I took them for river people. They looked older than their long hair and dungarees suggested, and their presence evoked in us quite different memories.

Earl straightened the brim of his cap and hooted, "Look at the ponytail on that guy, would you!"

The comment touched some long-buried nerve. I didn't mind running down my own old affectations, but I wouldn't hear some Masonic redneck from Ohio doing it.

"So what?" I said.

"You remember the riots at the Democratic convention in Chicago? Well, a month later those same people were down in Columbus throwing rocks at us. Seems like everybody that gave us trouble back then had long hair."

"I had long hair. I didn't throw rocks at anybody. Look, it meant little then and it means less now."

This was a stupid argument. What was I trying to prove to Earl, anyhow? That the reasons for chucking rocks at him had been more complicated than the length of the throwers' hair, or that all of it, the rock throwing and the politics, had been only a fashion, now out of style? I didn't know the answer to that one myself.

The afternoon light was fading. In the circle of grass, people were swaying to an old song. The words came slowly back to me, something about a moon shadow.

Ancient history.

Below Eagle, the Yukon flowed in loose coils at the bottom of a twisting, sunlit canyon. Sheer bluffs anticipated each curve in the river. The most spectacular was Calico Bluff, a striped and folded torte of black shale and yellow-white limestone six hundred feet high and a mile long. The bluff cast a cool, damp-smelling shadow on the river. I turned a corner, and another segment of canyon gave itself away — pleated green terraces and serrated mountains, defined in shadow and sunshine and fading into a distant range of clouds.

Three tributary rivers entered in quick succession — the Seventymile, Tatunduk, and Nation — each the keel of a lateral valley leading back into overlapping blue mountains. Miles back, I had entered Yukon-Charley Rivers National Preserve. The preserve stretched a hundred and fifty miles from Eagle to Circle, an area the size of Connecticut. It had been withdrawn in the waning days of the Carter administration, scuttled, so to speak, to keep it from falling into the hands of oil conglomerates and developers. But so far I'd seen no signs of a preserve on the bank: no rangers in campaign hats, no designated camp-grounds, no evidence of a park but the shaded block on my map.

In the hot weather, the river continued to drop, exposing a submerged landscape of gravel bars and shoals. Green, willowy tops of islands poked up from the water like conning towers. At ten in the evening, I beached the canoe on a hump of damp gravel and pitched my tent on high ground in case a cloudburst far upriver should reflood the island. I cooked a can of beef stew on my small kerosene stove and slept that night on smooth river stones where days before salmon had hovered.

In the morning, an acrid yellow haze hung over the water. Smoke from forest fires burning upriver had drifted downstream. The smoke made my eyes water and the shore look distant and fog-bound. I broke camp and motored on, the haze growing thicker and thicker until a plume of smoke billowed from a mountain notch above me. The burning woods were second-growth aspen, leafy and green beside standing deadwood from an earlier fire. Lightning had sparked this blaze, and another storm would have to put it out. With no one to warn or tell, I canoed on, letting the mountain burn behind me.

Ahead, a rubber raft floated with the current. From a distance it appeared to have slipped its mooring, but when I got closer I saw a rower and several passengers. With its human freight of bare limbs and sprawling torsos, the rubber boat called to mind *The Raft of the Medusa*. A young man sitting in the center, his nose streaked white with zinc oxide, let the oars go limp in the oarlocks and threw me a line.

"Where are we?" he asked. "Have we passed the mouth of the Kandik?"

The rafters, two couples in bathing suits and sunglasses, had chartered a helicopter to fly their raft and themselves to Eagle; now they were floating back to Circle, where they'd left their car. Reaching into a cooler, the oarsman produced a bottle of rose-colored wine and poured me a glass. For a while we drifted in tandem.

Here were the sort of people the new preserve meant to attract, visitors who would "take only pictures, leave only footprints." For that matter, so was I. But the rafters were disappointed at the scarcity of game and blamed it on the hunting and trapping permitted in the preserve.

"All we've seen," one of the women griped, "was a wood frog on the beach."

Among river travelers such complaints were universal. They expected wildlife to appear with the tameness and predictability of park animals. In Denali National Park, for instance, moose and caribou have adjusted to the shuttle buses carrying tourists through the park. When an animal is spotted along the roadside, someone on the bus shouts "Caribou at four o'clock!" or

"Moose at twelve o'clock!" The bus driver brakes, and half the riders shift to the other side to take pictures. What's missing from these encounters, however, is the randomness of meeting an animal in the wild, neither party knowing exactly what the terms of the meeting are — a bluff charge, a quick retreat, death. When the rules are spelled out too clearly, the sense of surprise that delights or terrifies is lost.

When I told the rafters I was stopping at fish camps and cabins, they looked nonplused. They were interested only in animal sightings, in grizzlies and caribou, in nature insofar as it excluded human nature. But it was arrogant to think people didn't belong here. In subtle ways a park changes the landscape it's meant to preserve by objectifying it, setting it apart from human experience, making it no more than a backdrop for someone's vacation. The rationale for the park was not just a fear of haul roads and oil derricks but of people who might settle down and turn the mountain valleys into bits of Appalachia. Yet the few human traces I'd seen — tumbledown cabins and fishnets trailing in the river — were all indications that the land was alive. Indeed, the country left its own mark on people, and these were signs worth reading.

A clear apron of water spread out at the mouth of the Kandik River, splitting itself among delta islands and driftwood. A flock of red-breasted mergansers bobbing at the entrance of a channel swung about as I approached. They swam away with a neck-rocking motion, then broke into a skittering run to gain the air, wings beating black and white, black and white.

I landed on a mudflat that held a profusion of animal tracks: black bear, fox, raven, gull, and the touching, childlike impressions of porcupines. A cabin loomed in the patchy sunlight above the spruce bank, but nobody answered when I called out. Purple fireweed grew as high as the rope swing in the front yard. The cabin door lay propped open, so I went inside.

Even by my modest standards, it was a poorly built cabin. The walls bowed, and daylight showed through cracks in the chinking. A partially scraped moosehide was nailed to the wall.

Homemade furniture lay in disarray among tins of freeze-dried food, and over all this hung a constant insect buzzing, the music of entropy. This wasn't a gold rush relic but the remains of a more recent stampede. I lay down on a mattress and scanned the books on the shelf: *First Lessons in Bee-Keeping; The Hunter's Bible; Eating from the Wild; How to Know the Minerals and the Rocks; Field Guide to Butterflies; Brave New World; No Place to Hide*. It might have been the library of an austere and failed sect. Before, there had always been a comfortable gap of years between myself and the old cabins along the river. But this place gave me the strange feeling of picking through my own things, reconstructing my own past.

A child's drawings were tacked to the wall above the bed. One showed two stick figures beneath an enormous orange and yellow sun. In another, a rainbow-colored ship sailed away on the summits of mountainous waves. Only a child, I thought, could imagine winter in such bright colors.

I left the cabin as from a bad dream. Paddling to the other bank of the Kandik, I came upon a man tinkering with an outboard. The cowling was off, and he probed its innards with a wrench. A worn path led into the woods.

I asked about the empty cabin.

"That place?" he laughed. "Sarge Waller built it about ten years ago, when his kids were little shavers. First chance they could, they took out of there for Eagle and never been back. One year he rented it out to a guy and his girl from Ohio. Jesus, they were so unprepared. I helped them put up a bunch of meat and fish and stuff. They didn't know what they were doing. But they made it. Came in the spring and the Park Service kicked them out the following spring." He thought about it for a moment. "That was a pretty dirty trick of Sarge to send them out here so unprepared."

He laid down the wrench and wiped his hands on his pants.

"Come on up to my cabin and have a drink."

Rick Lawrence's cabin lay in a clearing of black spruce. It had a sod roof and was bunkered with earth. There was a small garden in front and a fishnet drying on a clothesline. In the back, a team of sled dogs panted in the heat. Bedded down on a blanket of their own shed fur, they looked like half-fleeced sheep and reeked of rotten salmon.

Lawrence brought out two Mason jars of homemade beer. The lids opened with a slight exhalation, like corked wine.

"It's not really beer, it's malt liquor. I start off with three quarts of malt, four gallons of Kandik water, use a bottom-fermenting yeast, and throw in hops for flavor. Let it set for a couple of weeks at least. After drinking good home-brew, a bottle of store-bought tastes like nothing."

I picked gnats out of the foamy head and drank. It tasted pungent and cidery. Another swig and my head was swimming.

Arranged on the cabin roof was a row of lynx skulls, bleached white and delicate as teacups.

"I'm mainly a lowland trapper," he said. "But now that the rabbit cycle's crashed, the lynx will quit breeding. You don't want to trap in a low cycle or you'll trap off your breeding stock. So I'm going to have to move up into the mountains. You have to get up in the higher country to trap marten. Good marten trapping starts about fifteen hundred feet."

With his bib overalls, blond hair, and thick arms, Lawrence looked like he'd been lifted from a tractor dragging a cloud of dust through a corn field. He'd grown up in the flatlands of Iowa. His earliest vision of the North and of his future life was a Hamm's Beer display mounted on a tavern wall. It showed a revolving electric tableau of peaked mountains and clear-running streams. The Land of Sky Blue Waters. For years he looked for that place, making intermediate stops in Southeast Asia, Oregon, Juneau, and Fairbanks before arriving at the mouth of the Kandik River. Now that he'd found the place in the picture, he was convinced the government wanted to take it away from him.

"First couple of years I was out here were really nice because the Park Service was just a word. Two summers ago was the first time they showed up. Until then it was just hearsay that there even was a park. The way I see it, they don't want people like us living out here. They'd rather have us in a factory, paying taxes. Some bigwig from Fish and Game told a friend of mine,

'I think how and where you are living is a privilege and not your right.' "

One summer a backpacker paddling down the Kandik in a collapsible kayak spotted Lawrence's cabin and his fishnets drying in the sun. He dispatched an angry letter to the Park Service, demanding to know why people were allowed to live in a national preserve. The sight of the cabin, he wrote, had ruined his "wilderness experience."

Rafting down the Yukon a hundred years ago, Frederick Schwatka located half a dozen log houses opposite the mouth of the Kandik but found the current too swift to land. The huts belonged to the northernmost band of Han, who called their settlement Charley's Village after the head chief's Anglicized name. Another report placed the village just above the willow-lined tributary known as *Kayndik,* or "willow creek." In 1914 a flood washed the village away, but even into the thirties there were roadhouses and wood camps and trappers' cabins in this vicinity. In the long tenure of people on the Kandik, few if any residents would have described what they were doing in terms as rarefied as a "wilderness experience."

"Right now," Lawrence said, "counting up the Charley River and up the Kandik, there are ten or eleven households on the Yukon between Eagle and Circle. But if you leave, you can't come back. You can't even have someone come out and live with you. There have been several married couples out here who've split up. And the Park Service told them they can't bring anyone else out. That's sticking their nose in too far."

He'd come here alone but had acquired a female partner who'd squeezed in under the deadline. She was in Fairbanks now buying their winter supplies. Most of their food they gathered themselves from the garden, the river, and the woods.

"Took me thirty-one years and I finally made it. And it took me losing my wife and daughter because if we'd stayed together I'd never have gotten here. And now it's questionable whether I'll even get to stay because they made it a park with all these damn rules and regulations."

We compared divorces. His losses were greater than mine, but he seemed resigned to them, as if divorce was a necessary entry fee to this life. Evidently he thought it was worth the price.

"Seems these days," he said, "it's the woman who decides she don't want to be married. My ex liked Arby's Roast Beef sandwiches and movies and jump in the car and go when you want to. The things she was brought up with. So we're each living the life we want."

Tacked to a wall inside the cabin was a hand-drawn card — "I love you Daddy — from Sarah" — and a department store photograph of a small girl dressed in a cowboy hat and red bandanna. She was seated on a pony in front of a false backdrop of trees.

"She'll be nine next week. She was only a year old when they left. I don't think she has any memories of Alaska at all."

He took a long sip of beer and looked out the window at the peaked mountains and clear-running stream.

"I'm looking forward some day to bringing her up here," he said quietly. "Not to live but to visit. With no kids around and nobody to play with, it'd be hard for her. It's real hard on kids."

A headwind stirred up the river, splashing spray over my bow. Farther below the Kandik, I crossed the mouth of the Charley River, tea-colored and slack after its plunging descent. For a quicksilver mountain stream, it looked unpromisingly wide and bleak. Gusts of wind trembled willow leaves on the gravel banks and blew the river back toward the mountains.

The light had gathered in the north when I landed below an old roadhouse. A dirt road led up from the beach to a timbered building. Nailed totemlike below the second-story window was a grim memento — the head of a grizzly bear, its fur faded to blond.

Three dogs, skinny as coyotes, watched me from the shade of a birch grove. They were spooky, wild-looking animals, who neither barked nor slunk away but stood frozen, staring ahead with alert, feral eyes, ready to bolt. Turning a corner around the roadhouse, I met the dogs' master standing over a blazing fire.

Barefoot and shirtless, he wore a bearskin vest and had tied his long greasy hair back with a sash of marten skin. He had the long-distance eyes of a flower child gone to seed. Strapped across his back with a rawhide sling was a battered bolt-action rifle. He offered me a cup of tea, and we stood on opposite sides of the fire, feeding it sticks and stealing furtive glances at each other.

When I said I'd come down from Eagle, he shook his head. "I can't handle that place, man. It's too fucked up."

He'd spent the Fourth at a gold mine up Coal Creek and was still nursing a tequila hangover. The miners had sent him home with a bag of gray meat scraps for his dogs. But the dogs were going to see none of it.

"Look at this stuff," he said, hefting the rancid meat bag as if it were a sack of gold. "They were going to throw it away. Can you believe that?"

Willis lived by himself far up a tributary river, coming down to the Yukon only in the summer to fish. He was a true loner, the exception rather than the rule in a country where people necessarily paired up to survive its rigors. In the fall Willis had to line his canoe forty miles up the swift tributary to his trap lines, pulling the boat with a rope and sometimes in water up to his waist when the bank got too steep to climb. Tomorrow he planned to set a gill net in a swift eddy downriver, a difficult task without an outboard. I told him I'd help in the morning after a good night's sleep.

The park rangers who lived in the roadhouse were away in Eagle but had left a note inviting travelers to stay on the ground floor. The room was bare, with tall windows that bathed the whitewashed walls in river light. Flinging myself down on a mattress in the center of the floor, I tried to sleep. Once, on the edge of a dream, I thought I heard the whine of an approaching outboard. I opened my eyes and looked out the window. The fire was still burning, and through the flames I saw Willis staring back at me.

I slept uneasily the rest of the night.

In the morning, a park ranger dressed in gray twill came down the stairs holding a steaming pot of coffee. He was on his way from Circle to Eagle; it was his boat that had woken me in the middle of the night. Over coffee, he filled in the story behind the bear head nailed to the roadhouse. A year ago, a bear had tried to break through the same large window under which I had slept.

"I shooed the bear off once," the ranger said, "but when it showed up again I had to shoot it."

I asked him about the trapper at the mouth of the Kandik.

"There's a lot of paranoia that's probably not justified, but it's hard to convince people of that. Most of the people up here have a strong streak of anarchist in them. Myself included."

Dave Evans had pale blue eyes and a beard going nicely gray. His voice was soft and precise, carrying traces of Boston and Andover. He would have looked at home in a club tie. Ten years ago, Evans and his wife picked Eagle off a map because it had lovely mountains and wild rivers. Looking over likely tributaries, they settled on Sheep Creek only to find another trapper already firmly in place. So they hired a boatman in Eagle to transport them and what they hoped was a year's supply of food up the Nation River. They didn't return until the following spring. They built a cabin, started a garden, hunted, and fished. There was talk of a park even then, but nobody took it seriously. Three years after Evans and wife settled on the Nation, the Bureau of Land Management, predecessor to the Park Service on the upper Yukon, tried to evict them from their cabin for trespassing. Evans wouldn't be budged. Then last summer, he surprised a lot of people on the river by joining the Park Service.

"Obviously, if you want to win the hearts and minds of people, you hire them. The hardest part was confronting friends and neighbors, wearing a Park Service uniform when I knew they'd be uncomfortable seeing it on me. But I'm in a good position to look after their interests, which are, in fact, my interests."

We coiled Willis's gill net in a washtub and carried it down to the beach. After looking my boat over, Evans tactfully suggested using his nineteen-foot freighter canoe instead. We loaded the net in the bow, and the three of us raced downstream to where Willis's fish camp lay in an alder thicket. As we drew near, a young black bear in cinnamon phase, lean as an Airedale, peered over the riverbank. Seeing our landing party, the bear turned tail and dashed into the woods.

"I hope the bastard hasn't wrecked my camp!" Willis cried. But climbing up from the beach, we found pathetically little to wreck, only cut poles, a few pieces of tin roofing for a smokehouse, and swarming clouds of mosquitoes.

Willis retrieved a chunk of rock for an anchor, and we headed upstream to set his net in a turbulent eddy where the cliff tumbled into the river. Willis tied one end of the net to a crib of boulders and then fed out the rest as the current carried us away. At the end of the line, he dropped the anchor overboard with a splash, and we cut the strings holding the weighted lead line from the float line so that the net descended like a mesh curtain into the brown river.

Back at the roadhouse, Evans reached into a kit bag and brought out a nearly full bottle of Yukon Jack that Willis had left in Circle on his last visit. It was a syrupy, amber-colored liquor, "a taste born of hoary nights, when lonely men struggled to keep their fires lit," according to the label. Willis sat splay-legged on the floor, slugging down drinks as if he was afraid he'd forget the bottle again.

I asked Evans if Willis would always be allowed to set his salmon nets in the park.

"Everybody out here is pretty confident they'll be allowed to stay as long as they live a subsistence lifestyle. But what does that mean?"

Subsistence, the rather simple notion of living off the land, had become an increasingly complex and political concept. The state of Alaska was attempting to define the parameters of subsistence, having affirmed the priority of food hunters and fishermen when shortages of game occurred. Sportsmen's groups in Fairbanks and Anchorage attempted in a recent election to have the subsistence provision repealed, arguing that the game belonged to everyone. The issue set white against Native, city against bush. The referendum failed in the end. In the Yukon-Charley Preserve, subsistence was tied to cabin use. No new cabins were allowed, and the Park Service monitored its resident human population as closely as its grizzlies or the peregrine falcons nesting on the bluffs. But humans were less predictable in their movements. If a trapper worked seasonally on the oil pipeline, did that compromise his subsistence status? If he divorced and remarried, could he bring his new spouse into the country? If he got the urge to take a hiatus, could he head south for the winter, like the peregrine, and still return?

"A lot of people," Evans said, "are afraid that sometime down the road the Park Service is going to tighten up regulations and move them out. The land is pretty near its carrying capacity now. I don't think there's another place from Eagle to Circle good enough to fish and run a sustaining trap line. The test will be when somebody leaves and his cabin is vacant and there's space for a new family to move in. That hasn't happened yet. What I suspect will happen, and what I'd like to see happen, is that when an opening arrives somebody be allowed to fill it. I hope that fifty years from now somebody is living on the Nation."

Willis was by now thoroughly drunk. He had sat quietly on the periphery of conversation. Now, at odd moments, he broke in, speaking loudly to no one in particular.

"I don't want to own the land!" he shouted. "All I want is the use of these cabins!"

"I wonder," Evans said when Willis quieted down, "how many of these guys will still be out here in ten years. What happens when their kids reach school age? Subsistence is a year-round, everyday job. You can't step in and out of it, unless you're independently wealthy. One girl did inherit some money, not an astronomical sum, but enough to free herself. She moved into town."

"Women are no good in the bush," Willis moaned. He slumped further down on the floor until his face lay next to the bottle. In a little while, he was snoring like a bear.

Working for the Park Service had done more than just double Evans's income; it broke the boundaries of a life lived by trap and gun. But not without cost. Last spring, he and his wife flew to Fairbanks and filed for divorce. The idea had been his.

"What do you plan to do now?" I asked.

He shrugged his shoulders. "Two years ago, I would have said I'd never leave, that I'd die here. But I can't anymore. I might move to Fairbanks, or I might stay here. It's kind of nice not to know. For some years now, I've always known exactly what I'd be doing."

Evans got up to leave. Already it was dusk, and he had the long haul to Eagle before him and many stops along the river to deliver mail and visit friends. Gently, he moved the bottle of Yukon Jack so Willis wouldn't knock it over in his sleep. Then I went too, leaving Willis snoring on the floor to awake alone.

A RIM OF BLUFFS encircled the river, intersected by the dark green alleyways of tributary streams. On one of these creeks lived a French-Canadian woman who, two summers before, had been mauled by a grizzly. It was late July, the tail end of the King salmon run. She and her husband had stopped for the night at a friend's fish camp on their way to Dawson. Everyone had stayed up late drinking coffee and visiting before unrolling their sleeping bags beside the Yukon. Early in the morning, the woman awoke to stars overhead. The beach, with its borders of spruce woods and river, looked washed-out in the silvery twilight. Something dark moved on the other side of a picnic table, and the woman raised herself up for a better look. It was not, as she first thought, one of the camp's dogs but a sow grizzly, swaying its dish-faced head back and forth, sniffing the air for a scent. She remembered passing a sow and cubs on the beach earlier in the day. This might have been the same bear, drawn into camp by a loose dog or the odor of drying salmon. Whatever; before the woman could pull back under the covers, the bear covered the ground between them with terrifying speed and seized her head in its jaws. She smelled the bear's rancid breath, felt the dull crunch of tooth on bone, even as the grizzly hauled her from the warmth of her sleeping bag. By now the rest of the camp had awakened. Were those her screams? Clamping a huge foreleg around the woman, the bear began to drag her toward the woods. In that blurred moment, she was aware of the cool night air, the shouts of her companions as they tried to save her, and the awful knowledge that she was being carried into the forest. She had lived in the country for several years and understood that very shortly, and quite literally, she was going to become a part of it.

What saved her life was a fallen tree. The bear could not heft the woman over a deadfall and so dropped her and fled. Why she had been singled out for the grizzly's fury was a mystery. Athabascan Indians traditionally believed that an enmity exists between bears and women, perhaps because a bear is so solitary and manlike a creature; a skinned bear resembles nothing so much as a human corpse. More likely it is the fact that a woman's menses will attract a bear. At any rate, hours passed before the woman could be motored upriver for help. Then came the long, agonizing flight to Whitehorse, where surgeons reconstructed her torn face.

I had heard this story told piecemeal along the river, until all the details lodged together into a single narrative. Part of the nightmare quality of such stories is that they remind us of our earliest fears, in which death comes as a wild beast. And the most terrifying aspect is that the victim knows, even in the midst of dying, that she is about to be devoured.

The woman who survived the attack was not averse, people said, to talking about it. But I let the creek where she lived slip past without stopping. I did not want to meet the woman. I did not want to see her face because I knew my eyes would search out the pale webbing of scars, a secret map to the old fear.

As the last bluff fell away, the canyon receded into low spruce banks. With the sun gone, the air quickly chilled, and I put on a windbreaker and cotton gloves. Evans had warned me to watch for three islands, then keep to the left or I'd miss Circle altogether and slip into the labyrinthine sloughs and channels of the Yukon Flats. Two ragged islands slid by in the dusk. I turned left into a narrow, misting side channel that curved inland. Mosquitoes descended from the tangled spruce banks. The only sound was the chugging outboard and a startled duck that whirred up from the bank and flew ahead into the darkness. I was nearly out of gasoline and beginning to suspect the slough would dead-end in a swamp, when unexpectedly it circled back to rejoin the river. A little farther on, arc lights illuminated a circle of metal roofs on the left bank, from which I could hear the steady drumming of a generator. I landed on a shore littered with flattened beer cans. It was two in the morning. A molten sun slowly floated above the spruce-green and khaki-colored islands of the Flats. A dog came out and barked at it.

Circle was a settlement that Amundsen, upon his reentry into civilization, had found depressing. "Circle City must be regarded," he wrote, "as 'quite a little town,' as witness its liquor shops and dancing saloon, to say nothing of the fighting and drunkenness."

It was still quite a little town. Most of it fit under one roof. The Midnight Sun Café was a rambling complex that housed as well a post office, liquor store, trading post, charter helicopter service, and saloon. What connected Circle to the rest of the world was a gravel road, open only during the summer, linking it to Fairbanks a hundred miles away. The road dead-ended into the Yukon behind some picnic tables and a sign.

WELCOME TO CIRCLE CITY
Established in 1893
Interior Alaska's Oldest Major Gold Camp
THE END OF THE ROAD
Most Northern Point
on Connected American Highway System

Prospectors had named Circle under the mistaken notion that it lay within the Arctic Circle, which was actually fifty miles due north. And with the completion of the Dalton Highway to Prudhoe Bay, Circle was no longer the most northern point on the highway system. But it certainly qualified as the end of the road.

A dusty camper rolled to a stop in front of the sign. The driver got out and squinted at the river, broad here as a lake, thinking: The Yukon. He looked at it with the same blank expression people reserve for ocean gazing, staring off toward China. But the river, dirty yellow and seemingly without banks, couldn't help but disappoint. There was nothing to tie the river to the name, with its heavy freight of evocations. So he took a picture of the sign instead, then climbed back in the truck and headed home.

Sitting at a picnic table, I watched this scene played out over and over again.

A blue Land Rover with California plates, the roof heaped with trunks and tires. A young, tanned couple disembarked. The woman wore a diffident smile, while her companion scanned the water with binoculars.

A Winnebago from Plant City, Florida. The driver called inside, "Hey, Marion. Get the camera and I'll take your picture in front of the Yukon." She emerged, fattish in shorts, and posed in front of the sign. After the picture was snapped, she climbed back into the camper.

A teenager on foot, his thick black hair tied with a red bandanna. Twice he walked by my picnic table, a six-pack under his arm, before sitting down.

"Want a beer?" He peeled off a can and handed it to me. "My name's Arthur. Why don't you tell me your name?"

I told him my name.

"John. Hey, that's my last name! I wasn't sure I should come over here because you were reading a book, but I thought I'd take a chance."

Arthur John was celebrating because he had just earned a thousand dollars fighting a forest fire in the Minto Flats near Fairbanks.

"Another fire and I'll be all set."

In the heat, the cold beer tasted wonderful. It had been the warmest, driest summer in years, and kids from the village were happily wading in the river. We watched them splashing and shrieking in the muddy water.

Arthur suddenly stood up and shouted, "Hey, you better watch that little one there!" He turned to me, his voice grown very somber. "Those kids don't know what they're doing. That river's fast. It took my uncle and it took my grandfather. My grandfather was a real Indian, you know, tough. He fell out of a boat and it took him right under. My father told me, 'Arthur, I'm only going to say it once — respect that river!' "

But Arthur said it twice for my benefit: "Respect that river!"

"I do," I assured him. "I never go out in the boat without a life jacket on."

"Funny thing," Arthur said. "No one around here wears one. None of these Indians."

A battered yellow pickup truck. It was late in the day and I was preparing to leave. Having driven from Fairbanks for the weekend, the two couples sat on the picnic table drinking whiskey and Coke, watching the river.

"Where you headed?" one of the drinkers asked as I loaded my canoe.

"Fort Yukon." From habit I mentioned the next downriver settlement. Giving the Bering Sea as a destination seemed too dramatic; it was like telling people you were driving to China.

He snickered. "I don't know anybody but mean people come out of Fort Yukon. They have a running ad in the paper for a state trooper because they can't keep one. You better watch your canoe the whole time you're there."

"Everything is roped in."

"Hell, they'll steal the whole damned boat!"

His name was Lonnie, and the sun and whiskey had fogged his brain and made his clothes an encumbrance. He peeled off a pearl-buttoned shirt to reveal a large, unhealthily white belly. Another drink and he took off his cowboy boots and waded ankle-deep in the water to look over my canoe.

"Many people upriver?" he asked.

"Along the creeks," I said.

"That's what I'm going to do one of these days. Maybe next winter. Go up and build a cabin, trap. How are the trees upriver? Big enough for cabin logs?"

I told Lonnie what Evans had told me: that the land in the preserve was closed.

"Who needs that park shit anyway. I'll just go downriver."

Then, I said, he'd be trespassing on land owned by Doyon, the Athabascan Regional Corporation.

"I got that beat," Lonnie shouted. "I married an Indian!"

His girlfriend, however, was an ample redhead with curly hair and a guffawing laugh.

"Hey," he asked, stroking her backside, "you want to take her with you down the Yukon? She'll make it worth your while."

"I'm overloaded now."

Lonnie laughed, took his red Budweiser cap off his head, and placed it on mine.

"Consider it a gift."

I took the cap, pulled the visor low to shade my eyes, and then shoved off before Lonnie could remove any more clothing.

The river split around a wooded island, then split again, unraveling like a frayed rope. In every direction, the Flats spread out into an enormous swamp. The mountains had fallen behind, except for a spur of peaks far to the west like a gray smudge on the horizon. I kept turning off into side channels that were themselves good-sized rivers, each channel presenting a new opportunity to get lost. A map was useless for navigation. My chart looked like a satellite photograph of the earth, mostly blue water broken by green islands. Old-timers used to tie rocks to their bowlines, heave them overboard, and let the current keep them in the channel. I looked for high cutbanks where the water ran deep and fast. Skirting past logjams and a swirling whirlpool where three channels converged, I watched for stranded driftwood, which the current always pointed downstream, like the needle of a compass.

The flatness of the terrain, the network of articulating waterways, everything but the furious current suggested a river delta. Rounding an island, I was almost surprised not to find a yawning river mouth blending into the sea. The Flats is, in fact, made up of many river deltas. Several large tributaries debouch into the vast alluvial basin that forms the Flats: the Chandalar, the Christian, the Sheenjek, the Big and Little Black rivers, Birch Creek, and the Porcupine. A cloverleaf of rivers. If the Arctic is an arid wasteland of shallow soil and little precipitation, then this is one of its great watering holes. Moose graze in the willow scrub, bears tramp the islands, and waterfowl by the millions nest in the myriad lakes and sloughs.

In the sixties, there was a scheme to drown the Flats beneath the backwaters of an enormous hydroelectric dam. Rampart

Dam would have generated two and a half times the power of Grand Coulee and created a reservoir larger than Lake Erie. In the process, the salmon run would have been lost forever, nesting grounds destroyed, and seven Athabascan villages flooded beneath the dam's rising waters. A group of local boosters called "Yukon Power for America" thought this a small price for progress. Alaska senator Ernest Gruening described the Flats as "about as worthless and useless an area as can be found in the path of any hydroelectric development. Scenically, it is zero." In its place he envisioned a great freshwater fishery, where relocated Indian guides and visiting sportsmen would troll over the reefs of drowned villages. But Rampart Dam was never built. Had it been built, the dam's reservoir would have taken twenty years to fill. It would still be filling.

There is a violent beauty to the Flats. For all the apparent flatness, the gradient here is as steep as in the canyon, the current unrelenting. With no confining banks, the muddy water rushes furiously over the sand and gravel plain like a desert in a spate. The Yukon sweeps through the Flats, overflowing its banks, cutting new channels, tearing down islands here to deposit them there, the land constantly in the process of re-creating itself. Traveling through the maze of islands, I felt the giddy sensation of riding a flood tide, soaring over a submerged terrain that would soon be dry again.

A pair of Arctic terns screeched and dived as I erected my tent on a small gravel bar. They flew in winnowing aerobatics, gray and white wings slicing up the sky. If I bothered to look, I might find their mottled blue eggs hidden somewhere in the coarse gravel. But first I had to unload the canoe and then build a driftwood fire, as much for company as to cook upon. Afterward, there was the river, heavy with silt, to listen to and the birds flitting overhead. At eleven o'clock in the evening, the sun had not quite set but circled low over the spruce horizon.

I had crossed or would soon cross latitude 66°33′N into the Northern Frigid Zone. The Arctic Circle, as shown by a broken line on most maps, is essentially a demarcation of light. Above this imaginary threshold, the year divides itself neatly into seasons of nearly continuous daylight or darkness. Because of the tilt of the earth's axis, the Arctic sun does not set at midsummer nor rise at midwinter. Greek astronomers had first fixed the Arctic Circle of the heavens where *Arktikos*, the constellation Ursa Major, skimmed the northern horizon and did not set. Two schools of thought emerged concerning the region beneath these stars. The more enlightened reasoned that far to the north lay an uninhabitable frozen wasteland. Popular thinking, however, held that beyond the Rhipaean Mountains, from which the cold winds blew, was the land of the Hyperboreans, a legendary race who lived in perpetual sunshine and plenty.

There were merits to both views, depending on the season in question. The extremes of Arctic weather result from the absence or plenitude of light. If I remained on this tiny island through freeze-up to the winter solstice, I would see unrelieved darkness and unimaginable cold. I liked the Arctic summers better. The days were desert dry, and the night sky had a luminous quality, a pale afterglow.

I let the campfire burn itself out and sat watching the terns swoop overhead. Circumpolar travelers, they fly from Antarctica to nest in the Arctic, a migration even greater than the salmon's but without the tragic overtones. Flying from summer to summer, they live in perpetual sunlight, like Hyperboreans. That the ultimate destination for such a long journey should be this patch of gravel filled me with affection for both the terns and this tiny island.

Winding through miles of braided channels the next day, I despaired of finding anything so small as a village hidden in the Flats. Then I spotted a fish wheel, and then another and another, until there was a fish wheel churning on every bend. Ahead, two enormous radar grids loomed above the trees, part of the DEW line facing Russia. They dwarfed the village that sat on a high bench above a slough, which was slowly silting in. Fort Yukon was the largest Athabascan village in Alaska. Like most villages, it had expanded away from the river so that the oldest, most weather-beaten cabins fronted the riverbank. Painted on the side of one old building was a faded epitaph: FORT YUKON FOR RAMPART — For a Better Future.

I stayed with the manager of the Alaska Commercial Company and his wife in the company house behind the store. A comfortable split-level, it had bookshelves filled with Alaskana and beaver pelt doilies on the sofa. The manager was a slight man who viewed Fort Yukon in terms of the Third World.

"My wife gets tired of this comparison, but this place is a lot like one of those little nations that has a bauxite mine and suddenly becomes independent with no experience. You're just exchanging one elite for another. Instead of whites, it's a few Indians."

Beri Morris felt at home in the Third World. He called the house his bungalow and liked to sit on the screened veranda overlooking the Flats; perhaps it reminded him of the African veldt. After college, he had emigrated to the last vestige of empire, Ian Smith's Rhodesia, and joined the British South African Police. He stayed two years, until rebels shot up his Land Rover and he decided to leave. Morris ended up as a store manager and fur buyer in Fort Yukon, a village that had its beginnings as a Hudson's Bay post.

The Alaska Commercial Company had taken over the trading post after Hudson's Bay was given its walking papers and moved across the border. "There's a lot of the same appeal working for the A. C. Company," said Morris, "— the tradition, the throwback to earlier times." As manager, Morris was in a direct line of descent from Alexander Murray, who founded Fort Yukon in 1847. He had learned the ropes of fur grading from Hudson's Bay employees, since most of the furs he bought eventually ended up at the Bay's headquarters in Toronto. The display tables at the Hudson's Bay auction houses were painted powder blue, a color that shows fur to its best advantage. But in the company posts, the buying tables were painted tan to bring out flaws in the pelts. When Morris haggled with a trapper, he laid the furs on the A. C. store's floor, which happened to be brown.

"You look for different things with different animals," Morris said. "The color of skin on the inside of the animal, whether it's dark or light. How it was taken off the carcass when it was skinned out. Sometimes if the skin is stored in a warm room, it can dry out like parchment. Sometimes the fur will be over-stretched, the neck long in relation to the body. You look at the overall quality of fur. You check for heavy guard hair, which is the outer or second layer. Foxes, when they've denned all winter, will rub off their guard hair. On a lynx, you want a good white color on the belly, with no spots. On beaver, size is most important. With fox it's color. Cross fox, silver fox, and red fox are all color phases of the same animal, cross bringing the most money."

Last winter, Morris accompanied a trapper on his trap line rounds to see the process from the beginning. It was 48 degrees below zero when they flew to a small cabin near the Canadian border. After checking sixty traps by snowshoe, they'd caught only nine marten. Two of the marten were still alive, so the trapper hit them each one good blow to the head.

In Fort Yukon, trapping is one of the few sources of income. It is a way for a man to earn a living without having to move to Anchorage or Fairbanks. The trap line binds a trapper to a particular landscape and traditional skills, so that he acquires not only cash but an essential knowledge of the land and its animals.

Trapping is also an inherently cold-blooded business. The animal that doesn't freeze to death in a leg-hold trap is bludgeoned or garroted to death. Yet if trapping is evil, as many people believe, then the blood is not just on the hands of the person who kills an animal so that someone in a distant city can wear its skin. The number of trappers out in the woods in any given winter is directly related to the worldwide price of furs and the vagaries of fashion. An Italian designer adding a lynx ruff to his fall collection sets in motion a demand that ultimately seals the fate of many northern lynx.

My only experience with trapping was amateurish and cruel. On frozen suburban streams, a boyhood friend and I set our steel traps beside the runways of small animals. The whole business seemed mysterious and cunning to me: reading the tracks in the snow, baiting the trap with some foul-smelling bit of meat, disguising the set, and then slinking home to wait. In the morning, we would race back to the stream to see what turned up.

The woods were a grab bag of small mammals, and we didn't care what we caught. Once we found only the gnawed-off leg of a muskrat. Another time we caught a snarling, spitting raccoon, which took forever to kill. We took turns clubbing the punch-drunk creature, still anchored to the trap, until it no longer raised its head to receive the blows. Then we hauled our prize over to my friend's house in a cardboard box to skin. His father, who otherwise encouraged our outdoor forays, looked at the poor dead raccoon and said we were a nothing but a pair of little ghouls, which put an end to trapping for me.

The Morrises had a dinner engagement, so I settled into a deck chair on the porch for the evening. A pallid twilight had spread over the Flats, the quiet broken only by barking dogs and motorcycles whining down the gravel roads. It was Saturday night, and a party was in progress across the street. The door opened and closed with an exhalation of voices and music.

Much later, when I woke up in the deck chair, the slate blue sky looked only a shade darker above the line of spruce. A man was pounding on the door across the street. "Lemme in!" he cried. "Hey, goddamn it! You can't lock me out of my own house!"

Sunday morning broke cool and overcast, the sky pealing with bells. We walked to St. Stephen's Episcopal Church, where the Morrises had been married. The bell ringer was a tall, dark-faced Indian who prayed like a Hindu, with clasped hands pressed to his forehead. The pews were old and hard, with wooden kneelers that creaked under our weight. Music welled from an electrified pump organ in the back of the church. With a flutter of hymnals we sang Psalm 25, heeding the instructions *"not dragging"*: "My eyes are ever turned toward the Lord/ For he will pluck my feet out of the net." The prayer books were in English, but there were also red Tukudh hymnals in the Gwich'in orthography developed in the 1860s by the Anglican missionary Robert McDonald. The writing system was little used today, but it had resulted in at least one remarkable conversion. Albert Tritt, once a powerful shaman, heard God's voice in these written words and led a nativistic movement in the early

1900s. In Fort Yukon he was remembered slightingly as "the Mad Bishop of the Chandalar."

Albert Edward Tritt was born around 1880 in a caribou-skin tent near Smoke Mountain on the east fork of the Chandalar. The caribou was to the Indians of the northern cordillera what the buffalo had been to the Plains tribes. The Chandalar Gwich'in were then nomadic hunters, doggedly following the herds' migrations. They lived, summer and winter, in lodges of bent willow poles draped with caribou skins and slept on mattresses of soft hides. They strung their bows with caribou sinew, and their children played a form of volleyball with a ball of caribou skin stuffed with hair. After a successful hunt, the people feasted on such delicacies as unborn calf or the head of a bull roasted slowly over a fire.

Late in summer, thousands of hooves clicked over the tundra as large herds of caribou migrated down from fawning grounds on the north slope of the Brooks Range. At this time the Chandalar Gwich'in constructed circular corrals of lashed poles, sometimes a mile in diameter, to gather the herd for easy killing. Women and children drove the caribou into the corral, where the men could shoot them at their leisure. As a child, Tritt remembered the terrible noise of the guns, "like a thunder," as the men fired into the herd.

One winter Tritt's father returned from a trading trip to Fort Yukon with one of the Bibles that Archdeacon McDonald had translated into Gwich'in. Reading aloud from the book, the elder Tritt took the words to heart. He marked the Sabbath by scoring the days of the week on a board and forbidding work or movement even if it meant going hungry. If he caught his children playing on Sunday, he took a willow switch to them. And he warned them not to steal lest Jesus put them in a fire, but as the younger Tritt later recalled, "What was there to steal?"

Some years after his father's death, Albert Tritt journeyed from Arctic Village to Fort Yukon to trade. Attending Christmas services at the church, he was impressed by the mission's success at teaching Indian children to read and write in their native language. Tritt purchased an English Bible and returned to Arctic Village convinced that the wellsprings of the white man's power lay in the written word and the God that dwelled there. Slowly he began to teach himself English by the laborious process of comparing verses from McDonald's Gwich'in translation with the King James version. He took the Bible with him everywhere, studying it by campfire when he went hunting. Perhaps he was moved by certain parallels with the Israelites: the tribal divisions, the wanderings, the strangers coming into the land.

I read Tritt's handwritten journal at the University of Alaska archives. It is a record of amazing faith. Tritt's English retains the cadence and phrasing of the King James Bible. The account begins: "And it came to pass . . ."

In the journal, Tritt describes long days of loneliness and introspection. He hardly slept. He would put out traps and then not remember where he had set them. He would make tea and cook a little meat and then suddenly find himself in tears.

"Praying and crying I go up on top of the mountain with holding prayer books. I hold it up to heaven crying. I put my tounge on it to and my lots of tears on it to and some of it I eat to."

The passage mirrors an encounter with a fiery angel in Revelations 10:25: "And I took the little book out of the angel's hand, and ate it up; and it was in my mouth sweet as honey."

In apocalyptic style, Tritt was struck to the ground by a blinding flash of light. Regaining consciousness, he came down from the mountain a prophet with a vision. He would preach the Gospel to his people in their own language, and, with it, reading and writing.

Tritt spent the following winter at the mission school in Fort Yukon, mastering the Gwich'in syllabary. In the spring he returned to Arctic Village loaded with Native Bibles, prayer books, and hymnals. But while preaching literacy, Tritt also advocated a return to the old hunting ways. He persuaded the people to begin building a great caribou fence around the base of a nearby mountain. The fence, many miles long, took years to finish and proved utterly worthless. The caribou refused to be corralled. Next, Tritt turned his attention to the construction of a log chapel, a replica of the church at Fort Yukon — no small feat at the northern edge of the timberline. A two-story schoolhouse was also begun but never completed, as some of Tritt's followers began to have second thoughts.

When anthropologist Robert McKennan visited Arctic Village in the 1930s, Tritt was a lean, upright man who wore horn-rim glasses and a stiff, bristling mustache. His influence was waning among all but his relatives. His dream of unifying the old ways with the new religion had been only partially fulfilled. But he had embarked upon a final effort: cutting a straight path, twenty feet wide, through the boreal forest to Fort Yukon so that travelers might follow it to his chapel. When McKennan asked why, Tritt quoted Isaiah: "The voice of him that crieth in the wilderness, Prepare ye the way of the Lord, make straight in the desert a highway for our God."

On Monday I went to see the chief of the village of Fort Yukon, whose office was in a palisaded replica of the old Hudson's Bay fort. The position was elective rather than ceremonial and carried real political weight. In the old days, a chief might be the best hunter or trapper in the village. Now he was likely the most politically savvy, a hunter of grants and proposals.

I'd been feeling somewhat remiss because I had talked to so many more whites than Natives on this trip. Part of the reason was that whites were so eager to talk. They were dying to tell their stories; indeed, you got the feeling that some of them had their stories pretty well figured out before they'd even arrived here. Natives, on the other hand, were less likely to cast themselves as the heroes in a wilderness drama. One man I'd talked to in Circle, an Indian in his eighties, had trapped and worked on steamboats, but he could recall only the wages he'd been paid for each job — that being the measure of success in the larger society. Rattling through the years and figures, he'd grown increasingly upset, as if a lifetime's receipts had somehow not balanced out.

I was waiting outside his office when Chief Clarence Alexander puttered up on a motorbike that was too short for his long legs. He sat down behind a desk while I scribbled notes.

"The biggest concern of Native people is jobs. Right now trapping is the economic base of Fort Yukon, but not everybody can be a trapper. I've been trying for three years now to catch a fox."

Alexander had written a proposal to buy a sawmill so villagers could build their own log houses. There was also an agricultural project in the works.

"Younger people are interested in building their own homes instead of buying HUD houses, which ice up in the winter and don't jive with the environment. The village corporation is also subdividing land so people can get their own lots. Creating business is what we're doing. The key to everything is that the people have to think business."

But despite all the federal programs and funds, Fort Yukon was struggling to jump into the twentieth century. Eighty percent of the villagers were unemployed. Few high school graduates went on to college. Villagers blamed the schools, and the teachers blamed the parents. Recently the village council had passed a resolution condemning the public school system for not sending corrected work home.

"Neither of my parents were educated. They didn't understand why we sat through school. But they knew it was for doing business. My father never went to school. He spoke English but he just picked it up. He lived off the land. They call that 'primitive.' But that's a funny word because you take a man from a village and he'll get along in the city, but you put a city man in the country and he's lost."

After his father drowned, Clarence Alexander helped raise his younger brothers. One day the youngest brother came home with a note from his teacher telling him not to return until he was ready to learn. The next day Clarence marched his brother back to school to confront the teacher. She was young and newly arrived from Washington State. If she felt intimidated by this tall, handsome Indian, she didn't show it. The boy was readmitted, and Clarence soon began visiting the teacher for his own reasons. Their marriage was a turnaround in an era when the only Indian-white marriages were between village girls and white soldiers. Clarence and Ginnie Alexander moved to Fairbanks, where he worked for the railroad and the highway department. In restaurants they typically got poor service and in hotels the worst room. "They'd look at you," he said, "like you were a different species." After eight years, they moved back to Fort Yukon.

Last month, Alexander began working for the Alaska Department of Fish and Game. In villages, subsistence is not a matter of lifestyle but a hard economic reality. There are few jobs, and the only alternatives to hunting and fishing are welfare or leaving the village. Alexander was mapping out traditional areas of subsistence activities. The maps, in Gwich'in, partitioned the Flats into domains of use, land used for a particular purpose in a particular season.

"Every family has an area, given boundaries where they have certain rights, 'grandfather rights,' to use the land. I come from an area up in the lakes where we fish for whitefish and pike, trap for muskrat and beaver in the spring, and do our moose hunting in the fall. Within the cycle, you know when to take certain animals."

Alexander had been downriver at his own fish camp the day before when he heard gunshots from the far shore. He put a rifle in his boat and went across to investigate. It was a white man firing a carbine into the air. He and his girlfriend had motored down Birch Creek in a canoe and ran out of gas. They thought they had reached the upper mouth when, in fact, they were miles from the lower outlet. Alexander gave the couple a can of gasoline and invited them to his camp for coffee. The couple took the gas but nervously declined the invitation.

"They must have thought I was crazy," he said with a rueful smile. "Sometimes I wonder if a white man knows what friendship is."

On my last day in Fort Yukon, Mary Morris offered to take me on a bicycle tour of the village. While we were getting ready to leave, two dark-eyed girls padded up the veranda in their bathing suits to ask if Mary would watch them swim. In her soft Carolinian voice, Mary suggested they try a neighbor. No, the girls said, she was busy as well. Mary suggested they hold up a

sign in front of the store, and they wandered off in that direction.

Mary and I pedaled down the grid of narrow gravel roads. The sky seemed enormous. After the high, confining mountains of the upper Yukon, Fort Yukon looked like a prairie of stunted spruce under billowy clouds.

Coasting past the state troopers and the Wycliffe Bible Translators, we stopped by the new school where Mary taught. In the playground was a jungle gym labeled U.S. LUNAR LANDER.

"We've had five principals in four years," said Mary, "and we'll probably have a new one this year. There have been four superintendants since the school came under the Alaska Unorganized Borough Rural School District. The acronym is ABSURD."

I liked Mary. She seemed genuinely interested in her students and tried hard to fit into the village. But she wasn't naive about her chances.

"It's a myth to think that two whites could ever be a part of this town. The friendliness increases the longer you're here, but I still feel like an outsider. Many whites come here thinking they can take all the values and really mix. But they can't, not even if they marry Natives."

I thought of Ginnie Alexander but didn't say anything.

At the airfield on the edge of town, C-119 Flying Boxcars were taking off with loads of retardant to bomb on distant forest fires. Across the road was the Native cemetery, plots bounded by finely carved palings. Mary pointed out the Celtic cross over the grave of Archdeacon Hudson Stuck, conqueror of Mount McKinley and author of *Voyages on the Yukon and Its Tributaries*. One of only two whites buried here, the missionary had long been lost to rootage. A thick poplar grew from the center of the grave, shading it with heart-shaped leaves.

After so many river miles, I enjoyed the sensation of dry land passing beneath me and the comfort of staying in a house. But I knew the feeling would be short-lived. The road gave out at a riverbank heaped with driftwood. From the shore, we watched the Yukon spread out among the islands.

"I think you're going to see a lot more bears from here down," Mary said quietly. "The Flats are full of them."

10 ▌ BEAVER

LATE IN THE AFTERNOON I picked my way through the phalanx of reefs surrounding Fort Yukon and headed downstream. I kept to the widest channel, veering from side to side, trying to stay in the current and not veer up some corkscrew slough that would dead-end miles from the river in a canopy of willows. Far to the south I could see the hazy outline of the White Mountains above the spruce horizon.

I made camp that night on a sand spit and fell asleep to the distant wash of riverboat traffic from Fort Yukon. I must have slept lightly because I awoke with a start to the sound of something moving outside the tent. Imagining the worst, I peered through the mosquito netting. A mist was rising from the river, and in the daybreak light I saw a sandhill crane stalking along the beach between the tent and my canoe. The crane walked slowly with a long-gaited, professorial stride, like a man lost in thought. Something about the early hour, the half-light, and this stilt-legged bird nearly as tall as a man made me want to get a closer look. I climbed out of the tent and followed barefoot down the deserted beach. Realizing it was being shadowed, the crane picked up the pace. I followed until the crane stopped, threw back its head, and bugled a warning cry, short air-horn blasts that reverberated in the still night air. Then the crane launched itself into the sky. Neck extended, legs trailing, it glided across the river with slow downward flaps and quick upstrokes of its long gray wings, looking for all the world like a pterodactyl.

In the morning I found the beach tracked with great trident footprints alongside my own. The sky was gloomy and overcast, the river deserted. Washing up my breakfast dishes, I heard an insistent drone and ten minutes later watched a strange-looking canoe edge into view. Winglike outriggers extended from the gunwales, and a toy trolling motor barely propelled the canoe against the current. Then I saw the reason for the outriggers: the boat was precariously overloaded with a young couple, a mound of camping gear, and an agitated Doberman riding figurehead in the bow.

As the canoe nosed ashore, the Doberman leaped out, charged down the beach, and gobbled up my dishrag. The dog was choking on it when his master chased him down.

"Hey, sorry about the dog!" he said, prying the Doberman's jaws apart. "Come on, stupid, cough it up!"

The man was blond and all teeth. He and his dog shared the same predatory grin and lack of sense. The Doberman, he explained, was their bear protection.

"He's already chased off a moose calf," he said proudly. "We got pictures to prove it!"

I told him he was lucky the dog hadn't brought bear into his camp, especially a sow with cubs. But he fancied the idea.

"Now that's a match I'd like to see!"

I have yet to meet a Doberman owner who isn't a knucklehead. While he pored over my maps, his girlfriend, looking cold and tired, managed a wan smile from the canoe. They were headed for Fort Yukon, and for three weeks had negotiated the meandering course of Birch Creek only to emerge at the wrong outlet, low on food and out of gas. They had counted on catching fish, but the creek was too muddied from placer mining upstream. They looked disappointed to find how little progress they'd made.

"When we reached the Yukon, I saw a fish camp across the river, so I fired my rifle into the air to get their attention. Pretty soon this big Indian zooms over with a gun in his boat. It looked like an M-14 or something. He asked us to his camp, but we just took the gas and split."

By now I realized this was the couple whom Clarence Alexander had helped out.

"Why didn't you have coffee with him?"

"I thought the dude acted kind of strange. I mean, why take chances?"

Rolling up the map, he fetched the dog and climbed back in the stern. The canoe inched forward against the current toward Fort Yukon. For a long time after it was out of sight, I could hear the woman grumbling and her boyfriend urging them on. "We're making it! Hey, we're going to make it!"

By afternoon the clouds had peeled away to a hard blue sky, but there was a cool edge to the air. Having gained the Arctic latitude, the Yukon began its great crescent curve to the southwest and marched into the teeth of a headwind. For hours I passed no other boats, no fish camps along the shore, only the monotonous spruce horizon. Yet the paisley pattern of lakes and islands on my chart was densely populated with names: Joe Devlin Island, Johnny Frog Island, Ed Berg Slough, Jack Uheen Slough, George Lake, Riley Lake, Argo Bill Lake, Tony Lake, and Annie Lake. Whenever I felt lonesome, all I had to do was consult the map.

The channel made a hairpin turn, and I spotted, a mile away, a line of cabins on the north bank of the Yukon.

A young man in a denim jacket pulled my canoe ashore on the beach below the village of Beaver. He'd been cooking up a big iron pot of fish heads and guts for his dogs. The smell was terrible. He was a short, compact fellow, with the flat face and oblique eyes of an Eskimo, features out of place so far inland. I asked if there was a store in Beaver.

"It closed an hour ago," he said. "Maybe I could get Francis to open it up for you."

He laid some sticks over the dog pot to keep the gulls out, and we walked up the incline to the village. A dirt road ran between the riverbank and the row of cabins. Kids were jumping their bikes over a homemade ramp while their parents stood around talking, glancing now and then down the river. Everyone was waiting for the barge to arrive because, among other things, the village was out of fuel oil. Yesterday someone had seen the barge eighty-eight miles downriver and headed this way. It was due today or tonight. Maybe tomorrow. Nobody could say for sure.

The storekeeper, waiting along with the rest, had a wispy voice, and long black hair tied back with a red bandanna. He took us to the store, a log cabin with a sign above the window — BEAVER INUPIAT COOP — and opened the padlock. The shelves were empty except for a few canned goods and some candy. I bought a box of Sailor Boy pilot bread and a can of pop and joined the others standing along the riverbank. The sun felt pleasant, and a breeze off the water fluttered the flag above the store. I didn't care if the barge took its own sweet time.

"I can hear it," the storekeeper said.

Downriver, I could see nothing.

"Vibrations," he said. "You can feel them through the ground."

"Nobody can tell when it's coming," a woman next to me confided. She pointed out her cabin. "There's tea inside."

It took me a while to realize that she was inviting me to go into her house and pour myself some tea. The cabin door opened on a single room, which held an iron bed behind a big-flowered curtain, a barrel stove, a day bed, a table and bentwood chairs, and a tiny kitchen with a saucepan cooking on the stove. At the table sat her son, the fellow who had pulled my canoe ashore. He poured me a cup of tea and invited me to stay for supper. We ate bread and butter, boiled potatoes, and chunks of lightly fried salmon, the heads of which had gone into the dog pot on the beach. I thought: What a friendly place.

His mother stuck her head in the doorway to say that the barge would land soon. The barge wasn't in sight, but I could hear a dull pounding like a factory at the edge of town. The wait grew interminable. Then, ever so slowly, I made out the white triple-decked tug against the spruce banks.

At last the ship drew abreast of the landing, big as an ocean liner, its wheel house towering over the bank. Pushing two steel barges toe to heel, the boat stretched the length of the village. She was the *Tanana,* one of the Yutana Barge Line fleet operating from the railhead at Nenana, and her bulk made the river, so vast beneath my own small canoe, seem to shrink considerably. This was the *Tanana*'s third trip to Beaver since the ice went out in May. Barges are a major reason why villages along the American portion of the Yukon River had not been abandoned after the steamboats stopped running. During the four-month season that the river is open, they bring in all the freight that cannot be flown in: fuel, machinery, building supplies — everything that must be stockpiled to last the winter. For a while we watched a top-loader balance pallets of blue fuel drums down a narrow ramp, and then we went back to finish our meal.

I asked my host why so many people in Beaver, in the heart of Athabascan Indian country, looked Eskimo. The answer, he said, was simple. His relatives were Inupiat Eskimos from Point Barrow on the Arctic coast who, at the turn of the century, had wandered down through the wilderness, across mountain divides and rivers, to live on the banks of the Yukon. It was a migration of Biblical proportions, and the leader of this exodus was a Japanese man named Frank Yasuda.

Kyosuke Yasuda was born in 1868 at Ishinomaki, a fishing port on the northern coast of Japan where the Kitakami River enters the sea. The youngest child in his family, he would often sit beneath pine trees on the deep green hills that ringed the port and watch the tall-masted ships as they sailed out into the great world. When Kyosuke's parents died, first his father, then his mother, he took his leave.

He sailed to San Francisco and shipped out from there as chief steward aboard the revenue cutter *Bear*. A triple-masted barkentine, the *Bear* departed the Golden Gate every spring, bound for the Arctic to collect tax revenues and hunt seal poachers. For four years, the Anglicized Frank Yasuda sailed along the southern coast of Alaska, through the Aleutian chain at Unimak Pass and into the Bering Sea. The ship followed the gray, dismal coast around Norton Sound, passing through the Bering Straits and the Chukchi Sea and finally entering the Arctic Ocean. The last port of call was the Eskimo village of Barrow at the northernmost tip of Alaska.

The ship never lingered long in Arctic waters, with the ice pack always threatening offshore. Late in the summer of 1894, Yasuda stood on the windblown beach and watched as the *Bear* steamed away toward home. He had elected to stay behind in Barrow to man a weather station and try his hand at trading.

Short and solid, his face well tanned, he got along well with the whale hunters and married an Eskimo woman named Nevalo.

Fewer ships ventured into Arctic waters as the whaling industry began to wane, and the recent gold strikes on the Klondike and the beaches of Nome turned Yasuda's interest to prospecting. In 1903, Yasuda, his wife, and two white prospectors named Carter and Marsh sailed east along the Arctic coast in an umiak, an Eskimo skin boat, to the mouth of the Canning River. They lined the umiak up the river to its headwaters and then proceeded on foot, bound for unpanned creeks. They crossed the Arctic plain and then traversed the Brooks Range. On the other side of the divide, they entered the headwaters of the Chandalar River. Short of food, Yasuda and Nevalo decided to head back to Barrow to resupply and agreed to meet Marsh and Carter on the same creek a year later.

Yasuda, Nevalo, and two Eskimos returned by dog team the following December for their rendezvous with Carter and Marsh. Weeks past the appointed date, they came upon two white men on snowshoes. One was Carter. After parting company with Marsh, Carter had wandered into rich-looking country by Chandalar Lake, convinced it would be their El Dorado.

The following summer, accompanied by more Eskimos from Barrow, Yasuda's party found the upper Chandalar valley, which proved as rich in gold as Carter had foreseen. The Eskimo hunters kept busy shooting caribou and mountain sheep on the nearby slopes. In one day they killed almost ninety caribou, rolling their carcasses down the steep hillsides to waiting dog sleds. Yasuda hit upon the idea of marketing meat to the mining camps of the upper Koyukuk.

But the game supply was too tenuous to support the growing population on the upper Chandalar through the winter, so Yasuda and an elderly Eskimo named Tolakana traveled due south to the Yukon River, where there was plentiful game in the Flats and salmon in the river to supply the camps. They came to a high bank on the north shore of the Yukon, and Yasuda asked Tolakana if the place had ever been flooded. The old man, who did everything with great deliberation, examined the bark of spruce trees on the bank for embedded river silt.

There was none. Yasuda had found the site for his settlement. He called it Beaver.

Yasuda sold his interests in the Chandalar mining claims, moved his family down to Beaver, and started a trading post and freighting station. He sent back to Barrow for others to join him. With the demise of the whaling industry, many Eskimos did. Whole families, their packs on their backs and on the backs of their dogs, trekked across the Arctic plain in a migration that lasted nearly two years. They camped for the summer at the base of the Brooks Range and then crossed over the divide through Atigan Pass to the headwaters of the Koyukuk River, where they lived on mountain sheep and fish from the creeks. People were born and died in the nameless valleys. The following winter, when it was possible to travel on the frozen tundra and rivers, they crossed the Smith Mountains to the Chandalar and followed the river down to the Yukon. The second summer they arrived in Beaver.

In this land of spruce trees, the Eskimos learned to build log cabins instead of the subterranean driftwood and sod houses of the coast. From the Athabascans, they learned to trap beaver and muskrat on the Flats and to hunt moose, which they previously thought good only for dog food. They netted salmon on the spawning runs, although, compared to the bland whitefish they were used to, the salmon seemed almost too rich and oily to eat. The women learned beadwork from the Indians, and the two peoples traded and intermarried.

In addition to Eskimos and Indians, there were two other Japanese in polyglot Beaver. James Minano, an old friend of Yasuda's from Barrow and also married to an Eskimo woman, had come down in the first group with Yasuda in 1906 and later moved on. George Oshima, a shy man with a painful stutter, lived by himself in a cabin below Beaver and subscribed to the *New York Times* so he could follow the stock market.

The territorial government built a winter wagon road from Beaver to the mining camp of Caro on the Chandalar, and every summer steamboats docked in Beaver to unload freight. Frank Yasuda was the hub of this activity, grubstaking prospectors and trappers, supporting them during the lean winter months. In the spring of 1913, when Yasuda mushed into Fairbanks, the first city he had seen in twenty years, the local paper wrote him up like Rip Van Winkle, noting that "the moving picture performance that he visited last evening in company with a friend was the first he had seen."

But Frank Yasuda was no hermit. He was well read and followed the news on radio broadcasts from Fairbanks. On December 7, 1941, his daughter Hanna, who ran the post office, heard over the radio that the Japanese had bombed Pearl Harbor. She ran to tell her father. "No!" he said, shaking his head. "It can't be true!"

That spring he received a letter from the marshal in Fairbanks saying that he would have to be interned along with other Japanese in a relocation camp for the duration of the war. The marshal, a friend of Yasuda's, added, "I'm going to come over because I don't want anyone else to bring you in."

When the plane arrived, Yasuda had his big black suitcase packed. Solemnly he said good-by to his family and friends and climbed aboard. He was seventy-four years old. The plane pitched down the short, bumpy landing strip and was aloft, droning south over the mirrored lakes and sloughs of the Flats.

Three years later, another plane brought Yasuda home. Along with George Oshima, he had been interned in a camp in the New Mexico desert. Oshima never came back; he died in a nursing home. Remarkably, Yasuda did not return a bitter man. He was glad to be home, but the camp had been a surprising experience. So many Japanese faces all in one place! He had not seen so many since he was a small boy watching tall-masted ships sail from the blue harbor at Ishinomaki and wondering what the wide world was like.

11

THE
ROAD HOME

THE FLATS ended abruptly as the Hamlin Hills rose up on either side and the network of river channels and sloughs coalesced into a single channel that funneled into a rock-cut gorge. The weather had turned cold and dreary. I passed scattered fish camps along the banks and kept hoping someone would invite me to come ashore and warm myself by the tent stove. Everyone was inside, of course. All the tent flaps were secured, and thin plumes of woodsmoke wafted from the stovepipes. When a drizzle began to fall, I hunched under my rubber poncho and pushed downstream. In the rain-streaked distance, I could see a bridge slanting across the river.

The Trans-Alaska Oil Pipeline crossed the Yukon directly beneath the bridge and slithered up the hillside on its eight-hundred-mile journey from Prudhoe Bay to the tanker port of Valdez. Antennas and sensors bristled from the concrete abutments as a precaution against sabotage. This was the only bridge across the American portion of the river, the only road link to the North Slope, and its completion had been foreseen as an ecological disaster — hordes of Winnebagos rumbling across this bridgehead into the fragile Arctic. I had once been of the same mind. Now I approached the bridge in all gratitude because the pipeline road was going to take me home.

I had already made up my mind to steal away from the river for a while. It wasn't just the bad weather. After a month's traveling, I needed a break from other people's pasts. I wanted a warm bed and someone else's cooking. Most of all, I wanted to see familiar faces, people who would ask *me* questions for a change. So I was taking a short vacation from the river, a side trip, a temporary leave of absence for personal reasons.

I hid the canoe under alder branches at the end of a cul-de-sac slough and then hiked out to the highway, trying out my land legs. A gas station, café, and huddle of white double-wide trailers stood on a gravel pad at the north end of the bridge. This was the village of the future, a town on wheels, uncluttered by history, facing the highway rather than the river and stinking of diesel fuel instead of drying fish. I set my duffel at the shoulder of the road and waited for a ride.

The first hint of a truck approaching was the whine of gears as it barreled down the north hill, trailing dust on its desolate journey from the Beaufort Sea. If the driver didn't eddy into the gas station, he'd highball it for the bridge, and I'd stick out my thumb and catch a quick glimpse of the trucker riding high in a custom-painted candy-apple-red or metal-flake-blue cab, his CB handle inscribed on the door — *The Beatnik* or *Rat Shit* — before the truck whooshed past, sucking me into its wash, and then I'd watch it climb out of the valley until the descending pitch of downshifted gears faded into the trilling of a fox sparrow in the ditch beside the road.

Ten hours later, an Indian with a silver goatee and aviator sunglasses gave me a ride in his pickup. He had a fish camp six miles below the bridge and was hauling a load of King salmon to Fairbanks. We crossed the bridge and gained the high bluff. The narrow road snaked along the crests of hills, and rain had turned it into a slick yellow river of mud. At nightfall we passed Pump Station Six, its arc lights looking sinister in the darkness.

Clouds hung below in the valleys. As we bumped along a ridge spine, I heard a pop followed by a long hiss. The truck shimmied, and the driver pulled off the road and began to jack up the flat tire in the drizzle. He had a stiff right leg, which he had to swing out in front of him when he stooped to loosen the lug nuts. I handed him a balding spare from the back of the truck and suddenly remembered who he was. Years ago I'd seen him at the sled dog races in Fairbanks — the stiff leg pumping his sled across the finish line, the sunglasses that never came off.

He was George Attla, "the Huslia Hustler," the greatest dog

musher in the world. As a boy growing up in Huslia, a remote Athabascan village on the Koyukuk River, Attla had contracted tuberculosis and spent his childhood shuttling between TB wards. The disease wasted his right leg, so the doctors fused it at the kneecap, thinking he could at least use the leg as a crutch. Later it became his trademark as a dog musher, the leg swinging out at an angle as, more often than not, he crossed the finish line first. It was an authentic rags-to-riches story; in fact, a movie had been made of Attla's life. That he still dressed in threadbare jeans and hauled salmon in the back of his truck when he wasn't hauling dogs made him all the more a local hero.

Another pop and hiss. After we changed the second tire, I took the wheel so Attla could sleep. He pulled his jacket over his head and fell asleep against the door.

The night was moonless, the road beyond my headlights lost in darkness except when the distant beams of a truck across the valley revealed its winding course. Sometimes, as I drove blindly through a fog bank, the truck briefly seemed airborne, and I'd anticipate the fatal impact that never came. Still, in all this there was the pleasant sensation of being warm and out of the rain and trusted enough to drive while someone slept.

Ten miles outside of Fairbanks, pavement began and the sudden loss of reverberation stirred Attla. He stood me breakfast at an all-night café. The Star-Spangled Banner was fluttering across a television screen. Before we left, Attla asked the waitress to fill a new stainless steel Thermos with coffee and add it to the bill. The girl looked doubtfully at his frayed, fish-smelling clothes.

"You're not going to want it when I tell you what it costs."

He paid cash and then she recognized him.

"Hey, I've seen you on TV! Wow! How does it feel to be George Attla?"

Attla dropped me on the outskirts of town. The rain had stopped and the sun was coming up behind me. In the flat valley below, the lights of Fairbanks flickered off. Far across the valley, the white pyramidal peaks of the Alaska Range shimmered above the early morning haze. I was dead tired and not exactly sure where I was, since the highway had been rerouted. I started walking downhill, then broke into a brisk run, footfalls echoing off the wet pavement.

In the stillness of dawn, I knocked tentatively on a friend's door. I hated waking anybody at that hour, and especially him, so I rapped ever so softly, even though all of his dogs were by now barking their lungs out. He owned huskies, mongrels, a three-legged Labrador, even a few Ainu, Japanese bear dogs — all of them howling like maniacs. So I knocked harder until I drowned out the dogs. A friend's home is the place where, I would have said, when you come pounding at the door at three in the morning, they have to take you in.

The dogs quieted down when the door opened. Russ Currier, my former colleague at the university, stood in the doorway in his underwear. He'd grown a salt-and-pepper beard since I'd last seen him, and he seemed amused to find me on his doorstep.

"Well, now, look who's here," Russ said, addressing the dogs rather than me. "Our old friend!"

I was the prodigal son returned. Russ had helped me a great deal during my first year as a teacher, and I'd done little to stay in touch. The year before, he'd retired and with his Japanese-born wife Kyo now puttered around a workshop and raised their menagerie of dogs and goats. I followed him to a spare bedroom, which was cluttered with stacks of magazines and mail-order catalogues on the floor.

"Kyo thought it might be you," Russ said, smiling. "When she heard the dogs barking and someone banging at the door, she said, 'It's probably John.' " He switched off the bedroom light and I heard him thumping upstairs to bed.

It was a private joke, a reference to another late-night visit years ago, one I'd truly hoped they'd forgotten. It happened the second year that I worked with Russ, on the day I came home from work and my wife announced that she was pregnant. I was stunned, not because the pregnancy was unwanted, just unexpected. "That's wonderful," I remember saying, "that's just great." And then I made up some excuse, drove to a friend's house, and got perfectly smashed. I drank until the room started spinning, because in some dim way I understood that my life was going to change.

This friend's wife was pregnant for the second time and he must have enjoyed watching me drink myself into oblivion. He was a dog musher in a small way, with a few huskies and a birch sled, just enough to compete in local races. One of his dogs had just had a litter and he brought in an armful of pups from the cold, thinking that in my condition I might agree to take one home. I did. But then, skidding home early in the morning, I hit on the idea of giving the pup to the Curriers, who didn't have kids but had, I knew, a real soft spot for dogs. The stars careened unnaturally overhead as I pounded on their door. The lights went on and Russ appeared at the doorway in his underwear, exactly as he had tonight except that that night was freezing and he didn't look at all amused. After a short, drunken speech, I took the pup, the runt of the litter, from my parka and placed it on the floor. But something was wrong with the way the pup moved, and at that moment I realized it was lame.

I can't recall getting home that night or what happened to the dog. I showed up at work the next day with a terrible hangover and tried to apologize. But Russ didn't get angry. Instead, he took out scraps of paper on which he had copied down the gibberish I had said the night before. "Now what exactly did you mean by this?" he asked, and read a passage aloud. I felt like a perfect fool. We never talked about that night again, and yet I'd come back ten years later to bang on his door, still feeling like a fool.

I spent a week in Fairbanks, looking up old friends and carefully avoiding those who'd known me only as part of a couple. I didn't want to put them, or myself, through a capsule version of our breakup, divorce being the kind of personal failure I didn't feel like owning up to. But I had it wrong. Divorce has become a new rite of passage for people my age, a chance to admit mistakes publicly and make corrections in midstream. I kept learning of the dissolution of old marriages and the new couplings; the children that I'd last seen in diapers now tooled around on bicycles and wore their parents' faces.

The town itself seemed the most changed. Fairbanks had slowed down since the hurly-burly of the oil pipeline boom, but the boom had transformed it from a linear river town with small-town sensibilities into a sprawl of shopping malls and developments. Like any city, it had become stratified. In the ring of hills were choice-view lots and joggers running along shady lanes. On the descent, the houses became smaller and meaner, interspersed between discount stores and fast-food emporiums. And in all this displacement there was the irony of trying to retain scraps of the past being displaced, subdivision streets bearing the names of Alaskan rivers and mountains.

I was feeling smug because I had journeyed here mostly by river. Fairbanks had no connection with life in the bush villages except for the weather they shared. Along the Yukon, nobody needed to remind himself where he lived, but in Fairbanks it required an act of imagination to believe you were living a few degrees off the Arctic Circle and not in Des Moines. So people surrounded themselves with reminders: the coffee-table books of Alaskana, the obligatory soapstone carving, the family dog named for an Eskimo village. Among exiles living in a faraway land, you expect to find reminders of the home left behind, but here the mementos were of the place not found.

I called an old friend, and his ex-wife answered the phone. She sniffled through a head cold while we chatted until the awkward moment when it became clear I was calling for Michael and not her. At the moment, she said, he was living in a camper. She was leaving for California, so he would have the boys for the summer with no address but the back of a pickup truck. Michael was the friend who'd given me the pup that drunken night years ago.

Later I met Michael, his new girlfriend, and the boys at a restaurant in one of the new shopping malls. The waitresses wore Tudor costumes and carried enormous menus written in Old English script. The dinner began badly. The two small boys had come directly from their mother and were hyperkinetic, full of complaints, and on the verge of tears. Their father, caught between guilt and love, couldn't decide whether to discipline his sons or embrace them. Watching him, I had the unnerving sensation that I was seeing how my own life would have turned out had I stayed here.

The next day we all drove out of town to Chena Hot Springs.

The cloudy sky cast an aquarium light over the green hills. Several times the road crossed the upper forks of the Chena River, the water shallow and clear and fast-running over white rocks.

At the hot springs resort, we rented bathing suits and soaked in progressively hotter pools until our pale bodies emerged pink-skinned and smelling of sulphur. In winter this might have been invigorating, but in the heat of July it only made me feel parboiled and drowsy. The boys, however, loved splashing in the water, yelling to hear their voices echo off the walls. We must have seemed like any family on vacation, although we were really a collection of odds and ends assembled for the occasion. For my part, I enjoyed the role of visiting uncle, rough-housing with the kids. When the pools closed, we drove to the small cabin that Michael's girlfriend had rented for the summer. To get there we waded across a shallow, ice-cold creek, and when I reached the other side my feet were blue.

We played touch football into the evening. Nightfall brought a corresponding shift in senses, the colors of green willows and purple fireweed along the creek fading into the sounds of running water and children shouting in the dark. Finally, the mosquitoes drove us into the cabin, where Michael's girlfriend fixed drinks for the adults and hot chocolate for the boys. She was a small woman, very direct, at times withering — just the sort of woman he needed at the moment. She managed everything and began packing the boys off to bed, but the youngest boy refused to use the outhouse because of the swarms of mosquitoes. He had been a baby when I left Alaska. Now he was skinny and dark-haired and in a certain light resembled his mother. Fiercely, he took the honeypot, walked into the bedroom, and squatted. Later, when Michael went in to kiss the boys good night, I could hear his soft whispering in the darkened room.

My last day in Fairbanks I crossed a bridge into Slaterville, an old neighborhood bounded by the Chena River and a deadwater slough. It was the one part of town utterly unchanged. The gravel streets, lined with birch trees and mismatched houses, were still narrow and elliptical. On Noyes Street I stopped in front of a small cabin trimmed with blue, a horseshoe nailed above the door for luck. The cabin looked even smaller, if possible, than when my ex-wife and I had lived there.

We had rented the place our first winter in Fairbanks from an old miner and his wife who spent summers there and lived the rest of the year in Washington State. He was blue-eyed and silent as a stone, while she was all nervous energy and jabbered for the both of them. In the back yard were concrete footings and a pile of rotting lumber from another house begun forty years ago. He had left it unfinished as a result of an argument they'd had, and neither one of them had backed down in all that time. If there was a lesson in that pile of boards, we were too young to understand it.

The cabin had only one room and a tiny bath, and by November the single window would glaze over with ice. Even though I had not imagined myself living in the heart of town, it was still a log cabin and sometimes I felt as if we were the only people in the world. There were late mornings in bed and the untimely visits of Jehovah's Witnesses, leaflets in hand, framed against the white doorway. I loved the rigmarole of dressing for forty below, the small adventure of immersing myself in the cold. Winter transformed the landscape so that even casual chores took on a surreal quality. In the ghostly ice fog, a trip to the grocery store seemed like a moon walk, the air ringing with silence. I remembered coming home in the dark and standing in this yard, oblivious to the cold, watching the green, columnar lights of the Aurora Borealis shatter and realign across the sky. And I remembered the winter drive home from the hospital.

It was January. I had picked up my wife at the school where she taught second grade. She complained of spasmodic pains but dismissed them as Braxton Hicks contractions — false labor — since she had three months to go. I had gotten over the initial shock of becoming a father, but the pregnancy still seemed a mystery to me, a well-kept secret to which I was not privy. Lying beside her in bed that night, I slid my hand up the slope of her stretched belly, trying to cup its circumference, wanting to feel a kick, anything. She had shown me a book with a diagram of the uterus in the third trimester. It looked like the cross-section of a den dug into a hillside. Drifting to sleep, I couldn't imagine what unruly creature would emerge from that warm nest.

The bathroom light was on when I awoke. Like a somnambulist, I shuffled in the dark toward it. As my eyes adjusted to the incandescent glare of white tile and mirror, I saw my wife standing naked, braced against the sink while a tremor shook her. Her skin seemed to shine under the light. I noticed that the floor was spotted with blood.

"It's happening!" she said.

"What is?" I asked in a daze. "What's happening?"

"I'm in labor."

The ride to the hospital was indistinct, the sky and horizon washed out in the winter half-light. I kept thinking that we didn't even have any names picked out. What I remember of the delivery is an airless room filled with lights and the doctor standing between the stirrups. Dwarfed in the doctor's grip, a tiny pair of legs appeared. Then the doctor pivoted quickly, his back to us so we couldn't see, and when he turned around again his hands were empty. But I knew.

Later, after my wife had been moved from the maternity ward with its mocking posters of mothers and infants, the doctor came around to explain. He was an emaciated man, and his voice seemed far away. The baby had been born, he said, with a massive rupture of the chest and could not possibly have survived. Normally my wife should have miscarried early in the pregnancy, but the baby's heart had been unexpectedly strong. My wife listened very quietly and then in an even voice asked: "What did we have?"

The question caught the doctor off guard.

"A boy," he said.

I don't think I ever loved my wife more than during those hours after the delivery when her life seemed fragile, a gift given back to me. But when she came home from the hospital, we began to grow apart. Flowers arrived in foil-covered pots that I placed by the window overlooking snowfields. We had little to say. I had never shared in the baby's life, could never know its secret wanderings within her. Now I gave myself over to the details of a death in the family. By inheritance, we became antagonists; I would bury what she had conceived, be the precursor of her emptiness. She had already made up her mind to leave in the summer.

One day I drove to her school to drop off lesson plans for the substitute teacher. The second graders were at recess. Breathing clouds of frost, they swept across the snow-covered schoolyard, chasing a large red ball. Inside, her classroom was stifling warm and smelled of wet wool and paste. Standing among the stunted chairs and desks, I felt like a giant. I dropped off the lesson plans, and the substitute teacher handed me a pile of sympathy cards the students had prepared. Back in the car I sorted through them, looking perhaps for something cruel. All of them, printed correctly in capital letters, said the same thing: Get Well. The substitute had written the words on the blackboard and the children had copied them. Some had illustrated their cards in crayon, and I found these drawings strangely moving. A stickwoman convalescing in bed. A stickwoman weeping tears in red dashes like tracer rounds. In one card, I found myself joining the hapless stickwoman in a transparent, rocket-shaped house. The chimney was enormous, the artist having a problem with perspective. Outside the house, beyond the view of its inhabitants, a smaller figure lay curled below the horizon, a stranger I recognized at last as my son.

The Curriers drove me back to the Yukon River bridge so I wouldn't have to hitchhike. Heading north, we passed in and out of rain showers. A downpour on one hillside, sunshine on the other. We stopped once to pick blueberries that grew ripe and plump on burned-over land. By midafternoon we had crested a hill and saw the Yukon below us, the bridge looking very small across it. I retrieved my canoe from the buggy woods, and we sat at the boat landing eating a picnic lunch. By now my trip seemed a succession of departures. I had become quite expert at leave-taking — the firm handshake and promises to write. Another thousand miles of river stretched before me, but I was not so anxious now to leave friends behind.

Bolting the outboard onto the transom, I pushed out into deeper water to make sure the engine would start. The current caught the boat, and by the time the outboard kicked over I had drifted far from shore. I realized I hadn't even told my friends good-by. Standing up in the canoe, I shouted and waved, but they were already fast receding from sight.

12

A DOG'S
LIFE

THE NEXT DAY I motored down to Rampart, a ramshackle village where no one would talk to me. "The people here are very shy," the storekeeper said, and knocked on a cabin door. He left me with a family of seven who sat around a table, pretending I was invisible. When I'd ask a question, they'd shrug and stare out the window at the vegetable garden. One by one, they filed out the door, until I was the only one left in the cabin.

Rebuffed, I headed downstream to the lower ramparts, where the Yukon cut a deep, narrow trough through a range of green summits. The afternoon was heating up. I lounged against the backrest and worked the tiller arm with my elbow. I passed a fish wheel and, farther on, a row of sled dogs bunkered in cubbyholes along the riverbank to escape the heat. A woman standing outside a canvas tent in a saddle of birch trees waved to me. She was tanned, sandy-haired, about thirty, good-looking, in an orange tank top and blue shorts. I waved back. When she brought one hand to her mouth, tipping an imaginary coffee cup, I swung the canoe about and made for shore.

She brought out strips of smoked salmon called "squaw candy" to eat with the coffee, and we lunched in the shade of a blue tarp. On the beach, a small boy and girl seined water through a butterfly net.

"We usually get a lot of people dropping in," she said. "But not so many this summer. River traffic is down."

Sheri Mitchell had deep-set blue eyes with only the beginnings of wrinkles at the edges. It was an appealing face, at once vulnerable and strong. She had set up the fish camp early in

June and ran it herself while her partner fished commercially in the rough water of the Yukon Delta.

Fish camps were traditionally a female province: men tended the nets while their wives prepared the salmon for drying. Now, with the men away for months on pipelines or fire crews, women often ran the entire show. In the village upstream I had sat lazily watching Indian women unload their fishing boats, a hefty King salmon on each arm. The "bush" was such classic male terrain that I was always surprised by the women it attracted. I don't know what I had expected, except possibly the extremes: mousy types bullied into someone else's fantasy, or Calamity Janes in buckskins. But the young women I'd met along the river were neither. They had chosen their own lot and, if anything, often seemed happier than their boyfriends, having less to prove.

After lunch Sheri and I walked up the cobblestone beach to see her smokehouse. Two stories tall and narrow as a chimney, the shed was made of corrugated metal sheets loosely hung over a log framework. A tarpaulin covered the entrance. Inside, it was dark and pungent smelling, cracks of daylight showing between the metal sheets. Sheri banked a smoldering cottonwood fire in a barrel stove greasy with dripping fish oil. She'd cut the salmon into long strips, dipped them in brine, and hung the strips in tiers above the smudge fire until they cured a bright scarlet. Gazing up at them was like staring into branches of blazing red maple leaves. A tree of fish.

Sheri grabbed a few salmon strips for dinner appetizers and we headed back to the tent attended by a horde of free-roaming puppies. They were a clownish bunch, all ears and nose, nipping at my shoelaces, constantly underfoot. The adult dogs were a different matter. Chained in tiers along the riverbank, they were sleek, wolfish creatures with deep, tapering chests and skinny legs. They had the perked ears and curved tails of huskies, but their faces and coloring were a cross-section of the dog world. Some cringed as we passed through their ranks; others probed us with wet snouts and wore a leering cleverness. Upwards of fifty dogs were staked on the beach, and they all belonged to Sheri's partner, an up-and-coming musher.

"This is Joe's empire," she said, and laughed. "You've got to meet Joe. He'll be disappointed if you don't stay for dinner. I'm sure he'll be back soon."

A chorus of howls went up when a gray shovel-nosed skiff raced downriver and landed on the beach. The dogs fawned, tails between their legs, in a ritual show of submission, as shirtless Joe Runyon, the alpha male, bounded up the riverbank. He had a boyish face, with shy blue eyes and a killer smile.

For dinner we ate macaroni salad, pork and beans, and roast haunch of bear. The haunch belonged to a black bear that had been raiding salmon from the drying racks of a fish camp across the river. Each night the bear would eat its fill, stopping in the middle of a row of fish, then reappear the next evening to resume the feast. After several nights of this, the bear got itself added to the menu.

Most of the dinner conversation centered on Joe's empire. Last year he'd entered the Iditarod Trail Sled Dog Race, a grueling thousand-mile run from Anchorage to Nome. He'd mushed his dogs a hundred miles a day over mountain ranges and frozen rivers and arrived in Nome two weeks later, twenty hours behind the winner. It was the second-best time for a rookie, although he knew he could have done better. But he didn't fault the dogs.

"It was me. I didn't know the trail and got turned around for four hours. And I was inconsistent in how I rested them. That was a big factor. The dogs didn't screw up. It was pilot error."

After dinner we took the kids for a hop across the river in Joe's skiff to unload some salmon. The sunset had plunged the north wall of the canyon in shadow and louvered the fish camp behind us in pinkish light. I jumped out of the skiff in my fireman's boots to keep the bow from smashing on the rocks and then carried the kids ashore. Cliff swallows swirled over a creek pouring out of a cleft in the timbered bluff. The creek cooled the air several degrees, so that approaching it was like stepping into a root cellar. Joe had dammed the flow with rocks to form a refrigerant pool for keeping salmon until they could be cut into strips and smoked. We carried the heavy Kings from the skiff by their gill flaps and slipped them into the clear pool, where they settled sideways, their silvery moon eyes glaring up through the mirrored sky.

Back in camp, Joe dumped the remaining fish into a blackened cauldron and boiled them into a steaming witches' brew of fish heads and comblike bones. He fed the pups from a common bowl, giving each adult huskie its own coffee can. Before ladling the stinking, hot slurry into the can, Joe felt the dog's hip, and if it was too plump cut down on the portions. He called each dog's name as it was fed — Blondie, Shogun, Yoko, Spanky, White Girl, Screamer, Bantu — and gave me quick anatomy lessons.

"This is a low-cadence dog," he said about a black dog with a white triangle at its breast. "The long, pointed snout indicates longer vertebrae, so the muscles of the scapula become fan shaped and the dog can really cover ground."

"Look at the angularity in those legs!" He pointed to Muscles, a white huskie with coiled springs for legs. "You see the set of the pelvis? How the ass end really curves in? That's what I call a racy dog!"

But he couldn't hide his disappointment with Shogun. "There's no legs under that dog, no angularity, nothing to stretch out. He might be good as a power puller, a draft animal, but not as a racer."

They were designer dogs, bred from a who's who of long-distance racers. There was a little of George Attla's lead dog, Scotty, a little of Don Honea's Hickey, a pinch of Gareth Wright's hounds, a hound being any outside breed, in this case Irish setter. Most of the teams facing each other in the big races were engineered from a common gene pool, and genetic disorders such as endemic mange and eye problems were beginning to surface. Some mushers experimented with exotic combinations, crossing huskies and greyhounds, for instance, but the resulting product lacked the proper mindset. It was a dog that would pull its heart out one day and loaf the next.

"Actually," Joe said, "the dogs I like best are the ones you can talk to."

The canyon walls darkened, and the river was split by a streak of moonlight. As we walked toward the yellow slope of tent, the dogs began to howl, their voices climbing several octaves into a long, hurtful wail that left me disquieted. It was a haunting sound, beautiful and disturbing, like some primordial country music played upon the listener's nerve endings.

Arranged inside the tent were a makeshift bunk bed, a metal cot, two cross-fox pelts, a cassette tape player, a carbine, and an envelope marked FISHING RECEIPTS. Sheri and the kids were already asleep. Joe lit a fire in the small tent stove against the chill rising from the river.

"Every other year I'd take a big trip," he said. "I'd get tired of this place, or the woman situation wouldn't be what it was cracked up to be. So I'd take off to Europe or South America or India. But after a few months my batteries started running down. The thing that you think you are, starts running out. Last few years I've been up here steady since I met Sheri and got into this dog thing."

Harnessing a dozen dogs to haul a man in a sled a thousand miles seems either cruel or funny until you see a team running mindlessly along a trail as if their whole lives were reduced to that single impulse. They run with something like pure joy, except for the lead dog, which is always a nervous wreck, bearing as it does the responsibility of staying on the trail, not to mention the strain of having a dozen dogs charging up its back. While some mushers instill discipline in their dogs with a short length of rubber hose, Joe said he simply tapped into energy that was already there.

"The dogs don't know they're racing. They run like birds fly. Some mushers think the only way is to brutalize their dogs. With male mushers, their egos are involved. They think the dog is personally disobeying them and they'll beat the shit out of it. Women usually won't. I think that's why a lot of these women drivers are good. The dogs are going to run as hard as metabolically possible, but you need to channel that energy. Whenever I get impatient, I just hold my breath and think, Balance and harmony."

Everyone else had already risen and stepped over my sleeping body before I awoke. After breakfast we loaded ten huskies into the skiff for an exercise run. The prospect of a boat ride threw the dogs into a collective ecstasy. When they had all been loaded and clipped to a snap line, we raced down the canyon. The kids and I rode on the heaving bow with our backs to the wind, watching the river unfold. It was a blue banner day, not a cloud in the sky, and we caught the jubilant mood of a school outing. The dogs hung their front paws over the gunwales and lolled their tongues in the breeze.

Rampart Canyon tapered to its narrowest point, where a reef of white boulders split the channel in half. The water made a sucking noise as it swirled past the rocks. Joe killed the engine, and we hurriedly unclipped the dogs from the line and shoved them overboard. They swam for shore, dog-paddling sideways to the current, arfing like seals. The brisk swim would limber them up for the two-mile race back to camp.

The advance huskies hit the beach running. Sleek and wet, the pack strung out along the shore, high-stepping over rocks and moving flat out on straightaways. At twenty miles an hour, the skiff was just keeping up with the leaders. A pair of ravens joined the chase and flapped overhead as if following a wolf pack to a fresh kill. Splish-splash across a creek, the dogs flew through a neighbor's fish camp, setting off a hue and cry from his chained dogs.

All the while, Sheri whistled and shouted encouragement from the boat.

"Good girl, Yoko! Come on, Screamer!"

She pointed to a white huskie traipsing along the beach, stopping to sniff the wild roses.

"See White Girl down there? She's not going to make the cut."

Loafing on these fun-runs could bring fatal results. One measure of the cost of sled dog racing was the number of dogs culled to develop a winning team. By summer's end, the fifty dogs in Joe's camp would be thinned to around thirty. A dog that lingered too often would be traded or shot.

"The process of elimination is a little tough," Joe said. "But that's the way it goes."

Bantu, a brindled malemute, had taken the lead with a mile to go. Neck extended, tail flying like a pennant, he ran stretched

out, back paws falling in the tracks of his front paws. A low-
cadence dog. As he approached the camp, the dogs still staked
to the ground began to yelp. Bantu checked his speed as he
cantered in, his jaw hung slack in a dog's version of a grin. Chest
heaving, he waded out into the river to cool off, then trotted
ashore, lifted his leg against an oil drum, and peed.

Friends arrived by boat for lunch, a couple and their six-month-
old baby. They lived up the Tozitna River but moved down to
the Yukon each summer to fish the salmon run. Families often
traveled great distances along the river to swap cassette tapes,
trade gossip, and provide their children with temporary playmates. The pups had gotten into the leftover bear meat, so we
ate smoked salmon strips, saltines, and celery stalks instead.
When a rainstorm moved up the canyon, we sat under a tarp,
watching the hills suddenly turn blue beneath the clouds. Then
the shower passed and we moved our chairs into the sunshine.

There was a restlessness among the whites who had come
north in high spirits a decade ago. They were having children,
getting older. As in other stampedes, the summer adventurers
had gone home, leaving only the hard cases, who shared a growing conviction that they were being squeezed out. Salmon prices
had fallen so low that commercial fishing on the middle Yukon
was hardly worth the effort. And since the Alaska Native Land
Claims Settlement Act, the whites along the river existed in a
limbo between federal and Native land. Joe's trapping cabin
near the Nowitna was on land owned by Doyon, the Athabascan
Native corporation, while his fish camp was on federal land just
below the Yukon's high-water mark. So the whites built only
makeshift camps because the land would never be their own.
The settlement of aboriginal land claims was only fair and long
overdue, but I also understood the frustration Joe and the others felt, looking out on the green hills across the river and the
hills and valleys beyond those, knowing that all of it, every inch
of it, was taken.

Much of the carping, though, disguised a wistfulness for by-
gone days.

"Check this out," said Joe. "When I first came here, everyone was in their twenties. All the old miners had died. Now we're all in our thirties and I keep looking over my shoulder to see if another group is coming. But they're not."

The afternoon dragged on until the visitors stood up to leave. It was time I left as well. I planned to catch a ride on the tugboat *Ramona* when it stopped in Tanana to unload freight.

We all walked down the beach to the visitors' boat. Their twenty-foot skiff dwarfed my canoe. It looked like the runt of the litter.

"If you flip over, stick with your boat," the man advised. "I'd think long and hard before trying to swim for shore. The river got a lot of people last year. Just swallowed them up."

I found this news upsetting because I considered myself on good terms with the Yukon. For over a thousand miles I had canoed on the river, drunk out of it, washed in it, and always the river had presented a benign face. To hear stories of the innocents it had drowned was like reading in the morning paper that your traveling companion was a murderer.

The conversation swung around to a mutual friend who had drowned in the canyon the summer before.

"Eric was a good swimmer."

"Eric was a real cerebral guy. He loved his radio and he loved his books."

"Eric was the first of us to crap out."

Eric Johnson's fish camp had been just downriver. He and his wife were checking a fish wheel when he noticed their boat had slipped its mooring. He told his wife he was going to swim for it. She begged him not to, but he dove into the icy water anyway, surfacing a short distance from the runaway skiff. He was a powerful swimmer, but the current kept the boat just out of reach, as if it were pushed along by a puff of wind. The woman took her eyes off her husband for a second and when she looked again he was gone.

Joe and the others organized a search party to drag the river for Eric's body. The scene reminded him of the part in *Huckleberry Finn* where Huck has faked his own death and watches as townspeople on the ferry shoot off cannons to raise his corpse from the river bottom. But there were no cannons and Eric was not ashore to watch the activities. Ten days later the body came up just downriver from the fish wheel, directly across from Eric's camp.

Joe went to Tanana to see who wanted to attend the funeral. An Indian clairvoyant told Joe that he'd seen the wind blowing a certain way the day Eric drowned and knew the river would take someone. The funeral was a cross-cultural affair. Women from the village sewed the lining for the coffin. One of the whites shot a bull moose for the potlatch and the Natives brought big soup pots to boil the meat. A funeral potlatch is a feast in memory of the dead, an occasion to sing and dance, a cheerful requiem to bind together the living and the dead.

"I have to admit I really enjoyed the potlatch," said Joe, "and the funeral when all the women were singing. What really struck me was that we had no ritual for dealing with Eric's death, but the Natives did."

It took two days to dig through the permafrost at the base of Moosehead Rack, a mountain with four distinct peaks like tines on moose antlers. As if by premonition, Eric had once mentioned that that was where he wanted to be buried. A trapper from the Tozitna who held a certificate of ministry in the Universal Life Church gave the eulogy, and each of the river people said a few words. Then they lowered the body in the gaping hole and, taking up shovels, planted it deep as if the frozen ground was their own.

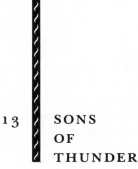

13 SONS
OF
THUNDER

BELOW RAMPART CANYON, the hills opened up and Moose-head Rack slipped past me in the darkness. I was in a hurry to reach Tanana before the *Ramona* did. I gauged my distance from the village by counting the wooded, elliptical islands in mid-river. Sixteen Mile Island. Twelve Mile Island. Six Mile Island. After the last island, the current slackened and the river widened into an enormous pool. The Tanana River, the Yu-kon's second largest tributary, had entered the main stream from the southeast behind an archipelago of sandbars and cot-tonwood islands.

Across from the confluence, I lashed my canoe to the river-bank beside a float plane that belonged to friends of Joe Run-yon. Mike McCann was sitting at the kitchen table eating dinner in his T-shirt when I knocked at the screen door.

"Don't stand in the doorway letting the bugs in, Rufus," he shouted. "Sit down!"

Claire McCann put their baby to sleep and set another place at the table. The first thing I asked was whether I had missed the *Ramona*. The McCanns smiled at each other and said not to worry.

A tugboat had sunk at Squaw Crossing at the mouth of the Tanana River. Shallower and siltier than the Yukon, the Tan-ana has shifting channels that make it trickier to navigate. The tug got only five miles above the confluence before running aground on a sandbar. In the tug's effort to rock free, its pro-peller came loose in the casing, so that when the boat did reach

deeper water it sank like a stone. The tug was not the *Ramona,*
but its sinking blocked the only channel of navigation and nobody knew when the next barge might reach Tanana.

"I flew over the wreck the other day," Mike said, "and all I
could see was the pilothouse sticking above the water like a
telephone booth."

The McCanns seemed an unlikely couple, each making up for
what the other lacked. He was a displaced New Yorker, swarthy
and muscular, keeping up a nonstop street patter. Claire, on
the other hand, was small and pale, that rarity, a white native-
born Alaskan. She was the better bush pilot, and he was a reg-
istered nurse. He had grown up in the dim canyons of housing
projects and kept his edges rough, boxing and lifting weights to
stay in shape. She was quiet, a no-nonsense woman, wary of
strangers at the door and fiercely protective of her husband. Of
the two, Claire was the one I'd least want to cross.

The McCanns insisted I spend the night because a liquor store
had opened in Tanana and they were convinced I'd wander
into trouble. They painted a picture of the village as a booze-
sodden and violent place. It was late and I was tired, so I bedded
down on their living room sofa. I had just managed to fall asleep
when their infant son cried for his 3 A.M. feeding.

The next day Mike McCann drove me into Tanana. But first
we bounced in his jeep out to the airfield behind the village.
Parked in the yawning shade of a hangar was a single-propeller
airplane with a radial engine and fabric-covered wings mounted
over the plane's cockpit that were slightly canted, like a seagull's.
The 1942 Stinson Reliant Gull-Wing, built as a lend-lease observation plane for the British, became a favorite workhorse of
bush pilots after the war because they were cheap and virtually
indestructible.

McCann had found the Stinson fourteen miles from Tanana,
lying on its back under several feet of snow, only the landing
struts showing. Finding a crashed airplane in the woods was
not, in itself, unusual here. The Alaska bush is a veritable museum of vintage airplane wrecks, Curtis biplanes and Ford tri-
motors still stranded where their pilots crashed them. But
McCann wanted the Stinson to fly again. He cut a trail through

the brush to the plane and then hauled it in sections — engine, wings, and fuselage — back to Tanana by dog team. McCann loaded the Stinson on the barge to Nenana, the plane's original destination, and then drove it down in a trailer to Montana, where a mechanic helped him put the Stinson back together. When the plane was finished, he flew it back to Tanana, the Gull-Wing's first flight in twenty-eight years.

The cockpit was as roomy as the interior of a Packard. We eased into the twin seats, and McCann fingered the controls.

"Some day I want to do the interior up right. You know, leather seats and brass knobs. Did you notice how the windows roll down?"

I asked how the plane had come to crash in the first place.

"Ran out of gas. They were flying from Galena when the plane went down across the river. The pilot and passengers all walked out."

There had been no passengers, I found out later. And to say that the pilot had merely "walked out" was the essence of understatement.

Joe Cook, a CAA mechanic, had taxied the Stinson off the runway at Galena on the cold, clear morning of October 30, 1952. He flew east following the ice-covered Yukon and then turned south at the confluence with the Tanana River. Running into a sudden snow squall, he changed course and headed for an airstrip at Lake Minchumina. But the visibility only worsened, forcing Cook to make an emergency landing on a riverbar to wait out the storm. After several hours, he took off again, only to be forced down on the top of a thousand-foot-high hill, damaging the Stinson's landing gear in the process.

For four days, Cook remained stranded on the hilltop. At first he could hear search planes droning overhead in the thick overcast. So he built a seven-foot brushpile and doused it with fuel from the Stinson, ready to ignite the next time a plane flew over. But the dense cloudbank never cleared, and he realized his bonfire would not be seen. The only way he was going to get off the hilltop was to fly off.

Using only a hatchet from his emergency gear, Cook began clearing a fifteen-hundred-foot runway through the dwarf spruce and aspen. When it was complete, he taxied the plane to the far end, peered down the slot of cleared hilltop, and gunned the engine. As the Stinson hurtled down the narrow strip, it began sliding sideways and finally crashed into the brush. The aborted takeoff had ripped the plane's fabric, exposing the wings' metal skeleton. Two more attempts ended the same way, each time the plane emerging more tattered. On the fourth try, the plane again started to edge sideways off the runway, but this time Cook kept the throttle wide open as the plane hit the trees, the propeller chopping through branches until, with a sudden lift, the Stinson was airborne.

Cook headed north for the Yukon River. But even as the hilltop dropped away, the engine began to sputter and the plane lost altitude. He was running out of gas. Within sight of the white band of river, the sputtering stopped and there was only the sound of rushing wind. The Stinson nose-dived into woods and flipped over on its back, throwing Cook twenty feet. Bruised and tired, he gathered emergency food and a rifle from the wrecked cockpit and set off on foot through the deep snow. He reached the Yukon's wide banks that day and followed it upriver toward Tanana. For two days Cook walked, the temperature falling into the teens at night, until he was directly across the river from the town. Too exhausted to go on, he lay down in the snow and fired his rifle into the air. A miner in Tanana heard the shots, flew across the river, and picked Cook up.

True to the code of bush pilot heroics, Cook brushed aside suggestions he stay at the hospital in Tanana a few days. Instead, he hopped a plane to Fairbanks to see his son.

"The Stinson is a total loss," he cheerfully told reporters. "But that sure was a good airplane."

In any case, Cook had already sold the plane. He had been flying the Stinson to Nenana to deliver it to its new owner when it crashed.

I liked Tanana despite the McCanns' warnings. I liked its ragged yards, the prickly rose and lupine growing wild between lots, the few vegetable gardens on raised beds like effigy mounds. The pace of life in the village was slightly slower than the river's current, so I felt no loss of equilibrium at coming ashore. With the more energetic souls away at fish camps or wage jobs, Tanana had sunk into a summer's drowse.

Joe Runyon had left me the key to his cabin on Third Street. Tall and narrow with vertical blockhouse windows, the cabin rose from a junkyard of provisions. Dog sleds, three army surplus trucks, piles of lumber, freezers, old canvas tarps, nylon salmon nets, plastic fish tubs, blue fuel drums — all assembled on a piece of land the size of a city lot. I settled in, happy to have a place of my own, to await the *Ramona*. Down the street was the new city-run liquor store, the Tanana Sand Bar, which was neither a bar nor much of a store, just a concrete shed heaped with cases of lukewarm beer. I bought a six-pack and listened to a country-western station on the radio play heartache songs. Maybe the *Ramona* would never come. What would it be like to live here, I wondered, to stop drifting and lay in provisions, maybe find a woman, watch the river freeze?

First Street, pockmarked and graveled, ran between the riverbank and "downtown" Tanana — a row of cabins, the Episcopal church, the A. C. store, and the post office. I sat down on a bench from which I could keep an eye on river traffic as well as the pickups and three-wheelers cruising along the main drag. In a short time a stooped-over man with silver hair and nut-brown skin sat down next to me. He talked about the good weather and the tug that had sunk at Squaw Crossing, never once taking his eyes off the river.

Lee Edwin lived in a green house across the street, but he had grown up in the old village below Mission Hill.

"I was born in Tanana in 1908, but I lived all over. Trapped and fished all over when I was young."

Tanana was a white man's town then, with false-front saloons and gambling halls. Indians weren't allowed in the city limits after dark, and it was against the law to serve an Indian a drink. But Edwin harbored no animosity toward the past. The old hunting life had been tough, and he belonged to that last generation of Natives to remember whites fondly for their marvelous gadgets rather than their get-rich schemes and diseases.

He remembered seeing his first outboard engine in the early

twenties, "that little engine pushing this big long boat." Every summer Edwin netted salmon in Rampart Canyon not far from where Joe Runyon's fish camp was now. In early spring, before the ice broke up, he would drive a dog team up to the Yukon Flats to trap muskrats — one year he trapped over six hundred — and when the ice cleared he'd build a raft to float his dogs, pelts, and himself back to Tanana. If he shot a moose on the way, he'd stretch the raw hide over a framework of willow on the spot, making a bull boat of the skin to ferry the meat home.

As a boy he traveled with his parents up the Tanana in a Peterborough canoe, turning off the Kantishna River to trap muskrat and beaver in the lakes north of Mount McKinley with the few Indian families who lived in the shadow of the great mountain year round.

"We lived on caribou, berries, and water when we were out in the woods. When I came back down the Tanana after months in the woods, we stopped in Manley Hot Springs, where a trapper gave us beans and bread, and I got sick."

The next year when the family returned to the Kantishna, they found only graves. A flu epidemic had raged up the river, and those who hadn't died had moved on. That was the last trip Edwin and his parents made up the Kantishna.

An old man now, Edwin complained of pains in his chest and blamed his poor health on the severity of that early life. He'd had seven operations, and his hands fluttered along his legs, stomach, and chest to show where the doctors had cut into him. He hadn't hunted or fished in years and relied on grandchildren to chop his wood for him. But finding help with the chores couldn't have been too difficult, as his kin seemed to be everywhere.

A woman carrying a bag of groceries from the A. C. store waved to Edwin as we talked.

"That's my sister-in-law. And over there is my granddaughter." He made a small gesture with his hand, encompassing the village. "Everyone you see is my relative."

One day I hiked out of town to see the house Mike and Claire McCann were building on Mission Hill. The trail zigzagged up the wooded hillside in a series of steep switchbacks. Jogging to stay ahead of the mosquitoes, I reached the top out of breath, my heart pounding. But the view was worth it. Through the screen of spruce trees, I could make out the wishbone confluence and the purple foothills of the Alaska Range beyond, and in the far distance the jagged white peaks of the cordillera.

Mike McCann sat astride a canary yellow D-4 Caterpillar bulldozer, rolling up the deep moss campion as if it were carpeting. He had brought the Cat down from a mine on Quartz Creek and used it to cut a road up the hill. When he'd finished leveling a spot with the blade, McCann would let out cable from a winch in the back of the bulldozer to snake logs up the hillside. Once the line was hooked around a log, I helped keep the cable from tangling as it wound back onto the spool. When a log snagged against a standing tree and sent it crashing to the ground, I decided to stay out of the way.

There was a time when such mayhem in the woods would have been anathema to me. But now I found the bulldozer, with its tank treads and baritone belch of diesel smoke, exhilarating, like spending a lunch hour watching a wrecker's ball tear down an old neighborhood. Building my own cabin, I'd been almost apologetic about the trees I felled, an attitude that now struck me as nonsense. I remember friends who'd built their cabin from dead spruce pulled from a berm pile rather than cut down a single living tree. It was a beautiful cabin on a lofty ridge above Fairbanks, but the logs were honeycombed with carpenter ants. Every morning tiny pyramids of sawdust appeared on the floorboards from ants slowly eating the cabin walls from the inside out.

When a warm rain brought a halt to the work, McCann and I huddled under a tall spruce to wait out the shower.

"For years we've been trying to own a piece of land," he said, "but we've had nothing but hassles. People here resent it if you try to accomplish anything."

The Tozitna Corporation, a village corporation established by the Native Land Claims Act, held title to nearly all the land around Tanana except for this high wooded promontory overlooking the confluence. Until recently, Mission Hill was owned by the Episcopal Church, which had operated a mission at the base of the hill. When the church began to liquidate its land holdings in Alaska a few years ago, a Fairbanks realtor contacted the magistrate in Tanana to see if any local people were interested in buying a chunk of Mission Hill. A group of prospective buyers, all of them white, held a meeting at McCann's house and agreed to put down earnest money on five-acre parcels.

The sale of Mission Hill to a group of newcomers created bad feelings in the village. Building sites were vandalized. The Tozitna Corporation threatened to sue the Episcopal Church, and the church, backpedaling from a public relations disaster, offered to give back the earnest money. But McCann and the others declined, unable to understand why the village corporation, which owned so much property, was upset about the sale of a paltry thirty acres on Mission Hill.

The point of land across from the confluence of the Yukon and Tanana rivers was for centuries the site of an annual trading rendezvous among Athabascan tribes scattered throughout the interior. In midsummer, Gwich'in from the Yukon Flats, Koyukons from the upper Innoko River, and Tanana Indians from far up the tributary gathered at *Nuchalawoyya*, "the place where the two great rivers meet." It was the farthest point reached by Russian traders from downriver or Hudson's Bay traders from upriver. As many as six hundred Indians would assemble to trade and barter, their pointed bark canoes lining the riverbank.

In 1888 the Episcopal Church built a mission on the old trading site, and an Indian village soon grew up beside the church and one-room school. A few years later, the U.S. Army built Fort Gibbon, a military post and telegraph office three miles below the village, creating a symbiotic white community of stores and saloons. Whiskey and wood were the mainstays of the white town's economy: whiskey for the lonely soldiers and wood to heat the post. Employment and public schooling gradually drew more Indians to the town, now simply called Tanana, until a measles and flu epidemic in the 1940s finished off the old village. For the older people who had grown up there or whose relatives lay buried in the mission cemetery, Mission Hill was not just view property but a part of the village and, by extension, a part of themselves.

The rain had turned the hillside to mire, so McCann and I took a short walk through the woods to see his building site. He'd chosen it for the singular view of the river juncture and because in winter a temperature inversion would keep the hilltop twenty degrees warmer than its base. But mostly McCann wanted to remove himself farther from the village. The Athabascans he dismissed as "a real death-oriented culture. A potlatch every weekend. They really get hung up on the grieving."

The building site had been cleared, and rising incongruously from it was an Indian tepee. It was High Plains style, white canvas stretched over a tripod of lodge poles, with a smoke vent and circular entryway. McCann had sewn it himself. In fact, he had put himself through college selling his tepees throughout Montana. The Indian tepee was one tottering end of a long love-hate relationship.

In the sixties a lot of young people stuck feathers in their hair and imagined themselves the last of the Mohicans. But McCann's infatuation with tribal culture ran deeper. A city kid, he studied nursing out West so he could work with an Indian tribe. He braided his long black hair in a ponytail, wore high-top moccasins and a fringed buckskin jacket, and carried a medicine bundle of herbs and amulets. Weekends he'd set up his tepee at the Crow Fair or other powwows, joining in the tremulous singing and the circular dances. He embraced the Native American Church and partook of its sacramental peyote.

After spending a winter with two Cree trappers, McCann moved to Alaska, reasoning that the farther north he went the more authentic the Indians would be. He settled in Tanana as a public health nurse, but a few years of muscling drunks into detox soured him on village life. He cut his hair, learned to fly a plane, and made plans to exile himself from red men, who seldom met his high expectations.

Frederick Whymper, an English artist on a similar quest more than a century earlier, observed the gathering of tribes at Nuchalawoyya in 1867 and was not disappointed. Of the Tanana contingent, he wrote: "They were gay with painted faces, feathers in their long hair, patches of red clay at the back of their heads covered with small fluffy feathers, double-fringes and beads, and elaborately worked fire bags and belts. They reminded me of the ideal North American Indian I had read of but never seen."

Sunday was the feast of St. James, so the morning's service at St. James Episcopal Church promised to be a celebration. The congregation, mostly elderly and female, had bottlenecked at the church's front steps behind an old woman stranded in her wheelchair. I and a slight man in a denim jacket, the only "young" men in attendance, bore the old lady up the steps in her wheelchair. The church was narrow and plain, not nearly as grand as the one in Fort Yukon, but I liked the floral designs on the stained glass windows and the way fragments of colored light fell on the floor when the sunlight shifted.

The Episcopal priest turned out to be my partner in good deeds. He had exchanged his denim jacket for a white chasuble, but with his fringe of long brown hair and a thin, bemused face, he looked less like a cleric than the owner of a second-hand record shop. He seemed tentative with his flock, not wanting to take the initiative. "What hymn shall we do now?" "Do you think we should have a church committee meeting after services?" "What time?" "Is that all right with you?" To all these questions, the congregation responded with silence, thinking perhaps that the priest should set the schedule and choose the hymns. He met each silence with an ingratiating smile.

The priest began his sermon at the Sea of Galilee and slowly steered it north.

"Once there were two brothers who were fishermen. They fished the rivers and they fished the lakes. When they were fishing, there was only the sound of the wind on the lake as they drew in their nets. But the brothers argued a lot between themselves, and so they were called the Sons of Thunder. Of course, I'm talking about James and his brother John. They argued a lot, but they always loved each other."

Here the priest paused to shift tracks.

"That seems to be the story of Tanana or any other town, isn't it? Lots of arguments, but as long as people still love each other they get along. I'm thinking of the new liquor store. The Tanana Sand Bar. That's what they call it, isn't it? But that's not a very accurate name. Why don't they call it the Weeping Mother Bar? [Scattered nods of approval from the congregation.] Why don't they call it the Crying Father Bar? [More vigorous head-nodding and whispered yeses.] Why don't they call it the Lost Children Bar or the Dying Family Bar?"

At this point, the flock seemed thoroughly incited, and I wondered what course the priest would set them on. He only smiled gently and shook his head.

"But we're not going to argue with those people because we love them."

After the offertory, the priest read through a litany of intentions, to which the congregation murmured back, "We pray to the Lord." Then he looked in my direction and, spotting an outsider, added, "For those traveling on the river, we ask that the God of the river grant them safe passage."

More than anyone else, Patrick X. Moore was responsible for turning Tanana "wet." He had started a petition to get the city-run liquor store on the ballot and successfully campaigned for its passage. When I dropped into his office at the new peeled-log city building, he had his feet up on the desk and was shouting into a phone. Moore terminated the conversation with a string of nos and slammed down the receiver. He wore faded blue jeans, a Tanana Dog Mushers Association cap, and red logging suspenders drawn tight over a bulging work shirt. Moore, thirty years old and white, was the mayor of Tanana.

When I suggested that he might be one of the "sons of thunder" in Sunday's sermon, Moore nearly fell out of his chair.

"That Episcopal priest doesn't even live here! He just flies in now and then! What puts a twist in my tail about these Bible thumpers is how they try to pour their morals on everybody else!"

Tanana had been semidry since the late 1950s, which meant that liquor was not illegal to possess, only to sell. Anyone thirsty enough could go down to one of the bootleggers in the morning, slap down twenty dollars, and have a case of beer flown in from Fairbanks on the afternoon plane.

"The only difference now," said Moore, "is that there's no waiting period and the money stays in town. Hell, I was a bootlegger myself at one time. I didn't see the light. I just couldn't make it work anymore."

The mayor saw no irony in using money generated from the Tanana Sand Bar to pay for the village's problems, most of which were alcohol related. He envisioned a golden age of progress for Tanana, ushered in by revenues from the liquor store. Perhaps the money would go into additional law enforcement and substance-abuse programs, or maybe cable TV. Maybe a park. Who knew? When he spoke of the staggering possibilities, the mayor's voice turned soft with wonder.

Moore was no stranger to village life. He'd grown up in Aniak, a small Eskimo village on the Kuskokwim River, where his father worked for the Federal Aviation Agency. After a few semesters in college, he moved back to Tanana and played his guitar sixteen hours a day. His future prospects had looked slim.

"There was a time when I didn't fit in worth a shit around here. About three people in town smoked dope, and I was one of them. I had hair down to the crack in my ass. But in Tanana you could do what you wanted. Hell, I didn't change — the town did."

We took a slow tour of the village in Moore's pickup truck, cruising past the community vegetable garden — "Our experiment in socialism" — and the new jail. We rolled to a stop by the barge landing downriver where Moore kept twenty sled dogs tethered in the willows along with a pig he was fattening up to butcher in the fall. The dogs were blue-eyed malemutes for the most part, sprinters rather than distance runners, except his lead dog, a skittish yellow half retriever.

"Guess what her name is," he smirked. "It's *gussuk!* You know what that means, don't you?"

"It means something like 'ofay.'"

Gussuk is the Eskimo corruption of "cossack," a term first applied to Russian fur traders and later extended to any white.

We drove east along the river, past birch woods and berry pickers, and stopped by the side of the road where Mike McCann was unloading blue drums of fuel oil. McCann seemed surprised to see me riding around with the mayor. Moore and McCann joked about how busy they were and grinned warily, each wondering if the other had given me his number.

"Now, don't go believing everything this guy tells you!" McCann shouted as we pulled away.

"Shanghai McCann," Moore called him when he was out of earshot. The nickname referred to McCann's reputation for hiring drifters rather than locals to work on his projects. Moore and McCann used to play together in a rock 'n' roll band in Tanana. McCann was on drums, while Moore played electric guitar and sang lead vocal. The band's big number was "Going up the River," which wasn't even a song but only a few guitar chords and a single refrain. The crowd loved it when Moore sang "Going up the River."

We rolled to a stop in a grassy clearing at the base of Mission Hill where the old village once stood. In the meadow stood one of the loveliest churches I'd ever seen. The Mission of Our Savior had a vaulted roof, Queen Anne gables covered with cedar shakes, latticework windows, and a high bell cupola. The city had a grant to restore the old church but so far had only shored up the sagging foundation. Inside, the church was as dark and empty as a barn. We walked past an old, white-picketed cemetery in a grove of birch trees.

"A lot of the animosity Indians feel toward whites," said Moore, "has been handed down from when they lived here and were treated as second-class citizens."

The sale of land on Mission Hill only widened the rift between Moore and his old friend. He thought McCann and the others had made the deal too exclusive.

"They kept it pretty quiet. Things would have been different if they had been completely in the open instead of trying to surround themselves with white people because they thought Indians were too rowdy."

He walked ahead through the tall grass, heading back toward the truck.

"I learned what to say and what not to say when I was a kid

growing up in an Eskimo village and getting the shit kicked out of me. You don't ever want to forget who's the minority here."

Mike McCann lay sprawled on his living room couch the next day, holding a bloody compress to his head. He had been chain-sawing through a nine-inch timber on Mission Hill when the saw blade bucked backward and tore a deep, ragged furrow down the center of his forehead. He'd managed to stumble down the trail holding a blanket to his head to keep the blood from running into his eyes.

I'd come up to the house to visit and found him staring pa-tiently at the ceiling. Claire arrived shortly with the ex–public health physician and his nurse wife. They were friends of the McCanns. The doctor had McCann lie across the dining table by the window, but there still wasn't enough light to operate, so I volunteered to hold a lamp overhead.

"Now this is going to hurt a little," said the doctor. He sewed the gash with a curved needle until the stream of blood running down the patient's forehead began to ebb. It took fifteen stitches to close the wound. By then my own head felt particularly light and drained of blood. I needed a breath of fresh air.

The doctor's young wife, sopping up the overflow, was Irish. She wouldn't be rushed when her husband snapped at her to hurry it up.

"Oh, balls, Bill!" she said in a lovely brogue. "You're such an asshole when you operate."

The great illusion of village life is that it is simple. A village is like an extended family, and village politics are a prolonged version of a family quarrel. One side of the coin is togetherness, the other lack of privacy. In a big city, you can afford to tell your neighbors off once in a while, having a surplus of them. But in a village you have to get along with the same hundred people, in the same way you kowtow to disagreeable relatives just to keep the peace. The river is an escape valve in summer, as people move to outlying fish camps. But in the isolation of a long dark winter, a village can become terribly confining, and slights, real and imagined, easily fester into blood feuds. Expatriates from the city, seeking the carefree life in a village, find themselves instead distant cousins at a large and unruly family reunion.

As a traveler, I enjoyed a certain neutrality, but my visa was fast expiring. For a week I lingered in Tanana, floating between factions, but the longer I stayed the more I felt caught in the bickering between camps: between boozers and teetotalers, between villagers and the people building on Mission Hill. Eventually I would have to choose sides, and I didn't feel like choosing. So every day found me waiting more eagerly for the *Ramona*'s arrival.

LATE IN THE DAY I moved my canoe down to the barge landing, after Mike McCann telephoned to say that he'd heard the *Ramona* rattling toward the confluence. Someone was already camped on the beach, an unemployed bus boy from Anchorage. He had troubled blue eyes and a scrunched-up face. His canoe partner had deserted him in Circle, so he'd paddled on to Tanana by himself, pilfering salmon from fish wheels along the way. Now he was trying to sell his canoe so he could fly home.

We heaped together a big fire on the beach and watched the sun go down. Soon the sky was dark and the first stars came out. When a skiff labored upriver, the glow of the driver's cigarette looked like a running light. A cool breeze blew off the water, and we huddled closer to the circle of firelight.

At first I felt sorry for the bus boy because nobody in Tanana would have anything to do with him. But after a while, I understood why. He was bad luck. If I boiled water for coffee, he'd spill it. Or he'd accidentally kick sand in my cup. He also had a nervous habit of looking at his wrist watch every few minutes and then asking me what time it was. Finally he pulled off the watch and flung it in the river.

"Wasn't working anyhow," he said.

Then he took a wrinkled dollar bill from his wallet and showed me the side with the one-eyed pyramid.

"Ever look closely at the words underneath? *Novus ordo seclorum.* That's Latin for "the new world order." That's what the Rockefellers want, a new world order!"

Now I was worried.

Like any route to the far edge of a continent, the Yukon attracted its share of end-of-the-road types: the perennial losers, the harmless screwballs, the crazies. The river was often the last step on the gangplank. In villages along the Yukon, traveling without a motor was taken as a sign of lack of destination and common sense. An individual drifting with the current was either a tourist or a madman. I'd heard plenty of stories about such people; they were called "floaters."

One floater rode into Tanana on a door bolted to four gas cans. He had driven nails through the soles of his shoes so that they dragged along the ground like bear claws. He demanded emergency food and, in particular, margarine. Another floater announced himself as King David and said he was on his way to Siberia to test the theory of gravity. One summer a fellow rafted to Tanana wearing a long overcoat with machetes and meat cleavers hung from the lining. He stole a boat, fell out of it a few miles downriver at the mouth of the Tozitna, and started a forest fire trying to warm himself. But not all of the stories were funny. In late spring of 1984, a young drifter murdered seven people at Manley Hot Springs and dumped their bodies in the icy Tanana River before being gunned down by state troopers pursuing in a helicopter.

At midnight there was still no sign of the *Ramona*. An owl hooted across the road. I brewed another pot of coffee and prepared for a long vigil.

"Look at all those stars!" the bus boy exclaimed softly, his back flat against the sand. "There must be more than a million of them! Doesn't it make you think we're not alone?"

"Alone?"

"What if there's another planet just like this one, and the people on it are just like us? Identical twins! Everything we do, they do! Like right now they'd be looking up at the sky and saying, 'What if there's another planet just like this one?' " Just thinking about this idea made his head spin from the overload.

The bus boy asked my opinion on the origin of life on earth — the hand of God or random chemicals? — then ranted about his own theories of alien spacemen. Odd as he was, I kind of enjoyed having a voice to keep me awake through the night. A beach is a kind of no man's land, and we were both a little river-struck; we were both floaters. After he crawled away to his tent, I decided he was harmless, but I stayed up and fed the fire just in case.

READING
THE
RIVER

THE *Ramona* didn't arrive until the next day. In the afternoon,
she slipped into view — a boxy tug stacked three tiers high and
painted white with lime trim. She looked like a wedding cake
set adrift. A sign over the pilothouse read: RAMONA. Pushing
tandem barges, the tug chugged down the far side of the river
as if she had no intention of stopping, then swung against the
current in a U-turn and angled toward shore. As the barges
nosed onto the landing, a skinny deck hand leaped ashore and
tied a dock rope to the thickest cottonwood he could find. Two
metal gangplanks clanged down, set just wide enough to fit the
wheelbase of a forklift. People drifted down from the village to
watch as the crew began the balancing act of off-loading.

The operation lacked the crisp chain of command I'd seen
aboard the Yutana Barge Line in Beaver, where orders were
relayed by walkie-talkie from the bridge to the crew. Here
everybody pitched in. When a car on deck failed to start on its
own power, Claude Demientieff, owner and operator of the
Ramona, climbed onto the forklift and snaked the stalled car
over the gangplanks as bystanders cheered. A short, thick-
chested man with a high-pitched voice and a hearing aid, he
looked Italian but was Athabascan-Russian. He seemed to know
everybody at the landing by name and moved among them,
working the crowd — pumping hands, joking, inquiring after
their families — as if these were his constituents and the river
one long whistlestop.

I asked him where I should put my canoe.

He scratched his ear. "Oh, anywhere. Just haul it up on a barge and tie it down."

Weighted down with freight, the barges rode only a few inches above the water. I hauled my canoe onto a vacant ledge and lashed it to a load of lumber. Then ropes were cast off, the *Ramona*'s diesel engine churned in reverse, and we were under way. I ran to the shoreside of the barge to wave good-by. Most of the people I'd come to know in Tanana seemed to be at the landing. Patrick Moore had come down to pick up a shipment of fuel drums. The bus boy's troubled face stared back at me, alone even in a crowd. A familiar, beat-up truck pulled up to the landing, and Joe Runyon and Sheri Mitchell jumped out and waved. After spending only a week here I was touched that someone would see me off. I felt like a baton being passed from one benefactor to the next. Then the landing slipped behind a screen of willows, and we moved downstream.

There were no sleeping quarters for me on the *Ramona*, but I had the run of the barges. Far from the engine's throbbing, they slid quietly along the river, pushing a breeze. I wandered about, squeezing through the narrow alleyways between loads and reading our itinerary stamped on the sides of freight: fuel drums to KALLANDS, a freezer truck-trailer to RUBY, lumber marked CITY DOCK—KOYUKUK SCHOOL HOUSING, and cases of beer and liquor sheathed in plastic and ominously labeled LAST CHANCE. I enjoyed the sensation of traveling without my arm bent around a tiller. I could stretch my legs or loaf, read or take a nap, and all the while watch the river unfold.

The Yukon opened up into a broader, less defined valley, the shoreline elevated where the current pressed against the right bank. Spruce woods along the shore gave way to light green hills of poplar and birch and distant mountain ranges. As we passed a creek mouth, a golden eagle flew downriver and alighted in a lofty spruce. When we caught up, it flew off again and landed in another treetop, playing tag with the boat until the eagle lost interest and soared away.

The deck hand I had seen jump ashore at Tanana crouched on the foredeck, lathering his hands with a bar of soap in the muddy Yukon. Scarecrow thin and bearded, Steve was one of two deck hands and the only non-Indian of the crew. He did double duty as cook, so he was washing off the grime from one job before tending to the other. Steve had first canoed down the Yukon on a lark a few summers ago, then hitched a ride back to Nenana on the *Ramona*. He enjoyed the trip so much that the following winter he wrote Claude to ask for a job. He loved working on the river, marking the summer as a series of villages between green hills, each trip an extension of that first joy ride.

To get to the galley, I stooped through the machine-shop racket of the engine room, plugging my ears until I was on the other side of the door. In the galley, plates and glasses tinkled in the cupboards from the pounding of the 225-horse diesel in the next room. There was coffee and the beginnings of a stew on the gas stove. I wasn't the only passenger along for the ride. There was the younger pilot's girlfriend, a redhead named Jo-Ann, who sat in a chair peeling potatoes. In the corner, Claude's twin teenage daughters played cards and watched the stove. They were quiet and exclusive as twins. When they leaned together to whisper a secret, their long raven hair closed like a curtain. One of the twins noticed that the coffee water was running low, so she went on deck with an empty bucket. The tug swung close to a creek mouth, and when the twin returned, her bucket was filled with clear drinking water.

I climbed the stairs to the balustraded upper deck, ducked into the crew's sleeping quarters, where one shift lay dozing, then climbed an open hatchway to the pilothouse. Perched three stories above the water, the glassed enclosure looked down upon the barges cluttered with freight and out to the river, a mile wide and shimmering in the late afternoon sun. At this height, the engine's din was muffled; the only sound was wind gusting against the sliding glass window.

Paul Starr steered the boat from a bar stool, his hands wrapped loosely on the spoked wooden wheel. We were steaming downstream at twelve knots with the current to our back. For the better part of the afternoon we had been tracing a line along the high right bank.

"You need good eyes to pilot a boat on the Yukon," Paul said over his shoulder. He was a pleasant, talkative man, heavy jawed, with the sloping build of an Indian heavy in a horse opera. "See that?" He pointed to the river's oily surface along the left bank. "There's only six inches of water there. The surface is too still."

The main channel of the Yukon runs to a depth of thirty feet, but there are bottomless eddies as well as hidden shoals too shallow to float a bar of soap. Because of the Yukon's glacial silt, a pilot must imagine the bottom terrain by reading the river's surface. The rise of shoreline is one clue, deeper water tending toward high cutbanks. Sandbars give themselves away with feather riffles or an icy smooth sheen.

As we entered an S-bend, Paul handed me a pair of binoculars so I could see the channel marker, a reflective metal sheet nailed to a spruce tree on the right bank. He tracked straight for the marker until he could see another metal sheet on the opposite bank; aligning with that, he steered the *Ramona* through the curve by connecting the dots. Paul spotted a black bear shuffling along the beach and turned the throttle down to get its attention. The bear snapped out of its reverie and backpedaled into the woods.

Our first stop was a squat homesteader's cabin on the right bank that belonged to an immigrant nicknamed "Herman the German." A raw-boned man dressed in fatigues and wearing a pistol strapped to his belt supervised the off-loading, but he wasn't, I was told, "Herman." Not wanting to be too much a tourist, I helped the crew wrestle thirteen fuel drums down the ramps to a waiting pickup truck. As we worked, Paul teased his shift mate, who had just removed his cook's apron, by singing, "Steve the cook! Steve the cook!"

Claude had gone to the cabin to visit, and when he returned, a small boy ran after him with a head of cabbage and some rutabagas from the homestead garden. Then we were off again on our voyage, and the people onshore drifted back to their chores.

The vegetables went into the stew, which we had for supper along with coleslaw, bread and jam, and endless cups of coffee. Claude, whose shift had begun at six o'clock, came down from the pilothouse to eat, leaving Ali Starr, Paul's brother and the

other deck hand, at the ship's wheel. I asked Claude about the
tug that had sunk at Squaw Crossing.

"They thought we were making millions up here and wanted
to get in on it! But they didn't know the river. As soon as they
entered the Tanana, they got stuck on a sandbar. Their boat
was too deep for that river. It drew four feet, and that was
empty."

The *Ramona*, drawing three feet fully loaded, had taken two
days to descend the Tanana. Because the river's shifting sandbars and constantly changing channel were treacherous in the
dark, the *Ramona* tied up along shore at night. In daylight, a
deck hand stood on the bow of the barge, sounding the channel's depth with a graduated pole, then lifting it high enough
for the pilot to see the high-water mark. Even so, the *Ramona*
twice grounded on sandbars, and the barges had to be shifted
around to free her.

The *Ramona* went anyplace on the river between the delta
and Fort Yukon, making the milk-run stops the larger, Seattle-
based barge lines couldn't afford to service. Once Claude had
steered the *Ramona* four hundred miles up the winding and
shallow Koyukuk River to the village of Allakaket to deliver well
drilling equipment, but he had needed a rainy summer to do it.
Claude's business card read: "Demientieff Barge Service — If
it's wet we go there."

As we talked, Claude kept glancing uneasily out the galley
porthole at the passing shore. We must have strayed too close,
because midway through his stew he put the spoon down and
hustled upstairs. A little later, a sheepish-looking Ali came into
the galley and lost himself in a Louis L'Amour western. Of all
the crew, he was the hardest for me to draw into a conversation.
He had the flat nosed, wary look of a prize fighter, and a speech
impediment that made him sound childlike and perhaps ac-
counted for his coolness with strangers. Still, he enjoyed teasing
the twins, who obviously doted on him, and he was perfectly at
ease as long as I wasn't in the room.

After supper, I climbed back to the pilothouse. Claude stared
straight ahead, every so often pushing down on the big-spoked
wheel or pulling up to adjust course. The river lay gilded in

dusky light. The crow's-nest view scaled the Yukon down to a more manageable size. Wind-driven waves looked no more threatening than ripples, and back eddies that would have swiveled my canoe around like a leaf couldn't even get a grip on the *Ramona*. From this lofty vantage point, I could view the river with a certain detachment. It was like watching a commotion in the street from a tall building without the slightest risk of being involved.

The Yukon split around a large island, the south channel washing against high cutbanks of frozen mud sheared from an enormous tableland. This was the Boneyard. As the high cliffs thawed in the intense summer light and calved into the river, the bones, teeth, and tusks of Pleistocene animals were sometimes exposed. According to Claude, the Boneyard was an ancient swamp that had dried up thousands of years ago and delivered the fossils of extinct animals a summer at a time.

I wanted him to steer closer so we might see the scimitar tusk of a woolly mammoth protruding from the bank. But a falling chunk of the huge cliffs could have easily swamped the *Ramona*. Even from a distance I could smell the dank, cellar odor of thawing humus. Natives in former times called these palisades "the cutbank of ghosts" and formulated a more intriguing theory to account for the fossils that eroded from the cliffs. They were the remains of terrible beasts that dwelled underground and could emerge only one night a year to roam the outer world. At all other times, the outer atmosphere was poisonous to them, which explained why only bones were found.

About nine-thirty in the evening, we passed the mouth of the Nowitna River, partially hidden behind a small phalanx of willowy islands. Earlier we had passed the Tozitna and would soon pass the Melozitna — "-na" being the Athabascan suffix for river. The sun had sunk downstream, and night was overtaking us.

Standing behind Claude, I tried to imagine the Yukon as he saw it. In the long daylight hours of summer, a novice might steer a ship like the *Ramona* down the Yukon by reading its surface. But in the lengthening evenings of late summer and fall, a pilot has to know the river by heart because, except for hairpin turns, the Yukon is unmarked. Some riverboat pilots keep elaborate navigation charts of shoals and reefs, revised each year as the river rewrites itself. Claude, however, worked without maps. He knew the river's contours by memory and could fix his position in the dark by the silhouette of hills.

The challenge of running a ship in autumn is knowing when to quit. Slush ice starts running on the Yukon in early October, stopping for a brief respite as tributaries freeze over, before ice seals the main river shut. But if a customer needed supplies — and this was typical — Claude would press his luck with a last trip, heading back to home port in Nenana with ice closing in behind him. The greatest danger is that the engine will fail and the boat ground on a sandbar, swamping as the pressure of the ice inexorably builds.

"One year we couldn't make it back to Nenana," said Claude. "The ice was running so badly we had to park the tug and barge in a slough at the mouth of the Nowitna. Then we took the pilot boat to Ruby. Got a loaf of bread and a quart of whiskey and drifted all night to Galena. We flew back in late April and landed on the ice. Oh, we had a great time living on the boat! For a month we hunted ducks and set nets for whitefish and waited for the river to clear."

Because he was hard of hearing, Claude sometimes guessed what my question had been, a tactic I'm familiar with, being partially deaf myself. Finally I gave up asking questions; just watching the river unfold over his shoulder was a singular pleasure. If you asked villagers along the Yukon who the best riverman was, the answer was always Claude Demientieff. Like the musher George Attla, another local hero, he was admired not just for being expert at what he did but for not changing in the process. Claude had grown up on the river, and for him every stretch was a kind of homecoming.

The Demientieffs were a well-known family on the lower Yukon. Orphaned as a boy, Claude was sent to the Catholic boarding school at Holy Cross, where he met Martha Au Coin, another orphan and his wife-to-be. The nuns ruled with a firm hand, and when a girl came to discuss a marriage proposal, the sisters might dismiss the suitor as "shiftless" or push another boy who was "a hard worker." Claude had fallen into the latter category. At fifteen he'd worked as a "flunkie" on the steamboat *Nenana,* washing dishes, making beds, and seeing, if not the world, at least the rest of the Yukon.

After the wedding, the Demientieffs set up housekeeping at Flat, a has-been mining town on the Innoko River, where Claude worked on a gold dredge. The population consisted of aging miners, the remnants of earlier stampedes. A clannish bunch, they watched for smoke rising from each other's chimneys on winter mornings to make sure a neighbor hadn't died overnight. But they could be quite feckless as well, especially when it came to young Natives. Two miners once hired Claude to take them by dog sled to their diggings, and before setting off, one of them gave him a packet to hold. Thinking it was the man's watch, Claude kept the packet inside his parka. At the end of the bumpy ride, the miner asked for the packet back; wrapped inside were blasting caps.

Claude piloted harbor craft in the Aleutian campaign, then moved to Anchorage and worked construction during the postwar boom. He was often away from home for months at a time. Once, after a particularly long stint, his three-year-old daughter failed to recognize him, and Claude decided he needed a family business. He built a covered wooden barge, stocked it with groceries, and towed the floating store from village to village for ten years. The transition to barging freight was easy since people were always asking him to bring something down on his next trip. So he welded together a steel barge and built a plywood tug to push it; the tug he named for his oldest daughter, Ramona, the one who had failed to recognize him.

I climbed down from the pilothouse to the galley, where the twins were playing rummy. Moving through the engine room din, I stepped into the cool night air. Ali was smoking a cigarette on the foredeck and we passed in silence. On the barge I found a niche among some roof trusses that smelled pleasantly of pine and was just large enough for me to unroll my sleeping bag. Warm and sheltered from the wind, I watched the river rolling past. It was wonderful, like having a berth on a night train rolling across the Great Plains: there were no bumps; you could doze off and wake the next day in mountains. The river had taken on the drab green of the hills. The willow and alder along the shore looked impenetrably thick, the only lights a sieve of stars — Polaris and the Big Dipper. This might have been the Mississippi River two hundred, three hundred years ago. In the vast, unlit expanse there was nothing to suggest that the landscape was not untouched and primeval. The age of steamboats came and went, the boom towns fading into the woods. Time seemed to flow backward and I could imagine hunters huddled over campfires on their long trek inland, their heads bent to the sound of beasts trampling through the darkness.

The roar of the diesel engine gearing down woke me in the middle of the night. The *Ramona* was angling toward electric lights strung in a saddle between hills. It was a cheery sight, like landfall after an ocean crossing, the contours of land defined by shore lights. Ruby was the only village below Circle on the left bank of the river. Terraced into the hillside, it had taken its brief turn as the largest settlement on the Yukon before sinking into obscurity.

A pickup truck held the landing in its headlights as the *Ramona* eased the barges ashore. Helping with the heavy steel ramps, I smashed my finger and decided to stop playing stevedore and watch the unloading from shore. The twins were watching, too, silhouetted against the pilothouse window.

Claude couldn't haul the freezer truck-trailer up the steep landing with the forklift, so he borrowed a huge backloader to do the job. The remaining freight was moved to a single barge and the empty barge uncoupled and moored to shore to be picked up on the return trip. The entire operation took three hours. By then a rosy light rimmed the eastern hills; downriver still lay deep in night, and the sky in between was a gradient of blues.

The single, overloaded barge rode low in the river, a film of water running over its edges. The valley stretched into low swampland on either side, flat and monotonous. The topography was all in the sky, great black-bottomed cumulus clouds sailing upriver. In a drizzle, we passed the tin-roofed village of

Galena on the right bank and farther on a control tower rising from the willow flat. The air force base at Galena is only a few hundred miles from the Chukotsk Peninsula of Siberia. As the *Ramona* drew abreast of the runway, two delta-winged fighters streaked across our bow, climbed vertically, and then leveled off below the cloud cover, flying west toward the Russian Bear.

At noon we steered around a large island at the mouth of the Koyukuk River. The village of Koyukuk lay two miles upstream at the base of a wedge-shaped mountain. Steaming past rows of cabins, we arrived at the barge landing, a notch cut into the wooded bank. A reception committee came aboard to watch Claude unload lumber for new teacher housing. He had worked straight through the night and would sleep on the upriver run. One of the boarding party produced a pint of vodka. Claude went into the galley for cups and orange juice, but finding no juice he dipped the cups in the muddy river.

"That's good water," a tall man, owlish in round glasses, told me. "I've been drinking it for sixty-five years."

As we drank, two boatloads of GIs from the airbase at Galena motored up in camouflage fatigues and floppy jungle hats. They looked like a raiding party until I saw the fishing rods. They picked out the one white face on the *Ramona*'s deck, mine, and asked if this was Nulato. I said it wasn't.

One of the Koyukuk men, who'd drunk more than his share of the vodka, shouted back, "You missed the turn, cowboy! Nulato is eighteen miles downriver, cowboy!"

The soldiers, barely out of high school, looked at each other with chagrined smiles. Then they revved up their Evinrudes and peeled off, leaving a rolling wake. One of them turned around and gave us the finger.

When the *Ramona* headed downriver, two of the visitors who'd come aboard at Koyukuk went along for the ride. One of them snoozed on the nearly empty barge, and the other, a thin, beagle-eyed man, tiptoed around the deck. Claude told me to keep an eye on him.

"He steals things. He's a nice old fella, but you've got to watch him. It's like a compulsion. And he's smart, too. Once he tied up to the barge and I watched him the whole time. Well, he got back in his boat to leave, but the engine wouldn't start. See, he'd unplugged one of the spark plugs. So while I tried to start his engine, he went back and got a case of beer, telling the crew, 'It's all right. Claude said I could have this.' "

Claude laughed at this story even though the joke had been on him. Still, I didn't want the old man rummaging through the stuff in my canoe, so I shadowed him around the boat in a game of shipboard hide-and-seek. He had the floating walk of a pick-pocket and a guileless smile he used to great effect to show that he knew that I knew.

Our final stop was at the end of a cutoff slough, a cluster of cabins and a liquor store called Last Chance. For the remaining five hundred miles downriver, all the villages were dry, so this was literally the last chance to buy a legal drink. Judging from the stack of booze we unloaded, the store did a fire-sale business.

The crew members customarily took turns buying a case of beer before heading back upriver. I bought the beer this time, but the stowaways drank most of it. I was sorry to see my sleeping quarters disappear as the roof trusses were unloaded. The *Ramona* would return to Nenana soon, with a brief stop at Ko-yukuk to drop off two drunken passengers. I had enjoyed the luxury of being a passenger, especially on the *Ramona,* which in itself was a form of endorsement with the villages along the river. From here I was on my own again, and things could only get tougher. Like Steve, I wanted the barge ride to go on for-ever.

Unroping my canoe, I slipped it into the water and tied it to the railing. But when I went to pay Claude my fare, he refused to take any money.

"What for?" he said. "You didn't eat much."

I pressed him. "After all, I've taken up space like any other freight."

"In that case, we charge by weight. I'd have to weigh you. But first," he winked, "I'd dip you in the water!"

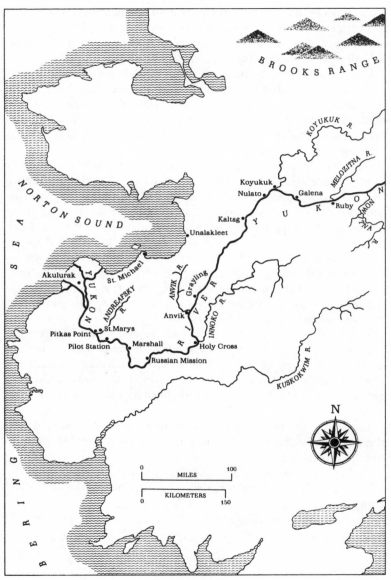

Lower Yukon River

SUNDAY MORNING.

A cloud of seagulls rose up as I rounded the point of an island where I'd camped the night. The sun caught their white heads as the flock took shape in the wind. Wheeling and crying overhead, they overtook my canoe. Their rookery must have been close by because the gulls were in a bad temper, diving halfheartedly at my head and making a terrible screeching that sounded one minute like bicycle horns and the next like children crying. Splashing down ahead of the bow, they formed a cordon of stern gull faces. I bore down until at last they flew off noisily, abandoning the river.

Coming upon Kaltag from the river, you see the old Catholic church steeple and the village sprawled below, suspended between gray water and blue sky. The gravel beach below the village was lined with skiffs, their engines tilted up, and racks of drying salmon the color of cured tobacco leaves. I parked my canoe and walked up a path to the village. At the far end of the beach a chained husky set up a forlorn howl.

The village looked deserted beneath the bright summer sky. The oldest buildings were jammed shoulder to shoulder beside the riverbank, squat cabins built in the Russian style, with the weathered logs dovetailed at the ends and chinked with moss, while down the road was a new pastel-colored high school. There was no one around except for three old men sitting on a bench. In every village along the Yukon there had been these old men, these sentinels, always looking upstream to see what the current would bring.

This morning the river had brought me, but the trio seemed

uninterested. They were waiting for the priest to come down from Nulato to say mass. I had known a student from Kaltag at the university but had no idea whether she'd come back home.

"Does Violet Esmailka still live here?"

"Yes," said one of the men. "But her name is Burnham since she got married. They live in that house over there."

He pointed across the road to a red frame house with a hipped roof. It was the biggest house in the village. I walked across the road and knocked on the door. Nobody answered.

"It's Sunday morning," the old man said, turning the words slowly in his mouth so I might comprehend the obvious. "They're sleeping."

So I asked about the portage trail to Unalakleet, the old trade route between the interior Indian tribes and the Bering Sea Eskimos. It was a short cut to the coast. By taking a ninety-mile dogleg inland and crossing the divide to the Unalakleet River, one could shave five hundred miles off the river route to the sea.

The old men just yawned and shook their heads in unison. The trail was very wet in summer, they said. A person would need hip boots to cross the swamps. When I explained that I only wanted to hike a little of the trail, this did little to shake the old men's growing conviction that the Yukon delivered up only fools.

"That's brown bear country," one of them said, smiling behind his sunglasses. "Lots of bears come down from the hills now that the fish are running."

His friend picked up the thread. "There was a fella that tried to walk over it last year. He came here in a canoe like you and asked a lot of fool questions about the portage and people told him not to go. He had canvas shoes and carried an ax. No rifle. He got lost in the swamp and a brown bear chased him. Someone from the village found him a few days later, all ragged and cold on the riverbank."

"Maybe that fellow was afraid," the man behind the sunglasses said with satisfaction. "You know, a bear can smell if you're afraid."

*

The portage trail began as a wide lane cut into the birch and spruce at the end of the airfield. The morning had warmed up, and the good, astringent smell of Labrador tea and sedge arose as I crushed them underfoot. After the first mile, the litter and empty plastic containers of snowmobile oil all but disappeared. The woods closed in, and I felt a long way from the village. From here the trail wound along the headwaters of the Kaltag River into the hills, crossed the divide near Old Woman Mountain, and descended the Unalakleet River to the sea.

In the spring, when the snow crusted over, Koyukon Indians had crossed this route with dog sleds, carrying fox and wolverine skins, beaver pelts, and carved wooden dishes; and when they returned from trading with the Eskimos, their sleds were loaded with seal oil, blubber from beluga whales, trade beads, and domestic reindeer hides from Siberia. That trade relations had been cordial could be seen in the villagers' round, Eskimo features.

Over this same route came the first Russians to open the great interior to the fur trade, although not without difficulty. The Koyukons, who had set themselves up as middlemen between the Eskimos and other interior tribes, were reluctant to bring in competition. For four winters in a row, the Indians had put the Russians off the trail by providing guides who led the foreigners over longer, more difficult routes. Finally, Vasiliy Malakhov, a trader with the Russian American Company, crossed the trail in 1838, and established a trading post the following year upriver at Nulato. A few winters later, Lieutenant Lavrentiy Zagoskin of the Russian Imperial Navy set off on the portage trail from Unalakleet one December morning with five sleds and twenty-seven dogs. Halfway up the Unalakleet River, he came to an Indian village he called Ulak. In *Travels in Russian America*, Zagoskin wrote of the villagers: "It is rare to find an Ulukagmyut who is not a shaman — every single one of them is an excellent trader. As it is a matter of indifference to them by what means they get rich, they take by force or buy at their own price what they cannot acquire by trade or shamanistic manipulation."

These days, Indians drive snowmobiles over the trail to the coast only when they want a change of scenery. The Russians have long departed, leaving behind only their names among the villagers.

Downhill, the trail got wetter and spongier as it gave way to muskeg. I stopped to pick blueberries along the way. Stooped over, I moved through the bushes, raking the branches like a bear until my fingers were stained a deep purple. I was in no hurry. A wind whipped through the birch trees, the trail moving in and out of shadow.

I wondered if fear, like sex, carried a perceptible cachet, as the old man said. I imagined it would smell sour and overly ripe, like something dying. On the Yukon, I never thought to be frightened because there was only the river itself to fear, and that would be like fearing the ground or the sky. But sometimes, walking into a new village or alone in the woods, I caught a whiff of my own quaking timidity. Bears may not be the blood-hounds of fear, as the old man said, but if they were, then sooner or later they'd pick up my trail. This was only a premonition, like wind trembling leaves, but as another breeze moved the woods into shadow I started back for the village.

The man who answered the Burnhams' door had a blond beard and carried a beer can in his hand. Behind him in the living room, two other men in their twenties crouched intently before a color television. One of them wore a baseball cap and motioned frantically.

"C'mon in, for Christ's sake. Guy here's going to sink a big putt."

Rushing inside, I witnessed a golfer in a pink sport shirt accept a putter from his caddy, hunch over the green, and tap a white ball in a curving trajectory toward the hole. He missed.

"Tough break!" my companion hooted. "Poor jerk just kissed fifty thousand dollars good-by!"

The golf tournament was telecast live via satellite from Palm Springs. To me, sitting in a log cabin village unconnected by road, the match could not have seemed more unreal had it been beamed from the dark side of the moon.

The man wearing the baseball cap shut off the set and got me a beer from the kitchen. He had a thin mustache with droopy ends, which he continuously flicked with his tongue. The Burnhams, he explained, were away fishing and wouldn't be back until late afternoon. He and his friends were only boarding here. They worked for an outfit called Tel-Com, laying telephone cable to every house in every village from Kaltag up the Koyukuk River. They had just finished in Nulato, where one potential customer threatened to shoot them if they persisted in digging a trench to his cabin. But for the most part, the villagers seemed pleased at the prospect of phone service. Then again, nobody had yet received a phone bill.

The Tel-Com men made the kind of fabled wages that lure young men north and can't help but arouse envy in the work-poor villages. In three months, they could earn enough money to take a flyer the rest of the year. The man in the baseball cap had spent last winter island hopping in the South Pacific and showed me a handful of raw opals wrapped in velvet that he'd taken from an Australian mine. "And the real beauty of this job," he said, "is that when it's over I can go back to Oregon and collect unemployment all winter!"

This being their day off and the weather so lovely, one of the phone men suggested a fishing trip. Why not? Rolling a few joints to keep the morning's momentum going, they rigged up fishing tackle, and we made a short parade down to the beach.

The clear Kaltag River enters the silty Yukon just above the village, and for a distance the two rivers flow side by side, unmixed, like vinegar and oil. Pellucid and lightly green in its depths, the tributary revealed a cutaway view of the river bottom: a drowned tree with schools of whitefish shimmering in its branches.

One of our party had outfitted himself like a bank robber, with a pistol-grip shotgun that rocked in its sling across his back as we followed a slick, muddy trail up the alder bank. I watched the dappled leaf light move across his shoulders until we stepped out onto a sunny gravel bar. Here the Kaltag River shrank to a good-sized creek, shallow and fast-running beside the tangled banks.

The fishermen began to flail at the river with their spinners, aiming at isolated Arctic char that hung in the smooth stretches of water between riffles. But mostly there were salmon — a river of salmon, each as long as my arm, their dorsal fins cutting the surface of the water. Nose upstream, they held steady in the current except for abrupt, lateral movements that carried them like cloud shadows over the pebbled streambed. These were chum or dog salmon, sea green with a batik of gaudy red splotches along their sides. Among Yukon salmon, the summer-run chum were the most numerous but the poorest eating; the Indians netted them only to feed their dogs. The chum salmon had begun to die as soon as they left saltwater. They disintegrated faster than other species of salmon, and by the time they reached the spawning streams they were rotting from the tail up. A few hook-jawed and battered males hung about, but most of the salmon in the river were females, hovering dutifully over redds, depressions scooped out in the gravel where earlier, swimming flank to flank beside a male, they'd spewed their load of eggs into a pale mist of sperm.

The blond-bearded fisherman snagged a salmon, and his buddies whooped and shouted as he horsed the fish to shore. The snagged salmon made one memorable run, the line slicing through the water as the fish shot upstream. But at last it came thrashing onto dry land, a treble hook in its tail. Pulling his lure loose, the fisherman pitched the salmon back into the river like a chunk of cordwood. He did not want the fish because its flesh would be soft and mealy.

I left the anglers and walked down the riverbank. The fish-market stench had brought a host of animals down to feast on spawned-out salmon that had snagged along the shore. I counted the tracks of fox, raven, porcupine, dog, and the man-like imprint left by black bears, the heel pad sunk deep in the soft mud like a person walking barefoot. The sheer diversity of tracks that converged upon the stream in radiating lines from the woods suggested, during the hours of darkness, heavy traffic.

In some riffles, I came upon a salmon swimming close to shore to avoid the fast water. It was close enough to touch, and so, a little guiltily, I did. My hand on its broad green back was just one more annoyance in a long series of trials unto death. If a fish could sigh, it would have. Instead the salmon wriggled to deeper water, and as the current caught it sideways, sweeping it back over ground it had gained, I could see how battered the fish was. A milky fungus covered its fins and eyes, and I realized the salmon was swimming blind.

All down the Yukon, I had been half conscious of this opposite movement, the upriver migration of salmon a fathom or two below the surface. The only salmon I'd seen had blundered into a net or fish wheel, ocean-bright colors faded, their eyes holding the astonished look of drowned men. But here, having navigated by some mystery of scent or taste five hundred river miles to their home stream, they seemed elegant in their spawning and dying. There was no panic. Like true believers, they fought the inevitable, downward sweep of current.

The river slackened as I followed it downstream, until it formed a deep, glassy pool so transparent I could see clear down to the bouldery riverbed. Then I realized that what I had taken for rocks were, in fact, windrows of dead salmon that had drifted downstream to settle on the river bottom. A fine gray layer of sediment covered the corpses so that the salmon looked fossilized, as if, having passed on to some further existence, they had turned to stone.

In the fading afternoon, the Burnhams returned, lugging camping gear and two small children up from their beach. I reintroduced myself to Violet. She had a pretty, roundish face, more Eskimo than Indian. I remembered her at college as bright and ambitious, illuminated by her own candlepower. After graduation, she'd worked a year as a bookkeeper and now, with a husband and two children, seemed a little world-weary. She would have liked to get back to Fairbanks for a visit but wouldn't because she hated bumping around in small planes.

The Burnhams kindly offered to put me up for the night in one of the upstairs dormers. My bunk mate was a quiet fellow who purchased salmon roe for the Japanese to turn into caviar. After supper, we all sat in the living room watching the evening news from Anchorage on TV. A tenement had caught fire in an eastern city; there was a garbage strike somewhere — all of it seemed very distant and unrelated, yet we watched with great interest. Television had come to Kaltag three years before, and, according to Violet, for the first year people scarcely ever left their homes. But the fascination with game shows and mini-series seemed to have worn off, and now everyone was visiting again. At the Burnhams' house, in fact, people dropped in all evening. One of them, a lean fellow from a village downstream, took a long, appraising look around the room. "Too many white people here," he said, and went out the door. For my part, I was glad to be caught up in a household again, even if only on the fringes.

While Violet put the kids to bed, her husband led the phone men and me to a shed beside the house. Inside were lumber, sleds, and a huge, palmated rack of antlers from a moose he had shot on the Innoko River. It was the only game trophy I'd seen in any village. The spread between the tines was as broad as a sofa. A tall, big-shouldered man, Richard Burnham had come to Alaska from Oregon for the big-game hunting, but now had to squeeze it in when he wasn't working for the village government. He seemed to have settled successfully into Kaltag, having married one of its daughters and started a family. Like Joe Runyon, he was a dog musher.

On a hunting trip the previous fall, Richard and his brother-in-law had chanced upon a black bear digging its den in the side of a cutbank ridge. The two men sneaked away but remembered the spot. In the winter they returned, and Richard's brother-in-law chopped through the frozen ridge top until he penetrated the bear's den.

"He jabbed a stick a long way down the hole," Richard said, "and we watched until the stick began to move by itself. The bear's breathing made it move up and down. So we knew a bear was in there. Chopping the hole bigger, my brother-in-law lowered himself head first into the den and shot the bear in the head with a pistol."

Then it was Richard's turn. He crawled through the entrance in the side of the cutbank, hoping the den held only a single resident. Inside, the air was warm and moist with the fetor of bear. Richard looped a rope around the bear's head, haloed in the shaft of light from above. Sliding out, he pulled on the rope with his brother-in-law until the bear, a glossy boar girdled with fat, emerged into the winter light.

Richard's story sparked a round of bear stories among the Tel-Com men, each more gruesome then the next. I didn't want to hear it. Saying good night, I drifted upstairs, where the egg buyer was already soundly snoring. I stretched out on the bunk and fell into a sleep heavy with the deaths of animals.

About three in the morning, I awoke. A window was open and the room had gotten very cold. Through the window, the noise of a domestic argument wafted up from the street below. I tried sleeping, but there was a painful familiarity to the recriminations and denials. For a moment, I thought I was home.

Looking out the window into the faint morning light, I saw a young woman walking down the road, followed at a short distance by a man. Her husband? Lover? Around the two of them a small crowd had assembled. The woman turned to face the man and screamed bitterly, "Liar! Bastard!" Stooping down, she picked up a stone and hurled it at the man, who stood with his arms outstretched, a penitent. The stone struck his chest with an awful, hollow sound.

Weeping angrily, the woman turned her back and walked off, the ex-lover and crowd following silently. They stopped after a short distance and repeated the scene as if it were the next station in some private agony. I lay back and listened to her shouts fade as the procession moved down the street.

By morning the weather had turned — a leaden sky and wind-slanted drizzle. While the other men of the house went off to work, I dawdled behind, drinking coffee with Violet and her younger sister. I enjoyed being a guest and staying inside with the women. Violet was giving her son a haircut at the kitchen table, while her sister and I watched the bland intrigues of a TV soap opera. Nobody mentioned the ruckus of last night.

Late in the morning, the phone men returned. They looked sober and shaken. The one with the blond beard poured himself a cup of coffee and sat down at the table trembling. Violet asked him what was wrong.

"We found a dead man on the beach."

They'd been laying cable to one of the cabins along the river-bank, he said, when they looked down and saw a body stretched out on the gravel beach. It was a young man, seemingly asleep, but his face looked strangely pale. Then they saw the shotgun clutched to his chest.

Violet's sister must have guessed who the phone man was describing because she clapped her hand over her mouth and ran out of the house.

Sad news travels fast, even without telephones, and soon everyone in the village knew about the suicide. According to Violet, the young man had been despondent for days and talked openly of taking his life. Last night he had not returned home. Apparently he had lain down on the gravel shore below the village, put a shotgun muzzle to his heart, and blown his troubles into eternity.

The suicide was apparently unrelated to the scene I'd over-heard from my bedroom window. Two random tragedies. Still, in my mind they were unalterably connected: the woman's screams, the muffled blast.

"Sometimes," Violet said, sweeping her son's hair clippings from the kitchen floor, "there's a wave of restlessness that goes through the village. You can almost feel it. There's no place to go, and people get restless." She shook her head. "It's so sad."

Already I felt restless. Dying men and dying fish. There were too many bad ions in the air, or a bad moon rising. Whatever; I wanted to be back on the river again.

Saying good-by to the Burnhams, I bought the gasoline I needed and headed back in the rain to the beach. On the wet road, I passed a crowd bearing the body in an orange tarp to the village hall. For the next few days, villagers would bring food to the family of the deceased, and a potlatch would follow after the burial. The following spring, the young man's death would be remembered at the Stick Dance, the traditional Feast of the Dead. The men would sing the thirteen ancient songs and the women would dance without moving their feet. After-ward the ceremonial stick would be taken down, carried through the village, then broken and thrown over the riverbank. In this way, the souls of the departed would be remembered and hastened toward reincarnation.

As I filled my gas tank, a small throng of high school boys wandered up the beach, shouting and stooping to pick up stones to fling into the river. Maybe they were upset about the suicide or restless or just bored, but I could see what was coming. As soon as one of them spotted me, the rest homed in because I was an outsider and fair game.

"What the fuck are you doing here, white guy?"

"Leaving," I said.

"Well, that's good because we were just about ready to wreck your boat!"

I gave them my best traveler's smile and shoved off. It was depressing to be razzed out of town by kids whose older brothers and sisters I might have taught in school. I wanted to knock their empty heads together and say they had no reason to hate me. But there were too many of them, and anyway this was their classroom, not mine.

August marks the beginning of the rainy season on the lower Yukon, and overnight the river had turned into a cold, gray sea. Idling the engine, I drifted away from Kaltag, the old church steeple passing overhead and then disappearing beyond the bank. I headed out into the middle of the river and opened the throttle. Out of nowhere, the seagulls rejoined me. Floating overhead on extended wings, they cried in harsh, urgent voices I could not comprehend.

THE WEATHER only worsened. The quick, lightning-shot storms of early summer were gone, replaced by a misting, wind-blown coastal weather that steadily ground me down. After the first hour at the throttle, I put on a wool sweater, then added a heavy woolen overshirt, a windbreaker, and finally a rubber rain poncho. Still I felt chilled to the bone. A monotonous gloom settled over the day. The more I stared over the bow at the bobbing horizon, the less distinct it became — gray river, gray sky.

For a hundred and fifty miles below Kaltag, the Yukon flows through deserted country with no intervening villages and very few fish camps. It is a perfectly bleak terrain, a Euclidean land-scape of bald headlands and muskeg swamps, all sharp right angles and planes. Across the river, the Kaiyuh Flats stretches in an unbroken line of alder and willow, while to the west a stark range of coastal hills soars above the river, their summits disap-pearing into the thick cloud ceiling.

The river was a mile and a half across, split into channels by wooded islands that went on so long I often mistook them for the shore. I kept to the leeward side and ran below the terraced banks, dodging in and out of the wind. Crossing an open stretch between islands, the canoe would buck in the whitecaps, climb-ing a green swell only to pitch forward when the bottom of the wave dropped out and drenched me with spray.

Late in the day, running in a light rain, I startled a flock of sandhill cranes on the point of an island. The birds nested in the Flats and were gathering now in large numbers to prepare for their autumnal migration south. A rush of gray wings, a few tentative hops, and the cranes went aloft with a great clangor. They flew across the river at a slight incline — long necks extended, legs trailing — breaking into three flights against the backlit sky. Then they headed back, circling to gain altitude. Higher and higher, the cranes kettled into the sky, a great wheel turning on the axis of the clouds.

Not being a naturalist, I'm interested more in my own species, but traveling through a long stretch of unpopulated wilderness I often wondered where all the game was hiding. Except for the occasional moose or black bear tramping along the beach, what wildlife I'd glimpsed on this journey had been in the sky above or the river below. These great migrations went on for the most part unseen. The birds and the salmon I did encounter always seemed to be in a crowd, always in a hurry, and always headed upriver. As the long summer days dwindled, I often got a sinking feeling that I was going in the wrong direction.

After ten hours at the throttle, I killed the engine and glided onto a sandbar, a teardrop Atlantis recently emerged from the falling river. Without the outboard's constant droning, an immense silence settled on the water, broken only by the interior ticking of my own brain. I sat on a log in front of a driftwood fire, my heels dug into the sand, and watched the brown river move past without a sound. In the west, beyond the headlands, a dull light was dying.

All day I had passed no other boats and seen no tents in the woods along shore. Only the land itself seemed alive — trees bending in the wind, the fluid movement of the river — all part of a world that lives and breathes without men. In such a landscape, who wouldn't feel peripheral and alone? Perhaps to make the land less lonely, Natives had invested the natural world with spirits, believing that animals and even plants possessed something like a soul. Setting off on a hunt, a hunter might address his quarry in song so that his prey, when he encountered it, was more than a stranger. The soothing words also assuaged any lingering guilt he might have felt at killing a fellow spirit. Even the animal's death was governed by ritual and social obligations. I remember a Yupik Eskimo from the delta, a bright student and natural leader, who grew unaccountably glum during his wife's first pregnancy. Later he explained that he had failed to share the first seal he had killed with the rest of the village, as was the custom, and so he'd been worried that if his wife bore a son, the boy would be physically marked by the father's transgression. His wife delivered a baby girl, as it turned out, so the matter was laid to rest.

I don't know how much currency that very old view of the world has in villages today, or how long such beliefs can withstand the daily onslaught of soap operas and satellite-beamed golf matches. It's easy to lament the passing of such traditions even though I cannot bring myself to believe that animals have spirits. If we were ever on speaking terms, we've long since forgotten the words or run out of things to say. When I've brought down a deer in the woods and crept up to finish the job, following the wounded animal's hemorrhagic breathing, the last thing I'd want to do is speak to it, or worse, have the deer speak back. Still, the tribal hunter rarely felt lonesome in the woods, which was how I felt at the moment. Marooned on this sandbar, I hungered for conversation, for contact with a soul other than my own.

Swimming out of sight, great schools of whitefish and salmon kept their own company in the river. Beluga whales, I knew, sometimes lost their way in the labyrinthine channels of the Yukon Delta and strayed far upstream searching for an outlet to the sea. The nineteenth-century naturalist William Healey Dall mentioned a white whale that was killed a few miles below Nulato, at least four hundred miles from saltwater, its appearance an ominous sign to the villagers of something clearly out of place. But I think such a visitation would be marvelous: Out on the river in the twilight, the canoeist feels something rubbing against the hull as if he had run aground. Looking over the side, he sees a ghostly shape breach the surface, exhaling mist from its blow hole. The head is pale and fetal, eyes set back beneath the high, intelligent forehead, the mouth a droll curve. Beluga and river traveler stare at each other across the vast evolutionary gulf. In a high-pitched tremolo, the whale speaks. What it asks is how to get home.

*

Through the rain, I saw a steam shovel, monstrous and wet, scooping gravel from the beach. The huge mechanical jaw hovered above a dump truck as though about to devour it, then unclenched, emptying its load with a resounding crash so that the truck bounced twice. I followed the dump truck up a puddled road past new frame houses built on pads of gravel torn from the same beach.

Grayling was the only village I'd seen along the Yukon that did not overlook the river. A half mile back from the beach, it occupied a flat tongue of land flanked by birch-covered hills. Behind some trees, a helicopter was landing and taking off with a jet-age whine. On the front porch of the Native Store, several loose-limbed teenagers stood out of the rain and looked me over.

Off the river, I was quickly reduced to the role of tramp, dependent upon the charity of others and, in bad weather, the shelter of public buildings. So I went to mail a letter at the small post office. The mail plane had just landed, and the tiny foyer was jammed with people. The postmistress stood on the other side of an open Dutch door, dispensing mail. She wore an oversized cardigan sweater and a crumpled man's hat, set cockeyed on her head, which gave her a coquettish look. By the time I bought my stamps, everyone else had left.

"You look like you've been standing in the rain all day."

"More like three days," I told her.

The run-off from my rain poncho made a small puddle on the floor. I must have looked pathetic.

"Wanna come inside and warm up? I've got a stove in the next room. I'll put on some tea."

She locked the Dutch door behind us. She'd made cozy quarters for herself adjacent to the mail room. There was a big potbellied stove and a television set blaring a game show. She'd decorated an entire wall of the room with pictures clipped from fashion magazines. Cover girls in various stages of cleavage and soft-focus lovers in fragrance advertisements stared down approvingly, although I imagined Grayling offered few opportunities to test out the wisdom of *Cosmopolitan*.

"Why don't you take off your wet clothes," she suggested, "and I'll get us something to eat."

She disappeared out the back door while, a little uneasily, I stripped down to jeans and a T-shirt, setting my rain suit and layers of wet wool beside the stove, where they began to steam. The postmistress returned with a loaf of spongy bread and a tin of cocktail sausages to eat with our tea. The room was already stifling, but she stoked the stove for my benefit until I felt flushed from the heat and the rose-scented cloud of her perfume.

Behind the stove was a wall map of Alaska. Tracing my finger down the Yukon River, I was perplexed at not being able to find Grayling on it.

"That's an old map," she said. "This place wasn't even a village until twenty years ago."

The people at Grayling had once lived far up the remote Innoko River at a place called Holikachuk. Since salmon didn't migrate up the Innoko, each summer the people would travel to the Yukon by way of an interconnecting slough to fish. In the early sixties, the Bureau of Indian Affairs convinced the people to move permanently to Grayling, where they would be less isolated. Now nobody was left at Holikachuk.

"I'll tell you something if you promise not to laugh," the postmistress whispered. "A long time ago, maybe a hundred years ago, people who were living way up the Innoko River killed a shaman. Before that shaman died, he told them that one day there would be no one living on the banks of the Innoko."

She pulled back a little. "Maybe you think that's a stupid story, but it's coming true! Nobody lives at Holikachuk anymore or at Iditarod or Flat. That leaves only Shageluk. And a lot of people are dying of cancer at Shageluk."

I didn't laugh.

"It's still pouring outside," she said, munching on a sausage. "Do you like games?"

She brought out a Scrabble board. The television still blared unwatched as background noise.

"P-E-R-T," she said, spelling out each letter as she laid the little wooden tiles down on the board. "A triple-word score. That's eighteen points!"

In no time at all, she was trouncing me. But then she came

up with words I had never thought of before, hyphenated terms and misspellings and her own original compositions. But I didn't want to seem rude by pointing these out, especially since it was still raining.

While I tried forming a word without vowels on the board, a teenage boy came by (her son?) and gave me a hard-eyed look. After he left, the postmistress's knee brushed against mine. I said I had to be going.

"Are you married?" the postmistress asked me.

"Yes," I lied.

"Then maybe you can give me a little advice on married men," the postmistress said. "There's this helicopter pilot who's a real fox!"

I told her I was the last person to ask for romantic advice. Putting on my damp clothes, I thanked her for lunch and headed for the door.

She asked where I was going next.

"Anvik."

She laughed. "That's a wild place! Two families got into a shoot-out not too long ago in Anvik. They call it Dodge City!"

It was thirty miles by river to Anvik. The rain had stopped, but a mist hung in tatters over the low mountains separating the Yukon from Norton Sound.

The Anvik River came in from the west behind a long point of land. I motored up the clear, dark tributary until I came to a village sheltered in the lee of a wooded bluff. The small houses hanging on the hillside and the damp smell of woodsmoke made me think of Appalachian hollows and feuding families locked in a deadly crossfire.

The Anvik general store had a plank floor and shelves stocked with hardware and a few groceries. When I asked the manager about the gunfight, he said the quarrel had begun over salmon stolen from a fish wheel. He was young and white, and I could see he didn't want to talk about it.

"Things have quieted down since the shooting," he said. "One of the people is in jail. Nobody got killed. Someone just took a little buckshot in the hand, is all."

He was less interested in Anvik's recent doings than in the safely distant past. From the back room he returned with a cardboard box and set it on the counter. The box held a collection of Indian artifacts: milky blue trade beads from Siberia, bone awls and combs, serrated ivory arrowheads, crescent-shaped slate *ulus*, or women's knives, and a bear-tooth pendant.

The storekeeper had found these things across the Anvik River on a point where the old village had been. As the Yukon ate away at the riverbank, it exhumed old graves, spilling bones onto the beach, as well as possessions placed with the dead to sustain them in the afterlife. Just the other day the storekeeper had seen a coffin hanging over the river, ready to drop, and surmised a double burial since it held two small skulls. He was quick to point out that he never disturbed the bones that tumbled onto the beach, only the trinkets and tools buried with them. Otherwise they would be washed out to sea.

"I'm only keeping them temporarily," he said, "until the village gets around to building a proper museum."

He replaced the lid on the box.

"If you're really interested in the past," he added, "you ought to talk with my in-laws."

The storekeeper's wife made a telephone call, and a few minutes later her father came to fetch me. He was small and slight and appeared to walk without putting any weight on his feet. Joe Jerrou lived near the store in a frame house with sturdy, dark furniture and a needlepoint sampler on the wall. His wife, Alta, was waiting for us in the living room. She wore a high-collared blue print dress, sturdy black shoes, and rimless glasses. A tall and graceful woman, she was old enough to have grown up speaking Ingalik Athabascan and now taught it to children in the village school so the language wouldn't disappear entirely. She spoke with the slow solemnity of her years.

"There was a trail to St. Michael when people used to trade with the Eskimos for seal skins and seal oil for their lamps," she said. "The Indians always went to the coast in the spring when a crust covered the snow. They traded wolverine and wolf skin and 'made things,' like wooden bowls and snowshoes. The Eskimos also liked the punk that grows on the sides of birch trees.

Indians took baskets of it over, and the Eskimos mixed the punk with ashes to make a chewing tobacco."

The winter portage followed the Anvik River to its headwaters, then went over the divide to the Golsovia River and down the coast to St. Michael. It was the same route used by the Russian creole Andrei Glazunov when he crossed from Norton Sound in 1834 to become the first white man to lay eyes on the Yukon River. The last time anyone from Anvik crossed the portage to trade with the Eskimos was in the late 1920s, although ten years before that the route had been used regularly.

"The village used to be on a point across the river," Alta said, "until the mission built the church and people started coming over. I attended the mission school, but I didn't live in the boarding school because I lived right here in Anvik. The boarding school took in children from up and down the river, mostly orphans."

Joe Jerrou excused himself to get his hearing aid. When he returned, he recalled seeing the first plane to land in Anvik, a biplane that skidded onto the frozen river on skis and brought a precious cargo of smallpox serum.

"That was the first plane I ever saw. The pilot had to stay two days because a thaw made the ice too sticky for him to take off."

Two years before, Anvik had been hard hit by a devastating influenza epidemic. The outbreak had come in late April, while snow still lay on the ground and the Indians were preparing to leave for their spring camps.

"I was a little girl then," Alta recalled. "When the flu came, people scattered. Some of them made another village two miles below Anvik. Others just lived in the woods along the river. A lot of people died. They'd come down with the flu, then catch pneumonia, then die. Afterward the mission school took in many orphans. In June a hospital boat came down, but by then it was too late."

The epidemic struck particularly hard at the elderly and those already weakened from tuberculosis. As many as four or five people died in a single day. Because the ground was still frozen and most of the men sick, coffins were heaped upon a scaffolding until graves could be dug.

"Doctor Chapman did the best he could with the medical supplies at the mission," Alta said. "But he wasn't an M.D. He was a doctor of divinity."

She was six years old when John W. Chapman left Anvik after a lifetime as its missionary. A picture of Chapman's son and successor hung on the Jerrous' living room wall. He was, she said fondly, the image of his father.

John Wight Chapman was a soft-spoken New Englander who had served his Episcopal diaconate in New York City before embarking for the Bering Sea under the direction of the Domestic and Foreign Missionary Society. On June 26, 1887, Chapman landed on the rain-drenched coast at the old Russian fort of St. Michael to begin his efforts. Walking on the beach a few days later, he chanced to see a squad of marines from the revenue cutter *Bear* escorting the shackled murderer of Bishop Seghers aboard. The Catholic missionary had been killed in his sleep by his lay assistant, now a baying lunatic. It was an inauspicious beginning.

Chapman and another missionary, Rev. Octavius Parker, purchased an old boat and hired a steamboat to tow them through the boggy delta and upriver to Anvik. Approaching the Ingalik village, Chapman saw old men sitting on the cutbank, hands drawn into their parka sleeves, watching impassively. "Something of a sense of loneliness came over me," he wrote, "as I landed among a strange people, who spoke or understood hardly a word of English."

Ingalik was the term given the Athabascan Indians of the lower Yukon by their Eskimo neighbors; it meant "louse-ridden." The Indians called themselves *Deg Hit'an*, or "the people from here." At the time of Chapman's arrival, they lived in underground hovels, relished spoiled fish eggs, and bathed in urine. They believed that when a man died his soul journeyed underground to a village of the dead located in the mountains at the source of the Yukon. Thus they regarded the pale strangers coming into their country as reincarnations of their deceased ancestors who had somehow lost their way.

After the first winter in Anvik, Chapman and Parker moved

the mission across the Anvik River from the village to be more autonomous. For thirty yards of ticking, fifty pounds of flour, and some tea and sugar, they purchased land at the foot of Hawk Bluff. Indian families were not allowed to live on mission land unless they converted and paid a yearly rental of one dollar. The Anvik River then became the dividing line between the "mission Indians" and the unreconstructed, a wide Jordan between heathen and saved.

Parker departed the second summer, leaving Chapman on his own. He stayed more than forty years. He built a church and a boarding school, but, despite the steady trickle of Indians across the river to the mission, he felt himself losing the battle for souls with the village shamans. How was he expected to compete with men who conversed in dreams with animals or rescued the sun from being devoured by an eclipse?

To make his case, Chapman undertook to learn the Deg Hit'an language. He found an extensive vocabulary that wedded the Indians to their country and particularly to the great river running through it. To fix their position, for example, the Deg Hit'an chose from a string of riverine adverbs corresponding to our cardinal directions. Thus, there was *ngido'* for "downriver," *ngine'* for "upriver"; *nginiggi* for "back from the river," and *ngitthing* for "to the river."

With the help of an Indian named Isaac Fisher, Chapman began translating the legends and stories told in the *kashime*, or men's house, to pass the long winter nights. It was not an easy task. He wrote: "The one word which translates 'I thank thee' is an example of Ten'a spelling. It is *hoxwoqourcrigudastcet*. A page of this writing has something unfamiliar about it at first." Chapman found in the Deg Hit'an genesis a Creator specified only as someone being above. The first of his creations was a porcupine, followed by a white bear, a man, and a brown bear. Afterward, the Creator retreated to a distant heaven from which he punished people for wrongdoing by taking away their food. A more vital character was Raven, who is called *Yoqgitsi*, or "Your Grandfather." Always wandering, hungry, and oversexed, Raven introduces confusion into the world and makes death permanent by blazing a trail for the dead to take so that they do not return. Chapman may have searched in vain for moral equivalents to the Gospels, but in the stories he preserved the face of a culture he had dedicated his life to undoing.

A hazy sun had broken through the clouds when I left the Jerrous'. Walking along the riverbank, I found the prim New England chapel with its white belfry and shake-covered walls that Chapman had built in a style to remind him of home. The mission boarding school next to it had fallen on harder times. The three-story building was painted chocolate brown, the windows boarded up, and a sign hanging over the door said WHITEY'S CAFE & POOL HALL.

At the store, I'd bought a copy of the folktales collected by Chapman and recently retranscribed by Deg Hit'an speakers, Alta Jerrou among them. Sitting beside the old church, I read the book into the late afternoon. The stories were marvelous, full of humor and wisdom, with characters certainly truer to Indian life than the cruel savages of Jack London's fictions. They spoke of a life spent in the woods and on the river in a constant search for food. The plots were a curious blend of the mundane and the fantastic: a jealous wife who transforms herself into a brown bear to destroy her unfaithful husband; a lonely spinster who hears a singing fish and realizes too late it is a man. (Since men and beasts share souls, characters changed form as easily as slipping an animal skin over their own.) One story put me in mind of the box of relics at the store. A young girl who lives alone with her grandmother unearths a string of beads from an abandoned village. She brings it home to her grandmother, who guesses where the beads came from and instructs the girl to return them. The next day the girl goes down to the river to fetch water and meets a man driving a big sled. She gives the beads to the sled driver, who turns out to be the ghost of her dead grandfather.

I thought of the stolen beads as I trolled slowly off the point of the old village, looking for the exposed coffin the storekeeper had mentioned. But I never saw it. Perhaps the coffin had already tumbled into the river and begun a new journey.

THE MOUNTAINS walling off the Bering Sea from the Yukon shrank to a low range of forested hills. And the current, a race-horse on the upper river, had diminished as well, down to a sluggish two knots, which counted little against the stiff head-wind trying to blow me upstream. With the end of the trip in sight, the river and I were both running out of steam. The weather had turned dismal, most of my clothes were soaking wet, and the casual warnings dropped about the next village downriver ("Don't stop there. The people are shy and don't like strangers") wore at my nerves. If there was a short cut at hand, I would have taken it. But every journey needs a desti-nation, if only to know where to stop running your finger along a map.

What kept me going was the single-minded thought of reach-ing saltwater. Yet the river, following the path of least resistance around the mountains, was actually moving farther from the sea before bending west to meet it. The Yukon flowed toward its own indirect, inevitable conclusion, that point, I imagined, where the shoreline would disappear altogether and the hori-zon merge into a brackish, even vaster river.

Near the mouth of the Bonasila River, I interrupted a black bear feeding off a rack of dried salmon. Standing on hind legs, like a circus bear, it worked methodically down the row, head partially hidden behind a curtain of scarlet fish. Nobody was home at the fish camp to scare it off, so I gave a shout. The bear stared myopically at the river and sniffed the air. It was a year-ling, lean and gawky, with disproportionately large snout and feet. Catching my scent, the bear dropped to the ground, "bad dog" written all over its face, then skeedaddled into an alder thicket.

The Yukon below Anvik seemed a highway for bears. Twice I stopped on islands to make camp, only to find a beaten path of tracks pressed into the gray sand. Bears are ardent swimmers and in the spring will swim to islands to chase molting birds. Now they were looking for spawned-out salmon the current had lodged against the shore like driftwood. Late in the day, I pitched my tent on an exposed spit. The only other inhabitants were a colony of mew gulls that launched into the wind at my approach, leaving behind fish bones and a white-splattered beach. For hours they hovered in the sky like kites. A blood-red sunset had earlier raised my hopes for a sunny day, but when the gulls quieted down I heard the first raindrops on the tent.

Next morning I trailed a pair of skiffs, loaded to the gunwales with passengers hooded against the rain, around a large island. The boats turned up a narrow slough, and I followed blindly until a short time later when we pulled up to a landing. I didn't know it then, but I had joined a procession of mourners on its way to a burial service. In the funereal downpour, we formed a melancholy parade down the road to Holy Cross, a jumble of houses at the foot of a high, peaked hill. The smell of wood-smoke mixed with rain hung in the air like incense.

There was a run on plastic floral wreaths and decorative crosses at the Holy Cross Mercantile. I bought a quart of motor oil and explained to a throng of kids that I was not their new fourth-grade teacher. In some respects, Holy Cross was a cosmopolitan village. This was the demarcation line between the upriver Athabascans and the downriver Eskimos, with the Russian influence thrown in as well; the children's faces reflected this mixture of races. I wanted to linger in the warmth of the store, but the owner was closing up to attend the service and locked the door behind me.

After the funeral mass, the mourners moved above the village to the cemetery, with its crosses and white picket fences. Athabascan graveyards are almost always located on the slopes of hills so the dead overlook the village and river, and thereby are kept in the heart of things. I could see the funeral party from the road, a line of black umbrellas moving up the steep hillside in the pouring rain.

At sixty, Betty Johnson was still a strikingly beautiful woman. Her dark hair was streaked with gray, and she had deep brown eyes. I sat on a couch in her living room while she brought hot coffee and a plate of smoked salmon. She was Claude Demientieff's cousin and with her husband had run the store in Holy Cross until they'd retired the previous year to build this house. Outside, her husband hammered away at a new back porch.

"I went to the mass this morning," she said, explaining why she wasn't at the cemetery, "but I really didn't want to stand in the rain."

"Someone you knew?"

"Yes. But it wasn't a sad death, if you know what I mean. He was ninety-six years old. So many of his family and friends came that the mass had to be said in the community hall instead of the church. What more could you ask?"

When I told her about the suicide a few days before, Betty Johnson shook her head. "I don't understand it. When I was growing up, people might fall out of a boat or shoot themselves accidentally, but never on purpose. Now you hear about young people taking their own lives all the time. It's like an epidemic."

She brought out a scrapbook from a glass cabinet, and we leafed through old photographs of Holy Cross as it had been when she attended the mission school. The pictures showed black-robed nuns, their faces framed in horseshoe-shaped wimples; a picket-fenced vegetable garden of turnips, cabbages, and potatoes; and smiling Native children, girls in pinafores and kerchiefs on one side and boys in starched shirts on the other, assembled beneath a flag with forty-eight stars.

"It was a good, good school. The nuns were very tough. Most of them were French or German, so we knew more French or Latin than Eskimo or Athabascan. We weren't allowed to speak our own language in school. I remember when we'd have retreats the church would be all dark and lit by candles. The priest would scare us with pictures of the devil pitching people into hell with a pitchfork."

The church, a great ship of a building with a cross-bearing cupola overlooking the Yukon, had been built largely by her grandfather, Ephraim Demientieff, and his brothers. Skilled carpenters, they carved all of the pillars, side altars, and tabernacles. She had been a little girl when Ephraim died but still remembered him clearly.

"He had the softest, bluest of eyes. He never raised his voice. The old-timers were all like that. They never raised their voices to children."

I studied an old photograph of Ephraim, his brothers, and two of his sisters. The women wore squirrel-skin parkas trimmed with ermine tails. The men were strongly built, with sandy hair, pale eyes, and brooding Russian features.

Nicholai Dementov, Ephraim's father, had been banished from Mother Russia as a young man for committing a crime that nobody now could remember. He was exiled half a world away to Sitka, the dreary colonial capital of Russian America, a log city crowded with Siberian *promyshlenniks*, creoles, Indians, and a garrison of soldiers sitting out the Crimean War. A few years later, in 1861, he was dispatched to manage a trading post far in the interior. The journey took Dementov two hundred and forty miles up the muddy Kuskokwim River, the second great river of Alaska, to Kolmakovskii Redoubt. The trading post was built on a steep bluff on the south bank of the Kuskokwim, where it was joined by the Kvygym River. Within the palisaded walls, Dementov found a store with a veranda, two company houses, a small Orthodox chapel, and a hexagonal blockhouse, all built of spruce timbers roofed with sod. Beyond the compound, the country stretched off into willow and the hilly tundra of the Kuskokwim Mountains.

Nicholai brought with him a wife, Axina, a creole from the Russian redoubt at Nushagak. She bore him four sons and three daughters, whose voices filled the lonely outpost with the language of his childhood. On Sundays they gathered in the log chapel to pray for the health of the czar.

Every spring after the ice broke up, Indians paddled down the Kuskokwim to trade their winter furs. Nearing the redoubt, the Indians discharged their muskets into the air, a greeting they'd learned from the Russians to show that their muzzle loaders were empty. The trading went on for days, until the riverbank along the post was lined with bark canoes and a thick gauze of white musket smoke hung over the water. Nicholai would stand in front of the store, stacking up pelts of beaver and otter to measure against the length of his rifle; a new flintlock cost its height in furs. After all accounts had been settled, he locked his daughters in the inner fort and then rolled out barrels of vodka. Inside the walls, the children could hear the gaiety and riot far into the night.

When Russia sold its Alaskan holdings, Nicholai declined repatriation. He remained behind in the employ of a Finlander who sent him even farther up the Kuskokwim River to trade at Vinasale in the foothills of the Alaska Range. When the Finn died, Nicholai replaced him at the old redoubt, staying there until his own death in 1893. An outbreak of influenza and famine gripped the Kuskokwim at that time, and Evan, Nicholai's eldest son, moved the family a hundred miles north to a bend in the Yukon River where Jesuits were building a mission. They left Kolmakovskii in the spring while there was still snow to travel. Having no dogs to harness, the brothers took turns pulling a sled heaped with their belongings across the frozen tundra. When they reached the mission on the north bank of the Yukon, there were only a few crude log buildings. Ephraim, an excellent carpenter and woodcarver, and his brothers helped the black-robed priests build a grand church with an imposing belltower that dominated the river.

When the rain let up, Betty Johnson took me for a walk. "The river used to run right past town," she said, "but the channel silted and the steamboats couldn't land. Now there's just the side slough. This used to be the mission gardens, but it's all willows now."

The church her grandfather and his brothers built had been demolished thirty years before when a new priest had declared it a fire hazard. Betty was living on the Kenai Peninsula at the time, but her mother had watched as a bulldozer hooked a cable around the cupola and brought the church crashing down in a cloud of dust and splinters. "Too bad," the priest had told her. "Such lovely memories."

Betty unlocked the door to the new church and we went inside. It was neither new nor elegant: simply a long hall with a dropped ceiling and paneled walls.

"We had so many artifacts in the old church," Betty said. "Sanctuary lamps and a baby Jesus carved of wax. All gone."

The only grandeur left was the flowered altar cloth embroidered by her mother in glass beads on white calfskin. A beadwork birchbark basket and salmon were sewn in the center to symbolize the loaves and fishes of the Sermon on the Mount, a parable about deriving plenty from the little at hand.

Back at the store, I ran into the new teacher for whom I'd been mistaken earlier.

"Of course," he said with a self-mocking laugh, "all *gussuk*s look alike."

Some kids were hanging out in the store, and though the teacher was having great fun with them, he kept a distance from me. He'd skipped the funeral so as not to appear too pushy as a newcomer, and I guessed his aloofness with me was only discomfort at being seen with another *gussuk*.

When the kids left, he warmed a little. He was a lay volunteer at the Catholic school; he'd stopped himself from saying "missionary," a word that suggested white cassocks and colonialism. We talked about my trip, and he corrected my pronunciation of the Eskimo villages downriver. "Say it from the back of your throat."

"Sometimes," he confided, "you have to remind yourself that this is the United States of America. You have to keep telling yourself: I am a citizen of this country and I have a right to be here."

He'd spent ten years teaching in Eskimo villages in the delta. He spoke Yupik Eskimo fluently and had married an Eskimo girl. He would have liked to have been an Eskimo, but it was beyond him and he knew it.

"I'll tell you a story," he said. "Once there was a teacher in a village where I worked who tried for years to be an Eskimo. She was a good teacher and well liked for a white, but she was never going to be accepted as an Eskimo. When she finally realized that, she left."

I spent the night with a Bureau of Land Management survey crew camped in a meadow that had been steamboat moorage before the Yukon changed its course. The camp was a separate village. The crew's Quonset-style tents had plywood floors and were huddled together on the willow flat like wagons drawn in a circle.

At six-thirty in the morning, I lined up with the survey crew for breakfast. Apologizing for having overslept, the bullcook rubbed his eyes and heaped my plate with fried potatoes, ham, and scrambled eggs. The rest of the crew, young and boisterous, wore college sweatshirts, lending the mess tent the air of a training table. While I hungrily wolfed down food, the chief surveyor talked about his job. He was surveying land allotments under the provisions of the Alaska Native Land Claims Settlement Act, which entitled any Native born before 1971 to claim up to 160 acres of land. Working within a sixty-five-mile radius, he was sending three-man crews by helicopter as far downriver as Russian Mission and as far north as the Bonasila River.

"We've got the helicopter contracted until the twenty-third of August," he said. "After that, the weather's usually no good."

When the BLM crew first arrived in Holy Cross in late May to survey the land allotments, they were met with remarkable indifference. Notices were posted around the village announcing a meeting at the community hall at which maps and survey packets would be distributed and any questions answered. Nobody came. So the meeting was rescheduled for four days later. This time two people showed up.

If the villagers seemed unenthused, it was because the land had always been theirs. In essence, the government was asking them to pick and choose, to codify their fish camps and trap lines into a formula of section-township-range on a quad map, a system that would make it easier to tax and ultimately dispose of the land. When Russia ceded its Alaskan holdings to the

United States in 1867, the treaty made no specific provisions for the Native inhabitants. The question of aboriginal title to the land was ignored for a century, until the discovery of North Slope oil made a land settlement expedient. The Alaska Native Land Claims Settlement Act of 1971 gave title to forty million acres plus one billion dollars to be divided among thirteen Native regional corporations in return for extinguishing their claims to the land. But I'd seen no oil-rich Indians in the villages; either the settlement money was invested elsewhere or it's gone. In 1991, Native corporation lands will lose their tax exemption, and shares on their stock will go public. One future scenario has *Fortune* 500 companies buying controlling interest in Native corporations' stock and thus their land, at which point aboriginal claims would be permanently extinguished. The more cynical observe that perhaps this had been the idea all along.

The chief surveyor, a tall, bearded pipe smoker from Anchorage, understood this.

"What good is a hundred and sixty acres? That's peanuts to people used to running a trap line on hundreds of acres. What happens to a guy's land when there's a bad ice jam and the river cuts two hundred feet off the bank?"

The surveyors didn't measure by pulling chain but used an electronic transit that bounced microwaves off reflecting prisms to calculate distance. In a few summers they would parcel out one of the last great wildernesses in bite-sized chunks. Most of the selections were along the Yukon River.

"Some people pick places they remember being as a kid. Others pick where they've always had a fish camp or trapped or picked berries. One guy wanted a place downriver so he could get out of the village when things get too crazy."

The survey party was fairly autonomous. Their food was flown in every two weeks by helicopter; they had their own generator, hot showers, and a VCR. They avoided walking the half mile into Holy Cross, although things hadn't gotten crazy there since the village had gone dry. It had voted to go dry shortly after the village corporation's new bookkeeper was shot dead. The twenty-seven-year-old Fairbanks man had gone to a

Saturday night dance at the community hall. Shortly after midnight, a young local pulled out a .44 magnum pistol, a caliber usually reserved for killing bears, and shot the bookkeeper in the head at close range. The bookkeeper had arrived in Holy Cross only three days before.

Behind the mess tent, the helicopter started up with a shrill whine, scattering willow leaves in the air. Singly and in pairs, people drifted away from the breakfast table to be lifted into the bush. I wiped my plate clean with a piece of toast, put on my rain suit, and headed for the river.

By afternoon patches of blue had broken through the misting, gray-flannel sky. For the first time in days I saw the sun. Stripping off my wet gloves and woolen watch cap, I set them steaming on the thwart to dry. What a difference a little sunshine can make in one's mood! Bad weather had cast much of the lower Yukon under a pall, but now, having shed my raincoat and gloomy thoughts, I whistled in high spirits and set my course for the Bering Sea.

Twenty miles below Holy Cross, a skiff roared out from the right bank to overtake me. Almost as a reflex, I wondered if I'd done anything wrong. But the skiff was too fast to outrun, so I cut my engine and the boat drew alongside. Its driver was a quiet-spoken Eskimo named Evan.

"Haven't seen anybody for a couple days now," he said. "That's my fish camp over there."

Following the angle of his arm, I saw a white canvas tent dwarfed against the far hillside. After being storm-bound for days, Evan had raced to the first passing boat simply to visit. Like myself, he'd grown tired of being alone and wanted a little company. Grasping on to each other's gunwales, we drifted side by side beneath the blue sky.

When he wasn't fishing, Evan lived in Holy Cross. The run of silver salmon had begun and would keep him busy until September. His skiff was high-prowed, with flaring sides and plenty of freeboard; bolted in front of the steering wheel was a car windshield. Like most of the fishing skiffs I'd seen, Evan's was painted the same steel gray as the river, while the interior hull was a bright aquamarine, a cheerful delineation to keep you from stepping overboard by mistake. Traveling down the Yukon, I had noticed a change in the configuration of boats. In the mountains and narrow side streams, canoes had been the rule, but on the breezy, open expanses of the lower river the boats were big-chested dories built to take a pounding from ocean-sized swells. Next to Evan's boat, my fifteen-foot canoe looked like a toy.

"Any problems with bears?" I asked.

"Only little black bears. There's a brown bear living up the hill with his family, but he never bothers me." The tone was respectful; he might have been talking about a reclusive neighbor. "In the fall, he comes right past my camp and moves up another hill."

As we pushed off, he mentioned an odd-looking raft with big sweeps on the side and a tall cabin. It had floated past a few days before without stopping.

"Maybe you'll catch up with it," he shouted over the water.

The Yukon bent steadily south. This was nearly the western limit of the tree line, as spruce forest gave way to a fringe of cottonwood, willow, and alder. The pyramidal Ilivit Mountains rising from the right bank were green at the base and buff-colored and bald at the peaks. Across the river, the landscape was as flat as the sky, a smooth plate for wind in any direction. The low left bank marked the start of the delta, a vast alluvial fan of tundra and thaw lakes circumscribed by the Yukon and Kuskokwim rivers. Depending on your point of view, it was the beginning or the end of the continent.

"How you like this weather we're having?"

The storekeeper at Russian Mission was a big-bellied man with a marine haircut and a secret affection for stormy days.

"Not very much," I told him.

He would only open the store a few hours today because it was Sunday. A single, bare light bulb dimly lit the place, perhaps to obscure the sparsely stocked shelves. Outside, the wind howled.

"Good duck-hunting weather though," he said, looking at the

empty shelves as if remembering to order more ducks. "They don't like to fly in weather like this, so you can really sneak up on them. But I guess you're not duck hunting, are you?"

Outside, I walked past two boys dribbling a basketball around puddles on an open-air court and followed a winding road to a green, windswept bluff to see the Orthodox church. The older section of the village lay sprawled below, tin-roofed cabins and clusters of blue oil drums crooked in the lee of the bluff. Russian Mission had once been an important trading post for the Russians and the site of an icon-laden "cathedral," mother mission for all Orthodoxy on the Yukon. Kerchiefed women were leaving the door of the alcove, putting on raincoats over their calico *quspuk*s, or summer parkas. The church was painted rust red and topped with two gold onion domes; a cemetery of Byzantine crosses surrounded it. Inside, sad-faced icons stared down from the dark panels of the iconostasis.

Closer to the bluff, an abandoned church stood knee-deep in fireweed. Its walls were stained dark with rain and a windblown spruce grew beside it, a yardstick of the building's age. The church looked ancient and almost certainly built by the Russians. I got directions to the deacon's house down the hill and banged on his door. The man who answered was no bearded patriarch but an Eskimo man my own age, relaxing in his shirtsleeves after the service. His daughter was on his knee, and immediately I felt foolish for intruding. He said the cathedral had burned down a long time ago. The "old" church had been built in 1938. In the delta any structure that withstood forty-five years of bad weather was a relic.

The rain did not start up again until evening, but then it lasted for three days.

19 | ALONG
THE
DELTA

THE WIND BLEW from the southwest, from the sea, tilting the river into a billowy expanse of whitecaps. I kept the bow windward to quarter the waves so they swept past without shipping much water over the gunwales. Sometimes a large swell heaved the front of the canoe out of the water and then dropped it into the lurch with a splash. I would sooner run Five Finger Rapids in a bathtub than face the lower Yukon on a breezy day. Rainwater collected in pools in my lap and streamed down my back until my lower half was soaked. Hugging the shore, I searched for a level landing. But sheer rock cliffs ran down to the water on the right bank, and the river was too wide and wind tossed for me to consider crossing to the leeward bank. Besides, I could barely see through the rain to the dismal far shore.

Tacking around a blind point, I landed on a pocket beach strewn with foam and driftwood. There is a great sense of relief at making landfall in rough weather, when each mile has been hard won. Quickly, I unpacked the tent and looked around for a smooth spot to erect it. Then I hesitated — fresh tracks led out of the bordering woods and made a transit of the beach. I'd seen plenty of black bear tracks before, but these were larger and more formidably spaced. Pressed into the soft yellow clay, each print was as wide across as the length of my boots and topped with five toes and radiating claw points just now filling with rain. The tracks belonged to a brown bear, a coastal grizzly, and they left no less an impression on me than on the wet beach. Faced with a choice of terrors, I debated whether to take my chances with the storm-tossed river or camp here and face a sleepless night. The river was an uncertainty, but the bearish nightmare was already fully formed in my brain: A sharp snort as claws rend the tent. A great, dish-faced profile sways overhead, so near I smell the close, rancid breath. The beaded eyes are set close together; the silver fur on its humped back glistens in the moonlight. I reach for the shotgun at my side, but the mechanism jams. I open my mouth to cry out but cannot. The bear pulls me from the sleeping bag into a terrible embrace as the dream dissolves around me.

I repacked the tent and launched back into the whitecapped waves.

Landing finally in a tiny grotto formed by projecting rock spurs, I set the tent on a narrow shelf of broken shale. It looked like a place for votive candles and miraculous springs. Out of the wind and safe from night-wandering bears, I fell into a deep, dreamless sleep. For two days I remained storm-bound on that ledge, protected from the storm and sealed off from the rest of the world. When I stuck my head outside the tent on the second day, I seemed to be in the middle of a cloud. The far bank was lost in fog, and the river's surface lay broken into gray waves like overlapping tiles on a slate roof.

The notes from my journal give some hint of my mood:

August 8. Still raining. Wind from the south. I am curled in a fetal position in my sleeping bag, head tucked under the covers, listening to the rain's patter and the steady lashing of waves against the shore. Finished last of whiskey yesterday, a small thing but one of those pleasures that civilize a camping trip. Did nothing today but memorize the tent's stitchery.

I boiled water over the small kerosene stove for tea and to keep the tent warm. Wet clothes were strewn everywhere. Some were trying to dry and others I used to plug the tent's leaky corners where pools of rainwater had formed. My journal entries were becoming more cryptic and full of complaints. I had reached that dangerous point on a long journey when things break down, when the essential organization on which you depend turns to chaos. Dishes are put away dirty, clothes don't dry out, meals are simplified to a few soggy crackers and tea. Mistakes wait to happen because your mind is set not on the tasks at hand but on getting home. I started making wish lists: dry clothes, a warm bed, a drink with ice. A few books remained to read, most having been given away on the journey in small payment for some kindness. Encased in my sodden sleeping bag, knees drawn to my chest, I reread a paperback *Odyssey* with a new sympathy for the shipwrecked Odysseus — "poor fellow, kept from his friends all this while in trouble and sorrow, in that island covered with trees, and nothing but the waves all about it, in the very middle of the sea."

In the afternoon the fog lifted enough to provide clearance between the river and cloud ceiling. I bailed out my canoe and started again. The Yukon reaches its southernmost point at Roundabout Mountain, near the abandoned settlement of Ohagamiut, having looped back to nearly the latitude it started at in Whitehorse. Rounding the horn, the canoe began to pitch and yawl in heavy chop. The wind had shifted and I found myself plowing north into stinging drizzle and the teeth of a thirty-knot gale. The river yawned three miles across where it swallowed an island. By ducking into side channels, I could run out of the wind until the slough rejoined the main channel and cast me back into the maelstrom. Shivering wet, my teeth chattering, I was determined now to motor on toward the next village. It was a fateful decision because soon I was too weak and thick-headed to think about putting up a tent in this wind. When my strength gave out, I would just tie up along shore and lie down in the rain for a long sleep. Each deserted bend in the river brought a new disappointment. I had nearly decided to moor the canoe to a cutbank and crawl into the alders when I saw a pair of strange lights burning ahead in the sky. They were the headlights of an airplane flying low beneath the clouds, descending upon the landing strip at Marshall.

I took a room above the store in Marshall. Few villages on the lower river have places for a visitor to stay, so it seemed great luck to find one here. The heat wouldn't come on, but I thawed out with a hot shower, my first since Tanana, and crawled ex-

hausted between the sheets. About six o'clock I heard the down-
stairs door slam as the store owner left and his teenage
replacement arrived. Immediately she put a love song on the
record player, something current and insipid. She must have
been heartsick, or maybe the record changer was broken, but
she played that dreary song over and over again until the lyrics
were etched in my brain. Even after she locked up for the night
and went home, the words kept returning like a bad dream.

I awoke in the morning to barking dogs and the whine of two-
stroke engines — the sounds of village life. Looking out a rain-
streaked window, I saw a man puttering down a muddy road
on his motorbike, a rifle slung across his back. Marshall sits at
the base of Pilcher Mountain on a high ledge over the Yukon.
Beyond the back yard clutter of woodpiles, oil cans, and clothes-
lines flying in the gale, the river lay puckered into whitecaps
beneath a slate gray sky.

The storeowner, a stocky, pleasant Eskimo named Leslie
Hunter, drove me around the village in his pickup truck.
Splashing down the road, Hunter pointed out the new fish-
processing plant. "Lots of fish this year," he said, "but not much
money." We passed a boarded-up hotel, bleached white as a
whalebone, a remnant of Marshall's past as a fledgling gold
camp. Two prospectors discovered gold on nearby Wilson
Creek in 1913 and named the creek for the current president
and the townsite for his running mate, Thomas Marshall, who
had campaigned under the bromide, "What this country needs
is a good five-cent cigar." The stampede to Marshall was the last
major gold rush on the Yukon. Most of the village, however,
seemed only a few years old. Set on barren tundra, the prefab-
ricated housing in poster-paint colors gave Marshall the look of
one of those instant Wyoming strip-mining towns. Hunter's
grandfather had come from Pennsylvania to be the mining
camp's first postmaster, but just as his grandson now favors the
Eskimo side of the family, so had Marshall changed complex-
ions over the years.

The truck rocked in the wind as we parked above a beach
littered with tethered skiffs and miserable-looking dogs curled
in the mud. I asked Leslie Hunter if any of the old miners had

stayed on in Marshall. There were a few, he said. One had just died at eighty-three, still chipping away at his claims. He'd hired a pilot to drop him at his cabin forty miles back in the hills. When the pilot flew back a month later to check on him, he found only a burnt cabin and some charred bones in the doorway. The prospector had stockpiled Molotov cocktails for bear protection because his eyesight was too poor for aiming a rifle, and the consensus was that the gasoline bombs, not the bears, got him in the end.

Hunter told me there was another old-timer who lived just up the road, and he dropped me at Gene Tetinek's cottage. Tetinek answered the door in a plaid wool shirt and bedroom slippers, a shock of white hair falling across his forehead. Stacks of newspapers and bundled magazines lay on the floor. He sat back in an easy chair and filled his pipe from a tobacco tin. A photograph of the paddle-wheeler *Nenana* hung on the wall. We listened to the weather forecast over the Nome radio station, first in English and then in Yupik Eskimo; another storm was spiraling up the coast from the Aleutians.

When I told Tetinek of my travels, he seemed unimpressed. I had arrived too late, he said, to see the real North. Old-timers were always telling me that.

"Used to be if you wanted to settle someplace, all you had to do was throw up a log cabin, and that was that. Not anymore. The country's changed."

In the summer of 1934, Tetinek was cutting cordwood in Fort Yukon when he got the itch to travel. He paid five dollars for a flimsy ratting canoe and set off down the Yukon, reaching Marshall just as gold hit thirty-five dollars an ounce on the open market. He was offered a job in one of the mines, but turned it down to spend the winter outside. Hiring on as a deck hand on the steamboat *Nenana*, he retraced his route upriver, hopped a freight to the railhead at Seward, and then took a steamship to Seattle, where he hitchhiked the last leg home to Cleveland. Tetinek returned to the America of the National Recovery Act, a country of soup kitchens and bread lines. The depression was in full swing, so he never even bothered looking for work. The next summer he returned to Marshall to operate a hydraulic hose in the Willow Creek mine. The hose shot stream water from the nozzle with enough ballistic force to strip the soil down to gold-bearing bedrock. When the gold mines shut down after the war, he operated a trading post until retiring.

I asked him why, with the price of gold so high, the large mines hadn't started up again.

"It isn't the price of gold, it's the price of everything else. Especially freight, if something breaks down and you need to have it shipped up. Last year I ordered a boat from Seattle, and the freight cost more than the boat!"

Once a year Tetinek flew to Anchorage for a change of pace, but when I asked why he didn't move there permanently, it was clear he'd soured on the city.

"What would I do there? You need a car to get anywhere. If you have a snow tractor, you need a permit."

One thing bothered me about Tetinek's story. I had seen a ratting canoe in a museum in Fort Yukon. Built of canvas stretched over a spruce frame, they are employed in the spring for hunting muskrat and look as tippy as a pea pod.

"Where did you stow your supplies?"

"Supplies?" The tone of his voice implied my own needs were extravagant. "Plenty of room for a sleeping bag, a rifle, some grub. What *more* could you possibly need?"

Before I checked out of my room above the store, Leslie Hunter warned me of three bad spots between Marshall and St. Marys, "stretches where the wind blows one way and the river goes the other." He had no map and so depended upon his words and the urgency of his gestures to convey the downriver landmarks, the islands and bends that I was to watch for. But I didn't pay much attention: I was in too big a hurry to leave during what appeared to be a lull in the storm. Immediately after leaving Marshall, I crossed a half mile of open water to a long island that broke the wind blowing off the main channel. I had completely forgotten about the first of the bad spots until, rounding the lee of the island, I stumbled into it. The wind was blowing a terrific gale. The waves broke with a sigh, lifting the canoe so that it teetered on the crest of a wave before plunging into the sea green trough. The major problem of small-boat navigation in heavy swells is keeping boat and waves on a parallel course. I would quarter the smaller waves, then align the bow to meet the oncoming rollers. Five inches of freeboard were all that separated me from the river. Yet as long as the waves didn't come from the side, breaking over the gunwales, the canoe would ride out the chop. Each roller rushing headlong toward the canoe seemed fated to swamp it, but each time the crest fell short, the little boat riding over the wave instead of beneath it.

The Yukon's course became more erratic, describing corkscrews and oxbow turns, as it cut away at the headlands. Changing direction, the river moved in and out of the wind, and for long stretches at a time I had smooth sailing. The second bad spot was Dogtooth Bend, a several-mile loop around a cuspid of tundra. At the bend, the channel I was following intersected with an even larger channel, and the waves, instead of charging at the bow, suddenly swept down from the stern. The canoe surfed forward on the crest of a wave heading for shore. Unable to change course for fear of presenting the boat sideways to the swells, I watched helplessly as the backs of green rollers rushed past to break in a line on the beach. Between waves, the prop scraped sand and kicked out of the water with an awful whine. Then the outboard stalled. The canoe lurched sideways and began to ship water. With no power or steerage, there was nothing I could do but tilt the engine up and paddle to keep the bow straight as the waves deposited me ashore.

The far end of the beach was not pounded nearly so hard by the surf. Lining the canoe to the sheltered end, I cast off again. The rain had stopped, and a sickly yellow light shone below the clouds. I turned into a leeward slough where the alder banks drew close, and the wind's tumult died as suddenly as if a window had been shut. A red fox trotted along the shore, tail unfurled like a pennant. For miles I followed this interior passage before stopping on a damp sandbar for the evening.

The edge of the sandbar was muddy, and as I carried gear ashore from the canoe my rubber boots pulled from the mire with a sucking noise. I shared the sandbar with an enormous spruce log propped up on its roots and pointing downriver.

Scoured from a riverbank by spring ice, its branches sheared off to nubs, the great log had rafted downstream in floodwater to be stranded here, smooth and polished. Its trunk sheltered my tent from the wind and its roots made resinous kindling for my fire.

Walking down to the river to wash my dinner dishes, I found that I wasn't alone. Voices and soft laughter carried faintly from a fish camp at the end of the slough, and somehow this discovery made me feel more forlorn. When you travel alone, it's not the strangeness of places that tugs at your heart but the way things are the same. The voices spoke in Yupik, but I could make out the peculiar cadences of family talk, the small jokes and affections. The few risky moments I'd recently had on the river only sharpened my sense of isolation. One of the most human of fears, I think, must be of dying alone. After a close call, we want someone to share our relief; we want to matter, not in any general way, but to someone in particular. I was tired of being a floater. When I could see past the bitterness of my failed marriage, I had to admit that, in balance, the good memories outweighed the bad. And, since memories were all I had at the moment, I wanted to cherish them. Crawling into the tent, I began a long-postponed letter to my ex-wife. I meant to finally clear the air between us, so it was really a good-by letter, but since we hadn't spoken civilly in two years it was a hello, as well.

The sky cleared the next morning. The sun felt warm against my back as I loaded the canoe and headed down the slough toward the main channel. Nobody was home at the fish camp except for a husky pup tethered to a stake.

The Yukon spread out windless and benign, a deeper shade of blue than the sky. Fishing boats bobbed in the distance — the truest measure of good weather. The rough water and bad weather behind me, I felt expansive, no longer in a hurry. The end of the trip seemed in sight. With the proper attitude, I thought, one could make a bargain with the river, stay on its good side.

I trolled up to a shovel-nosed skiff. An Eskimo fisherman and his son, perhaps the voices I'd heard the night before, were untangling a burbot from their net. The burbot had the head of a toad and body of an eel and glared malignantly from the bottom of the boat as it expired.

How far, I asked, to Pilot Station.

"You're almost there. You'll see it right around the next bend."

The Yukon formed a T as it bent sharply to the southwest and the Chuilnak River entered from the east. Racing around the bend, I saw the blue-roofed houses of Pilot Station in a saddle between two hills. The village could not have been more than a mile away, so I steered a direct course for it, cutting diagonally across the river.

Then everything went wrong.

A blast of wind caught me as I cleared the bend. Funneled down the narrow flume of the channel, the wind curled the river back on itself. Billowy waves loomed ahead like a range of green hills dusted with snow. Too late, I remembered Leslie Hunter's warning about the final bad stretch of river. It was here.

If I headed straight for shore, the waves would smash the canoe broadside and capsize it, so I had no choice but to steer straight into the green wall of water. The first swell lifted the bow into the air, the horizon tilted, and the canoe slid down the long valley of the wave. Climbing the next crest, I tried to count the oncoming rollers, wondering how they would break, trying to read the one that would finally crash over the bow and swamp the boat.

The sensation was of being propelled forward by a mob, a noise roaring in my ears, unable to stop or turn but only keep pace and stay alert. The shore lay a quarter-mile swim in either direction, but it might as well have been half an ocean away. If I capsized, silt would fill my pockets and boots and I would do the Australian crawl in slow motion to the bottom.

Seagulls careened overhead. Safe on two counts, the gulls pivoted their small white heads to see if I had any fish in the boat or if perhaps I was a fish. At first I felt a perverse thrill as the canoe smacked into a wave and still emerged upright. But knowing that I was almost certainly going to drown soon filled me with rage. At the fisherman for not warning me. At the river for letting me come this far only to drown in plain sight of blue-roofed houses. But mostly at myself for being so careless, so stupid as to ruin a perfectly good life by throwing it away. Shouting into the wind, I prayed the most basic prayer: Save me. Spare my life.

A roller swept the canoe up, then slammed it down into the hollow so hard that the gas tank nearly jumped into my lap. Between one terrible crest and the onslaught of another, I began veering ever so slightly toward the right bank, then straightening the bow before the next roller hit. Slowly, I edged farther from the foamy peaks until the canoe slipped into the sidewash. Then suddenly I was out of it, in calm water, the village shining ahead.

"I saw you in trouble out there," a young fisherman said as I hauled the canoe out of the river. He was bailing the bilge water from his skiff with a plastic pail. "But there was nothing I could do. You have to cross directly in front of the village to avoid those big waves. Lots of people drown where you crossed. It's a real bad spot."

On wobbly legs, I walked up the beach past the Russian church and up a hill to the little post office to mail the letter I'd written the night before. The mail plane had just arrived, and I had to wait in line while the mail was sorted. But it was a pleasant wait. People joked about the delay and enjoyed the sunshine. Standing there, among strangers, I found myself smiling too and thought: How amazing all of this is — simply being alive! I was elated because my life had been handed back to me when it seemed almost certainly lost. I felt the wind in my hair and noticed that my red baseball cap was gone, the one drunken Lonnie had given me long ago in Circle. It must have blown off in mid-river and was now drifting to rest somewhere in the delta.

20

STEAMBOAT SLOUGH

THE ANDREAFSKY RIVER entered from the east where the Yukon made a great bend at the foot of the headlands. Norton Sound was less than ninety miles downriver; already I could smell a sea breeze. But first I needed a few days to rest before going on. With the wind to my back, I ran full throttle up the tributary, skimming over seaweed that wavered in the clear, dark current. Two miles upriver, St. Marys lay on the green flank of the valley.

St. Marys is a full-fledged town, a hub to which smaller settlements in the delta are tied. There are two department stores, a cannery, two high schools, and a jetport. Compared to the tiny fishing villages I'd stopped at, this was the Big Apple. It was easy to feel anonymous here among the cannery workers, teachers, bush pilots, and others blowing through town. At Yukon Trader's, Inc., I read notices on the bulletin board and discovered that I wasn't the only traveler waiting around for a break.

> FOR SALE: Raft with cabin. Can be seen at Pitkas Point. Leave Message.

It must have been the strange-looking craft that Evan had described to me below Holy Cross. No messages had been left, so evidently the raft was still for sale. I decided to pay the rafters a visit.

A young trucker hauling aviation fuel to the airport gave me a lift out of town. The sun dropped beneath the clouds and lit the wet gravel road snaking up the bare hillside. The driver hunched over the wheel, his eyes feeling the surface of the road.

"What happens on this grade," I asked, "if a tire blows out?"

"I try not to think about it."

We crested the hilltop and rumbled across a high, treeless steppe, all grass and sky. The trucker dropped me where the road forked, then headed down the empty road, grinding through the scale of gears until the truck was just a speck on the horizon, its rumbling swallowed in the wind.

I picked up my duffel and started down the spur to Pitkas Point. The hill dropped off abruptly to the Yukon. Beyond lay the perfect geometry of the delta, equal parts water and land, the broad, flat plain broken only by isolated, volcanic mountains rising in the distance like islands. For as far as the eye could see, lakes and sloughs and islands stretched across the delta. Descending through an alder swale, the road led to the village on a high shelf above the river. The village had a new high school and an Orthodox church topped by a lime-green dome.

I found the raft bumping in the surf on the gravel beach below Pitkas Point. Buoyed up on empty blue oil drums, the raft had a plywood deck, projecting oar sweeps for steering, and a tall, windowed cabin fashioned from odds and ends. It looked like an ice fisherman's shack that had drifted loose in the spring thaw and lodged here. A pair of huskies poked their noses from cubbyholes beneath the cabin. But nobody else was home, so I walked back up the path to the village.

The social life of Pitkas Point centered around the community laundromat, where an electric sauna took the place of the traditional *qasgig*, or steambath. Quit for the day, salmon fishermen filed into the men's sauna. One of them held the door open and said, "Plenty of room." So I joined them. We stripped and showered, then entered the sauna's prickly heat, laying down wet towels on the slatted wooden benches to keep from scalding ourselves. One of the men poured a dipper of cold water on the hot rocks so that the steam hissed, searing my throat and nostrils. For the first time in weeks, I felt warm all the way through.

I sat in a dense fog of Eskimo conversation that parted at brief, unexpected moments when someone replied to a long, guttural speech in Yupik with "Okay with me" or "No kidding." As the heat became more intense, talk fell off, and first one man and then another retired to the outer chamber. There seemed to be an unspoken contest as to who could endure the burning heat the longest. I quickly retreated to the shower room, where naked men, their skin scorched red as a lobster, rolled on the cool tile floor. Then we wet down our towels and went back for another dose.

The heat in the sauna was nothing, they said, compared to the inferno of the *qasgig*. Built into the ground like a sodhouse, the *qasgig* had a tunnel entrance and a single hole in the roof for ventilation and light. Traditionally it was a men's club, from which women and children were excluded except on special occasions. Inside, men held their councils, danced, and told stories as a driftwood fire burning in the center of the dirt floor filled the *qasgig* with heat and smoke. A *qasgig* still survived in Pitkas Point, but the electric sauna was more convenient.

After my sauna, I walked down to the beach to cool off and found that the rafters had returned. They were a pair of shoe-string explorers from the north woods of Minnesota with haggard, sallow faces, and everything they owned on their backs. They had the lean, wild-eyed stare of men too long by themselves, and I wondered, My God, is that how I look? But their journey made mine seem like a Sunday picnic. For a year and a half they had been traveling by dog team across the high Arctic. They'd mushed down the Mackenzie River to its delta and then headed west along the Beaufort Sea coast into Alaska, where they finally ran out of snow in the Brooks Range and abandoned their sleds. At Bettles, on the headwaters of the Koyukuk River, they'd fashioned the raft out of sixteen empty oil drums and castoff lumber from the town dump. With their six surviving dogs, they had set off in late June, drifting down the winding Koyukuk to the Yukon. Pitkas Point was the end of the line for them. Now they were only waiting to sell the raft and air-freight their dogs to Anchorage.

Together we shared dinner on their floating home, mixing our remaining tins of food into a common slop. We talked late into the evening of trips and journeys. On the Yukon we had covered some of the same water, but we might have been talking about different rivers. They had the single-minded vision of explorers — churning out the miles, seeing the geography, but going out of their way to avoid people. (Later I would read that they mushed to the North Pole.) I had been more of a camp follower and latched on to others whenever I could.

Finally, the Minnesotans climbed into their bunks and I unrolled my sleeping bag on the cabin floor. A storm came up in the night and blew rain through the screened windows. The sled dogs kenneled in the space between the deck and the cabin began to whimper as the raft heaved in the surf. But I was too tired to care. I was only thankful to be sleeping on the river tonight instead of beneath it.

Rocked by waves, I dreamed that the raft had slipped its mooring and that I awoke in the morning between continents, bathed in shifting sea light.

"See that slough, how it winds back to those three little lakes? That's the first place I try. If that doesn't work out, I'll cross the Yukon to that big lake, over there."

Ray Beans leveled binoculars out the window of his plywood saltbox on a hill high above St. Marys. He handed the glasses to me. I saw only gray sky reflecting off a hundred thaw lakes and tundra potholes, each indistinguishable from the other. But to Ray, who was plotting his autumn moose hunt, the delta spread out before him like a deck of cards, alive with possibilities.

"Still too wet out there," he said. "I don't feel like getting drenched."

All morning and into the afternoon we had been waiting for the rain to stop. The silver, or fall chum, salmon were running. Although the day was closed for commercial fishing, Ray wanted the salmon for his own table and to feed the four pups he was raising for a dog team. We sat in the kitchen, which took up all of the first floor, listening to fishing reports over the CB radio. We drank coffee, rolled cigarettes, and explained away the past.

Ten years ago Ray had been my student in Fairbanks. I remembered him among the other Eskimo students — a quick, crooked grin, black hair down to the shoulders of his denim jacket. This morning as I had walked up in the drizzle to his house, he was chopping wood, still wearing a denim jacket. But there was less hair and a new gravity in the hooded eyes sizing me up. We had changed places. Now he was the family man with obligations and I the footloose bachelor.

Ray had outgrown the village when he left St. Marys for college. But after a few semesters, he dropped out to work on the pipeline as an assistant driller alongside Texans and Okies. Then he learned small-engine repair and met his pretty wife, Denice, an Oneida Indian from Wisconsin. They had a son and spent a year in a dingy city on the south shore of Lake Superior. But he missed the long sweep of the delta. The previous spring he had brought his family back to St. Marys and bought this plywood house. The foundation rested on thick willow stumps, cut back but still alive, so that the house tilted as they grew. Ray liked the view. From the window he could look down, not just upon the delta and the village where he'd grown up, but upon the whole wide world.

We waited another hour. By then the rain had turned to a fine mist, the sun shining through it. Berry pickers in calico *kuspuk*s stooped with their pails against the steaming hillside.

"Come on," Ray said, throwing me a pair of rain pants. "You'll be my partner today."

Doubled up on his motorcycle, we flew along the slick, wet road, leaning into the turns as we wound down the hillside to the river. His parents had built a new house next to their old one beside the riverbank. In the yard, braced up by sawhorses, was an Evinrude engine with its cowling off and parts strewn beside it.

"Haven't quite put that one back together," said Ray.

Pulled up on the beach below his parents' house was Ray's boat, twenty feet of marine plywood painted aquamarine with a slant front and a fifty-horse outboard and a small trolling engine mounted on the transom. Pumping gas into the line, Ray started up the big kicker and we rode a short way to the Beanses' fish camp to pick up a fifty-fathom net coiled on the beach. Then we headed downriver, picking up speed, the bow bucking against the chop.

A fog hung over the river. As we passed the mouth of the

Andreafsky, the bald hills on the right bank soared into the clouds and disappeared. There was a storm light in the west. I braced myself at the confluence, but the Yukon was strangely becalmed, a smooth, yellow sheet after the rain.

A few miles below Pitkas Point, Ray idled at the mouth of a long slough on the curve of the river. He tied a red buoy the size of a basketball to the end of the float line and fed out net while I ran the trolling engine in reverse, keeping a straight tangent from the bank. Over the bow went lead line and float line and three hundred feet of nylon mesh net. Ray tied the ends to the bow and took over at the tiller, throwing a slight belly into the float line. Then we drifted with the current, watching the muddy river strain through the net.

"Salmon like to stay to the inside bank," he said. "That way they don't have to work so hard."

One of the white plastic floats bobbed up and down in the water. Then another and another.

"They're hitting," Ray said. "Look at that! Every time you see a float go up and down, that's another fish."

I tried keeping count of the float line's undulations but soon lost track. Salmon were straining against the mesh. Then the salmon began to breach the surface as they tried leaping clear of the net.

"Looks like a good haul, huh?" Ray said excitedly. He'd been quiet with me so far, wondering if I was still just a teacher or could actually do something useful. Now he recalled once catching so many Kings in a drift that he couldn't get them all in the boat and had to cut the net.

After an hour's drift, the float line was fringed with driftwood and hung low in the water. Ray stopped the trolling motor and covered the bottom of the boat with a blue plastic tarp. Standing in the bow, we hauled the net glistening from the water and felt the live weight at the other end as if the river itself was tugging back. The first salmon dangled from the mesh, steel bright except where the scales flecked off to a cold blue. Ray untangled the fish and tossed it onto the tarp. The gunwale cut into my waist as I gathered in more net. Most of the salmon had already drowned when their gills caught in the mesh but a

few still struggled in the boat. I fumbled in a borrowed pair
of cotton gloves trying to uncinch a slippery salmon caught
by its gill flaps. A trickle of blood ran down from the gills
as I wrenched the salmon loose and flung it in the growing
pile at the bottom of the boat. By that time, Ray had untangled
three more.

We worked for half an hour picking the net, and when we
finished, the skiff was filled with fish. A hundred salmon piled
gunwale to gunwale on the blue tarp. They'd stopped thrashing
and come to rest at odd angles like victims heaped in a common
grave, jaws agape, and silvery moon eyes that followed you
everywhere.

On the way home, Ray stopped at a sandbar to collect driftwood for his father's steambath. As we landed, a pair of sandhill
cranes flew off and circled high over the river, their cries a
strange metallic bleating. We picked through cottonwood logs
to find spruce that would burn fast and hot. Supper was waiting
on the table when we got back to Ray's parents' house. While
the rest of the family watched television in the next room, we
ate our fill of duck soup, pilot bread smeared with butter,
salmon strips, and smoked seal dipped in mild-tasting seal oil.
Ray's brothers walked down to look at his boat loaded with
salmon, and later we heard them gunning their own skiffs
downriver.

After supper, Denice Beans and her son Olin came down to
help clean fish. "Pretty good catch, huh?" she said as we unloaded salmon onto the gravel beach. We cleaned them on a
makeshift table while waves lapped at our feet. Denice used a
crescent-shaped *ulu* to lop off the head and then slit the salmon's belly. From the females she pulled fat strands of orange
roe to be made into a kind of cheese. The cleaned fish went into
buckets of brine to be scored and hung to dry. Heads were saved
for the dogs, and the rest went into gut buckets, including the
salmon's swim bladders, which inflated and floated on the surface like white balloons.

While we butchered, Olin played at the edge of the beach. He
was a quiet little boy who got on his father's nerves when he
whined or clung to his mother. He was trolling a crude wooden

boat through the water with a string tied to the end of a stick. Far up the Yukon I'd seen other children play with just such a toy, imagining themselves fishermen.

Running without lights, we crossed the Andreafsky River beneath an indigo sky to dump the gut buckets into a leeward slough. Parked at the end of a side channel was a ghost fleet of paddle-wheelers. I could barely make out the rusted boilers and cogwheels of half a dozen wrecks outlined against the pearly night sky.

"That's Steamboat Slough," Ray said. "That's where all the old boats were left to rot."

A storm of squawking gulls flapped up as we heaved the buckets over the side. Wheeling at oblique angles in the sky, the birds followed in our wake until we outdistanced them. On the way back, Olin leaned over the gunwale, trailing his toy boat in the skiff's spray until his father told him sternly to sit down. Pulling in the line, the boy crouched in the bow and pouted for the rest of the crossing.

The rafters had pulled out when I got back to Pitkas Point the next day. The raft was stripped clean of dogs, sleeping bags — everything but a tin of tea and the flowers growing in window boxes. I moved my sleeping bag to the top bunk and tried to sleep, but the pale light and suspicious feeling of being watched kept me awake. Three pairs of dark eyes pressed against the raft's screened windows. They belonged to three small girls in calico dresses who wanted to know what kind of orange flowers grew in the window boxes.

"Marigolds," I told them, and sent each girl home with a blossom transplanted into a tin can. After I'd gone back to bed, the little girls returned with two friends. Did I have any more marigolds? What else was I giving away? The raft shortly became the village playground, with children clambering over the deck, climbing on the roof. When an older girl asked if she could have my sleeping bag, I sent everyone packing.

A rain squall tore up the river that night. Waves tossed the raft so it creaked and groaned against its mooring. The calm weather of the day before had been only a hole in the net of storms stretched across the delta. I worried that I had missed my chance to reach the sea.

In the morning I watched a skiff buck through the heavy swells, fighting its way upriver. When the skiff landed, I helped haul it out of the surf. The boatman was in his sixties, a thin-faced Eskimo wearing a Greek fisherman's cap. His wife had gone to St. Marys to play bingo, and he invited me to have coffee. We walked up the hill to a frame house with a big window looking out upon the windblown river. Pinned to the wall were family pictures, holy cards, and the blue insignia patch of the Alaska Territorial Guard.

As he poured the coffee, the fisherman talked in emphatic bursts.

"In the thirties, it was real tough living here. Eskimo was tough. No jobs. No money. No schools. Nothing. Real tough. Back then if children's parents die, somebody fed them, but not the government."

But life had become easier now, he said, so that "even a poor man is doing okay." There was steady work with the highway department and village corporation as well as seasonal fire-fighting and salmon fishing.

"Fishing is like gambling. You put out your net and the fish are there or you got nothing. But in the fall everything is fat. Ducks, moose, beaver — everything fat."

On his lips the word swelled with implications — plenitude, abundance, the fat of the land.

We were looking out the big window at whitecaps rolling up the river's backbone. The Bering Sea lay only two days' journey downstream, but it might as well have been on the other side of the world.

"When do you think it will clear?"

He frowned. "August is bum weather. Too rough. After Mountain Village the river really widens out. Here it's narrow but down there really wide."

My heart sank.

"You should have started earlier in the summer. Nothing but bum weather now."

*

After coming so close, it was disappointing to end my journey ninety miles from the sea, although the disappointment was not so keen that I was willing to risk drowning again. With time on my hands, I hiked to the Catholic boarding school to see an old German nun who had lived fifty years in the delta. She belonged to the Ursuline Order, whose patron saint had sailed up the Rhine to her martyrdom in a bridal convoy of eleven thousand virgins. As I descended the dim convent staircase, the familiar scent of waxed floors and musty books called up my own parochial schooling, with its mingling of mystery and guilt.

At the end of a long dark corridor, I found Sister Scholastica in the laundry, surrounded by baskets of wet clothes. A very old, very short woman, she wore a gingham apron over her habit and a short blue cowl that showed tufts of silver hair.

"The students will be back in another week," she said in a deep, accented voice. "I have forty-two boys to take care of. The girls do their own washing, except sheets and jeans, which I do."

She stopped folding clothes and looked at the clock on the wall. She had the German compulsion for hard work and cleanliness. "When I first came here, they needed cooks and people to work in the laundry, and I was strong at that time. Now I'm not so strong, but as you can see I'm still in the laundry."

She was born in Elberfeld, a small town east of Cologne. As a young girl she read the *Philothea* of St. Francis de Sales and daydreamed of African missions and shining black faces beneath the hot tropical sun. But her mother thought she was too young and kept her home. When the Great War broke out, she volunteered as a nurse in a military hospital. Having seen enough shattered young bodies, she signed on after the armistice to care for two elderly invalids. Nearly thirty when the last of her charges died, she'd almost given up the dream of mission work when she read an advertisement in a church magazine: "The Sisters of Saint Anne and the Ursulines are working with the Jesuits in the ice-fields of Alaska, and any generous girl who is not afraid of sacrifice should write Father ———." She dashed off a letter to the address in Bonn.

St. Marys mission was then located deep in the Yukon Delta at a place called Akulurak. Ten miles from the sea, the mission stood on the right bank of a meandering slough that joined two channels of the Yukon. *Akulurak* means "in between." Sister Mary Hargadon of the Blessed Sacrament kept the mission annals for 1934, the year Sister Scholastica sailed for the Bering Sea aboard the steamship *Victoria*. In a flowing hand, she recorded the progression of seasons and the migrations of fish and birds as well as of souls.

April	*13.*	*Sun.*	Girls walking on the tundra — better walking than river — rather bare. Few more cases of sore throat, etc.
May	*3.*	*Thurs.*	Saw Geese, cranes and a robin
	19.	*Sat.*	River open
	27.	*Sun.*	Snowing a little — ice on puddles. Very raw. Children back from church all shivers. (No stove there)

The bay at St. Michael was too shallow to accommodate a deep-draft ship like the *Victoria*, so freight had to be unloaded five miles out and barged to shore. Sister Scholastica was lowered in a basket down to the waiting boat. The next day, she boarded a launch that threaded its way through the winding channels at the mouth of the Yukon and deposited her at the mission fish camp at Aproka Pass, where fish wheels whirled in the current and drying fish hung from racks. Because the salmon were running, the priest at the fish camp hired a Native boat to ferry the new sister the remaining forty miles to Akulurak.

They left in the afternoon. The little boat's five-horse engine chugged along the winding slough at a snail's pace. The nun tried striking up a conversation with the four Eskimo women in the boat, but they only grinned and chattered to each other in Yupik. For the rest of the journey she silently counted the bends in the slough. There were forty-two bends between the fish camp and the mission. Rounding each bend, she could see the church and the string of mission buildings across the level tundra, but they never seemed to draw any nearer. Late in the evening when the boat finally landed at Akulurak, she was thoroughly discouraged. What possible use could she be to these people, she thought, when she couldn't utter a word of their language?

July 4. *Wed.*   "Glorious Fourth" Squakers for breakfast. Father distributed gum and tobacco in morning and spent an
hour with girls playing games in afternoon after which
he distributed candy. Flag raised.

   25. *Wed.*   Bro. Murphy home with three good rafts. About ten
o'clock at night a native boat (Olga Hunt's folks and
Mary Margaret of Cheniliak) came bringing Sr. Scholastica — a more than welcome addition to our little
community.

   28. *Sat.*   About noon Fr. Fox and his party returned. The doctor wrote that he can do nothing for Mary Bernadette
so she will come back as soon as possible.

A priest met Sister Scholastica at the landing and brought her
to the small convent where the five other sisters lived. The first
day she did nothing but wander around the grounds on a
boardwalk of lumber torn from the old paddle-wheelers at
Steamboat Slough. The mission stood on a slight elevation above
the surrounding tundra. For miles as far as the eye could see
there were no trees, no bushes, nothing to block the line between the sky and the waving grass. Changes in the weather
could produce strange mirages on the flat landscape. On a misty
day, the river below the bank would disappear, and leafy forests, lakes, and mountains appeared in the haze, only to vanish
when the sky cleared. Words spoken outside, even in an ordi-
nary voice, carried great distances over the open tundra, returning as an echo.

Sept. 3. *Mon.*   Girls had annual picnic at big hill. Srs. Laurentine and
Scholastica went along. So shallow that Amadeus [the
mission boat] couldn't get near bank and it was 11:30
before two loads were over and taken ashore in row
boats. The spread was bacon, greens, pancakes, fish,
rye crackers and tea with crackers and jam for lunch.
The weather held and pretty well tho 'twas sprinkling
when Bro. went for them around 4:00.

Sister Scholastica was put in charge of the bakery, baking fifty
to sixty loaves three times a week. She improvised a yeast from
sugar and hops and potato water. The mission raised turnips,
radishes, and a few heads of lettuce in its own garden, the dirt
brought down by boat from Holy Cross. Driftwood had to be

gathered far upriver as well and floated down in large log booms to heat the mission stoves.

Oct. 13. Sat.		Boys skating on walks.
23. Tues.		Feast of Our Martyrs — Sr. Laurentine's name day — seemed a bit cold and lonesome not to be able to give her any wee odds and ends, etc. but the new customs say "No." Benediction 7:15
29. Mon.		Much slush. River more or less frozen over these last few days.

Winter sealed the mission off from the rest of the world, except for mail, which arrived every few months by dog team from St. Michael. Winter was also the time of sickness. Most of the mission children had been orphaned by epidemics that periodically swept the delta. But tuberculosis was the major cause of death among the Natives, and the mission students were not immune.

Nov. 16. Fri.	Mary Bernadette died at 11:30 a.m. For a week one of the nuns remained with her all night, she was so weak and helpless. This morning at about 8:00 she had a choking spell. Father Lucchesi came over and about 8:30 read the prayers for the dying, during the course of which twice a really bright smile succeeded the body of pain and suffering. She seemed very slightly recovered about 9:30 but only for a few moments. At ten began the struggle and gasping which lasted till 11:30 without any sign of consciousness. . . . In school eleven years she was one of our best and most talented. She had wished to join the native sisterhood but the good God accepted her desire and took her home to her own. She was nineteen. R.I.P.
17. Sat.	Libera and absolution after requiem Mass for dear M. Bernadette. Burial at 11:00.

In the late 1940s, the mission began sinking into the tundra as the heat from the buildings melted the underlying permafrost. If that were not enough, the slough silted in, so that sometimes a high tide was needed to float the boats in or out of the channel. The bishop ordered the mission dismantled and the buildings barged up to their present site on the Andreafsky River. Most of the Eskimo families that had settled near the mission moved as well, until all that remained of Akulurak was the small graveyard on the tundra.

Sister Scholastica removed her steel-rimmed glasses and rubbed the bridge of her nose.

"What could we do? Either we had to move or build all over again. I was very sorry when we left. I liked that place very much. But it had to be."

She looked up at the clock. The talk was over. When she stood, she was not much taller than when she sat.

"Well, I must go back to work now. I have to prepare the sacristy."

Her story had deeply touched me. Washing other people's dirty clothes was an unusual form of altruism, although I'm certain she would have simply called it God's will. We walked together down the dim corridor to the stairs. Grasping both rails with her hands, she started up one step at a time. At the landing she paused to catch her breath. *"This* is hard work now — the stairs."

Saturday morning the weather hadn't cleared, and I resolved to sell the canoe. I went to see a man who had expressed interest in buying it. His daughter was playing jacks in front of the cabin.

"They're drinking in there," she said, as if commenting on the weather.

The cabin was dark inside, two sleeping rooms partitioned off with blankets. My acquaintance sat at the table smoking a cigarette, his sad, inebriated head propped in the palm of his hand.

"Have you had anything to eat?" he asked. "We were just about to eat supper."

A middle-aged couple rounded out the party. The woman sat alone and sober in a chair across the room, while her husband snoozed on the couch. I sat down, but nothing was cooking on the stove. The man on the couch roused himself. He was a pouchy, meat-faced man, with small, bleary eyes, set close together, that focused on me as if I were a hallucination. He seemed on the verge of tears. Slowly, he reached out to shake hands, and as I did so his hand clamped on mine like a vise.

"Who are you?" he bellowed. "Where did you come from? Why are you here?"

His wife tried to pull him off, but she hadn't the strength. Our host, unable to so much as stand, provided a running commentary as the drunk and I waltzed about the small cabin. "Don't mind him. He's my very good friend. One of the nicest people you'd want to meet. But he has this little problem. He's a sloppy drunk."

The oaf held fast to me as if grappling with a demon. He wanted a fight, but I explained very slowly that I didn't want to hit him. Drawing back his free hand, he threw a roundhouse punch that traveled in a slow arc, losing steam on the uphill grade, before it fell useless to his side. He was whimpering now. At last his wife peeled him off me with great effort, and he collapsed backward onto the sofa. Eyes red and teary, he sobbed, "Who are you? Where are you from? Why are you here?"

Part of the blustery revulsion of drunks is that they have no manners and speak the truth. I didn't belong here. The grace period for politeness was over, and in his clear-sighted stupor, the drunk was right. I had overstayed my welcome in this village. It was time to leave.

My canoe lay filled with rainwater where I had left it below the bank at St. Marys. The voyage may have been over, but there was one stop I wanted to make before selling the canoe. Shoving off, I headed across the Andreafsky into a stiff westerly breeze pushing white-topped swells up the middle of the river. On the far side, I ducked out of the wind and into Steamboat Slough.

Flights of merganser and gulls scattered before the bow. The water was shallow and pellucid, streamers of seaweed racing beneath the boat. The prop quickly tangled in weeds, so I shut the kicker off, pulled it up against the transom, and began to paddle. The ships were lined up in a row at the end of the slough, mothballed against better days that never came. The

wooden ribs had been cut off at the water line and the super-
structures cannibalized over the years, so that all that remained
of the great stern-wheelers were the boilers, winches, and cog-
wheel sprockets, rusted and gull splattered.

In place of the sea, this would have to do for a final destination. I had begun with the notion of following the river wher-
ever it took me, and this was it. Now I felt tired and pleased at
having seen as much as I did, knowing how quickly the North
was changing and how little might survive the next stampede
when it came. I knew I would never live off the country, but it
was enough to know that others did. At any rate I hadn't come
back to recapture the blind exuberance I'd felt when I first came
to Alaska. Now that I was in my mid-thirties, my own generation
interested me less than its predecessors. The reason I had
sought out so many old-timers along the river was not just to
record the way things had been but, selfishly, to see how I might
live. What impressed me was how so many of them still kept a
sense of drama and delight in just living, in letting time sweep
them along.

I thought about scuttling my canoe here among the wrecks at
the end of the line and swimming for shore. Instead, I paddled
inside the dark outline of the largest steamboat, stowed the
paddle, and let the canoe drift. Beneath the water line, the
ship's wooden skeleton was still intact and looked like some
immense fossil, seaweed wavering between the ribs.

Floating in the belly of the ship, I said my good-bys to the
river and headed for dry land.

21

SNOW
ON THE
MOUNTAINS

I MOVED off the raft and slept in an abandoned refrigerator trailer parked at the end of the airport. I had sold the canoe to an Eskimo named Fancybuoy for the price of a one-way ticket to Anchorage. He and his girlfriend loaded the canoe onto his fishing boat quickly, afraid I might change my mind, and caroomed away upriver. Swallowed by the skiff, the canoe looked very small as they took it away, and I did not so much dwell on the finality of the sale as marvel at how far the little boat had taken me.

Late in the afternoon, the Boeing 737 landed, full of teachers returning from summer vacations, a clean-cut group, all smiles and embraces. I felt the pangs of the solitary traveler surrounded by people who have someone to see them off or welcome them home, since no one would be waiting for me when I got back. The plane was air conditioned and tinkling with music when I boarded early. Having given up the river, I was anxious now to leave it behind and return to the life I had left months before.

There was some delay in taking off. My seat mate was flying to Anchorage to party and wanted to chat. When I tried explaining where I'd been and what I'd seen, the words came out flat. Still, the notion of a river trip fired his imagination. His own plan was to buy a riverboat, load it with liquor, and bootleg his way down the Yukon. "Not to make a profit, just to pay for the boat and gas. Oh, it would be a beautiful trip!"

The lights and music went out in the cabin as we taxied to the end of the runway. Just at dusk the jet hurled itself across the tundra and into the sky. The plane tilted to the east, and out the small window I saw the lavender hills fall away and the shining ribbon of the Yukon bending toward the sea. Then the plane righted itself, and when I looked again the river was gone.

The flight took less than an hour, crossing rivers and mountain ranges in the darkness, but the real distance covered was time rather than space. We might have been flying from the last century into the next. Then the lights of Anchorage glittered below like a carnival midway at the edge of a black sea, more lights in one place than in all the rest of the state. Late at night, the Anchorage terminal was crowded and unreal. Black GI's, tourists wearing flower leis and carrying boxes of pineapples, Indian and Eskimo kids, all of them shuffling like sleepwalkers past the Cheechako Snack Bar and a grimacing polar bear in a glass case. River time faded away, and I fell in step with the dull procession to the luggage carousel and watched suitcases revolve. Anchorage is the village where we all live now.

I rented a car and headed out Spenard Road to find a motel. The highway was a tunnel of arc lights through the dark city, the side streets and fast food restaurants looking shadowy and insubstantial in the peripheral light. I was having trouble driving, surging on the accelerator, looking at the curb to judge my speed as if it were a shoreline. Then a pair of headlights approached, grew larger until the glare became blinding, accompanied by a great blaring of horns, and I veered suddenly onto the shoulder of the road to avoid a head-on collision.

When my shaking stopped I realized I'd been driving the wrong way down a four-lane highway. I had no idea where I was going. I needed to cool off. Spend some time in a place of my own.

In the morning I boarded the Alaska Railroad northbound train. The train jolted forward, and we rolled slowly out of the Anchorage trainyard, past the backsides of warehouses and shopping malls and through the city's bedroom communities, the houses running right up the sides of hills. Then the tracks broke out into the open and ran alongside the tidal flats of Knik

Arm. From the window, I could see the moving shadow of the train racing along on the gray mud flats.

Over breakfast in the swaying dining car, I watched the spruce and birch trees drift past. The tinted window showed the late summer woods in a blue-green submarine light. A party of Japanese climbers in woolen knickers, headed for Denali Park, let out a collective shout when the mountain floated up like a great cloud. They rushed to one side of the train and clicked with cameras at the distant summit as if afraid it might float away.

For a long time we followed the milky glacial torrent of the Susitna River toward its head in the high peaks of the Alaska Range. The tracks kept crossing and recrossing lesser streams, clear with deep pools and white rents where the water piled up against the rocks. The train slowly labored up the divide, the spruce trees shrinking in proportion as we gained elevation. The train was crossing Indian River, a splashing bouldery stream with a gradient like a staircase, for something like the fourth time, when I looked down beside the trestle and saw, incredibly, fish swimming in a shallow pool. They were hump-backed salmon with olive green heads and fiery red bodies. The salmon had scaled the stream a pool at a time, wriggling forward to spawn high in the mountains. They were heading home.

The baggage man pitched down my duffel at Healy, and I watched the train pull away, following the river up the terraced valley. Below the depot, the Nenana broadened out into many braided channels on the wide gravel flats, white bluffs rising on the far bank. In the light rain, I could just make out the silty turbulence in each channel, the gray pulsing of arteries flowing north.

Shouldering the duffel, I walked past the depot and the boarded-up Healy Hotel to the spur road leading to the highway. Healy was a coal-mining town, and all the company buildings were painted the identical somber brown and tan. The place looked deserted except for a dog whose barking followed me out of town.

Hunched against the drizzle, I walked north along the highway. A bridge spanned Dry Creek, shrouded in fog. Even with the steady rain, only a trickle ran down the wide, empty stream bed. My first summer here, archaeologists were digging on the bluff above the creek because it was, and remains, a perfect vantage point over the valley. They uncovered five layers of hunters' campfires and pulled from the ashes microblades and the mandible of an Ice Age horse. Nothing much had changed at Dry Creek, except that the hunters were long gone, and now the archaeologists were gone, too.

At the clearing where there used to be a gas station, I turned off onto the Stampede Trail, an old tote road to the Kantishna gold mines. The road ran parallel to the outer mountains of the Alaska Range. As it climbed out of an aspen gulch onto the high tundra plain, more of the mountains showed and the clouds seemed closer to the ground. The road was muddy, its surface pocked with puddles, each of them holding a piece of sky. At any point I could head cross-country and hit Panguingue Creek, but the hiking would be murderous, bushwhacking through dwarf birch and willow, tumbling over sedge tussocks.

Coming over a rise, I saw two cabins along the road and the beginning of another that hadn't been here twelve years before. They were exceedingly small in the vastness of the landscape, but the country was different somehow, and I felt anxious to reach the creek. The road dipped slightly, and I veered off into the aspen woods, following a ridge crest where the creek valley fell away, and I descended in a hand-over-hand, tree-grabbing slide to the valley floor.

Bushwhacking through the alders, I could hear the creek, and then I saw it. The creek descended the gunsight valley in several tumbling pitches linked by smooth stretches showing clear to the pebbly bottom. I crossed the creek on a rock shelf where a feeder stream joined the main flow at the very center of the valley. In the small pool below the confluence, grayling held themselves against the current. A rock tilted under my weight, and my foot slipped. The grayling scattered like quicksilver, realigning farther downstream.

The willows were overgrown on the far bank and I lost the trail. The height of the willows depended upon the dynamics of the hare population, and since the hares were in a slump, the willows reached over my head. Without a shotgun, I felt a strong aversion to the willow thicket, where the light broke a dull yellow through the leaves and roots caught at my feet. In such close quarters, with branches closing overhead and behind, there was no room to maneuver.

There on the sandy ground was a moist heap of bear dung, heavy with crushed leaves and blueberries — the old fear. The spoor was fresh but not steaming; the bear could be anywhere in the thicket. He occupied this valley, possessed it more than my five acres allowed me to. That we would meet someday was inevitable. The creek valley was too narrow, too much a highway, to doubt it.

In a quaking voice, I began to sing, pitifully out of key. As birds will sing to define territory, I sang to define my swath through the willows and into the comparatively open spruce forest of the south slope. The falling rain filled the woods with its din. By the time I reached the cabin, I was soaked.

The cabin was set back from the river on a rise above the creek. Coming upon it suddenly in a birch clearing, I was surprised by its solidity. From this distance, it was impressive, given the tools and skills of its builders. Built up on creosoted posts cut from the butts of the largest trees, the log walls were snugly saddle-notched, the eaves framed in rough-cut lumber and shaded with a steep-pitched tin roof. Coming closer, though, I could see the mistakes, the gaps between the logs where the caulking had fallen out, the forward tilt of the cabin from using a tea cup as a level, the misjudgments suspended in time.

Seeing an ax propped against the door, the neat pile of firewood under the eaves, I wanted to call out. But that was my ax. There was no one here but myself. I was home.

I unlatched the door and pushed it open; the floor gleamed with bits of broken glass. A chair lay on its side amid the debris. A bear, perhaps the one whose spoor I'd seen, had broken in through the front window, taken a bite out of the chair, and departed. All else was as I had left it years ago. A magazine my ex-wife had brought along to read one summer lay yellowing on the table alongside a list of provisions never purchased. I set my duffel down and read through the list. The handwriting was my own, and yet I felt oddly intrusive here, like one of the archaeologists at Dry Creek, sifting through the effects of people I didn't know.

In a short while I had the cabin swept clean and a roaring fire in the sheet-metal stove. I fixed supper, and afterward, seated at the table, looked out where the window had been to see the Outer Range lost in the overcast hanging just below the summits. The valley was submerged beneath a cloud cover that seemed the rippled surface of another world.

Rain drummed on the roof. It was the same coastal storm, moved inland, that had dogged me on the river. The rain kept me stuck here just as it had kept me from reaching the sea. In the steady drumming, I heard the sad echo of my ex-wife's voice.

"But there's nothing to do here."

I never had come up with an answer for that. On the Yukon what had amazed me most was how people faced a landscape that was so utterly indifferent to them without bitterness and even with a lightness and gaiety about them, realizing that there was, finally, nothing to be done.

Snuffing out the kerosene lamp, I curled in my sleeping bag close to the stove, alternately roasting and shivering. The night was filled with starts, awakenings in the dark, the screeching of owls and imagined bears stalking close by in the woods.

Morning broke cool, the cabin floor sharply lit with sunlight. The rain had stopped, and in its place, awakened flies buzzed against the window panes. Stiffly, I dressed and began the fire in the stove, placing water on the top for coffee. Blueberry pancakes were the order for breakfast.

I walked slowly toward the creek, gathering up ripe berries in a tin plate. The day was heartbreakingly beautiful — blue-washed sky, raindrops glistening on the willows, the creek running fast and full. The Outer Range was plainly visible, talus slopes dusted with the first fine snow of the coming winter. Now in the warm sunlight the snow was melting, the run-off coursing down the green mountain slopes into the watershed that feeds the Nenana and the Tanana and the Yukon and flows finally into an ocean that covers the world.

SELECTED
SOURCES

Amundsen, Roald. *The Northwest Passage*. New York: E. P. Dutton, 1908.

Campbell, Robert. *Two Journals of Robert Campbell, 1808 to 1853*. Edited by J. W. Todd. Seattle, 1958. Limited edition.

Chapman, John Wight. *A Camp on the Yukon*. New York: The Idlewild Press, 1948.

————. *Athabascan Stories from Anvik: "Ten'a Texts and Tales."* Retranscribed and edited by James Kari. Fairbanks: Alaska Native Language Center, 1981.

Dall, William Healey. *Alaska and Its Resources* (1870). Reprint. New York: Arno Press, 1970.

Gilbert, Charles. "The Salmon of the Yukon River." *Bulletin of the Bureau of Fisheries*, 1920.

London, Charmian Kittredge. *The Book of Jack London*. New York: Century, 1921.

McKennan, Robert. *The Chandalar Kutchin*. Montreal: Arctic Institute of North America Technical Paper, no. 17, 1965.

Newman, Turak. *One Man's Trail: An Old Timer Tells the Story of His Life*. Anchorage: Adult Literacy Laboratory.

Osgood, Cornelius. *The Han Indians: A Compilation of the Ethnographic and Historic Data on the Alaska Yukon Boundary Area*. New Haven, Conn.: Yale University Publications in Anthropology, no. 74, 1971.

Oswalt, Wendall H. *Kolmakovskiy Redoubt: The Ethnoarcheology of a Russian Fort in Alaska*. Los Angeles: Institute of Archeology, UCLA, 1980.

Reed, Irving K. "Frank Yasuda: Pioneer in the Chandalar." *Alaska Sportsman*, June 1963.

St. Mary's Mission Annals. Oregon Province Archives of the Society of Jesus. Spokane, Wash.: Crosby Library, Gonzaga University.

Schwatka, Frederick. *Along Alaska's Great River*. New York: Cassell, 1885.

Tritt, Albert E. Unpublished Journal, 1900–1941. University of Alaska Archives, Fairbanks.

VanStone, James. *Ingalik Contact Ecology: Ethnohistory of the Lower Middle Yukon, 1790–1935*. Chicago: Fieldiana Anthropology, vol. 71, 1979.

Walker, Franklin. *Jack London and the Klondike*. San Marino, Calif.: Huntington Library, 1966.

Wright, Al. *Prelude to Bonanza*. Sidney, B.C.: Gray's Publishing, 1976.

Whymper, Frederick. *Travel and Adventure in the Territory of Alaska* (1865). Reprint. Ann Arbor: University of Michigan Microfilms, 1969.

Zagoskin, L. A. *Lieutenant Zagoskin's Travels in Russian America*. Edited by Henry Michael. Toronto: Arctic Institute of North America, Anthropology of the North: Translation from Russian Sources, 1967.

A note of thanks to Ronald K. Inouye and Katherine McNamara for sharing with me their unpublished manuscripts on Frank Yasuda and Frances Demientieff, respectively.